LEARN FRENCH

T0349426

TARGET:
LANGUAGES

LEARN
FRENCH
Beginner level
A2

Anthony Bulger

THE
TARGET: LANGUAGES
SERIES

THE COMMON EUROPEAN FRAMEWORK OF REFERENCE FOR LANGUAGES

When, exactly, can someone say they "speak" a foreign language? When can they claim to speak it "correctly" and fluently? Language mastery is an issue that has long exercised educationalists and linguists. It might have remained a topic of academic debate, and language acquisition just another subject on the educational curriculum, were it not for the fact that today's learners need to demonstrate or prove the skills they have acquired, especially when working in a professional environment, applying for a job, or even migrating to another country.

Various systems and scales have been developed to measure language proficiency, including the International English Language Testing System (IELTS), the ALTE Framework and, in the United States, the ACTFL Proficiency Guidelines and the ILR Scale.

In the European Union, which has more than 20 official languages (among the 120 or so spoken throughout Europe as a whole), the assessment issue was a particularly critical question. That is why the Council of Europe in 2001 designed the Common European Framework of Reference for Languages (CEFRL). The main purpose of this initiative was to provide a method for learning, teaching and assessing that applies to all European languages so that they can be learned and practised more easily. Another of the original aims of the CEFRL, in addition to encouraging Europe's citizens to travel and to interact with each other, was to put some order into the multiple private assessment tests that were in use at the time and that, in most cases, were specific to just one language.

More than 15 years after the CEFRL was rolled out, it has proven hugely successful, not only in Europe but throughout the world. Now available in some 40 languages, the framework is widely used by educators, course designers, human resource managers and companies, who "find it advantageous to work with stable, accepted standards of measurement and format".[1]

---

[1] "Common European Framework of Reference for Languages: learning, teaching, assessment", Council of Europe, 2001

CEFRL LEVELS AND CATEGORIES

The Common European Framework comprises 3 broad categories and 6 common levels of competency:

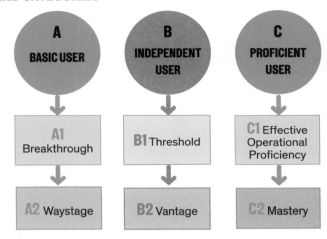

Each level of competency comprises detailed "descriptors" of language proficiency and communication:
• spoken and written production
• reception (listening and reading comprehension)
• spoken and written interaction
• spoken and written mediation
• non-verbal signals.

For this Target: Languages course, we have restricted the communication activities to reception and basic production. Interaction, mediation and non-verbal communication will be performed at a later stage by meeting and interacting with native speakers, either physically or online.

A2 LEVEL COMPETENCIES

At Level A2, the learner can:
– understand phrases and the highest frequency vocabulary
– read short texts and find information in simple materials
– understand short, simple personal letters
– communicate in simple, routine tasks
– describe in simple terms my family and other people, living conditions, my educational background and my job
– write short, simple notes and messages.

Most self-study methods refer to one of the CEFRL levels, generally B2, but few have been produced with those requirements specifically in mind. The Target: Languages collection has been designed using the descriptors and competencies outlined in the reference framework. The content of the dialogues has been enhanced with respect to the baseline specifications in order to meet the real needs of today's users. And, faithful to the Assimil philosophy, every effort has been made to make the learning experience enjoyable.

A word of advice to learners

By listening carefully to the dialogues, reading and understanding the grammatical explanations, and completing all the exercises, you will reach Level A2. There is no specific timeframe, so you can choose the pace that you feel conformable with. But when you reach the end of the course, that's when the work really begins! You must immerse yourself in the language, taking every opportunity to talk with native speakers, watch movies, read books, articles and blogs – in short, to take every opportunity for using the knowledge you have acquired. That is the first, important step on the road to mastery – however it is officially measured!

* Comparative competency scales

CEFRL	ACTFL	ILR
A1	Novice Low Novice High	0 0+
A2	Intermediate Low Intermediate Mid	1
B1	Intermediate High	1+
B2	Advanced Advanced Plus	2 2+
C1	Superior	3 3+
C2	Distinguished	4 4+

Courtesy of The American University Center of Provence

The author wishes to thank Marie Redondo, Assimil Publications Manager, for her invaluable help in writing and editing this course. Any remaining errors are strictly my own. Merci Marie !

LEARN
FRENCH

PRONOUNCING AND WRITING FRENCH

- PRONUNCIATION
- CONSONANTS
- VOWELS
- DIACRITICS

- CONNECTING THE SOUNDS: LINKAGE AND LIAISON
- STRESS
- INTERFERENCE

◆ PRONUNCIATION

Although many French words are similar or identical to English words when written (for example, **pardon**, *pardon*), they sound very different. Of course, the best way to acquire a good accent is by talking with French-speakers. But if you listen closely to the recordings that come with this method, taking care to repeat the dialogues and exercises aloud and check your pronunciation against the recorded material, then you will certainly be able to communicate effectively. You should also take every opportunity to listen to French radio, watch TV and films, and check out online media so that you become familiar with the sounds and rhythms of the language. More importantly, you should get into the habit of reading aloud, either by choosing a section of one of the dialogues in this book or by practising the groups of sounds explained below. (Remember that young French children also have to acquire these sounds, working from **un cahier de sons**, or *sound exercise book*.) Although French is an official language in nearly 30 countries, including Belgium, Canada and Switzerland, we have used the standard pronunciation found throughout France (the accent of the Touraine region is reputedly the "purest" of all).

One word of warning about the recordings in this section: the way a written word is pronounced will change slightly depending on its place in the sentence. Most of the examples below have been chosen from the course dialogues so that you can listen and compare pronunciations and detect any differences.

◆ CONSONANTS

Most consonants have more or less the same sounds in French and English. Listen and repeat:

a. **papier**	d. **femme**	g. **collègue**
b. **bien**	e. **professeur**	h. **vrai**
c. **merci**	f. **travail**	i. **directeur**

Final consonants, especially the plural **-s** and **-x**, are usually silent:

a. **magasins**	d. **réseaux**
b. **bateaux**	e. **femmes**
c. **professeurs**	f. **travaux**

There are four exceptions: **-c**, **-f**, **-l** and **-r**:

a. **sac**	c. **persil**
b. **tarif**	d. **car**

Other sounds that differ from English are **qu** [k] and **j** [zhe]:

a. **cinq**	d. **joli**
b. **quarante**	e. **que**
c. **jardin**	f. **jambon**

Some double consonants differ in pronunciation from English. For example, **ll** is generally pronounced [l], but if preceded by an **i** and another vowel, it sounds a bit like [y]. Likewise, **gn** is pronounced [nyeu], **ch** is [sh] and **th** is [t]:

a. **belle**	d. **oignon**	g. **chance**	j. **maths**
b. **bouteille**	e. **Bretagne**	h. **Michel**	k. **thé**
c. **travailler**	f. **ligne**	i. **enchanté**	l. **théatre**

(Note that **ville**, *town/city*, and **mille**, *thousand*, are exceptions to the [yeu] rule and are pronounced [veel] and [meel].)

— The letter **h** at the beginning of a word is silent, but there is a distinction between **h muet** (*silent h*) and **h aspiré** (*aspirated h*). Most words beginning with an **h** are of the first type and require elision and liaison.

For example, **un hôpital**, *a hospital*, is pronounced [eunopital]; with the definite article **le**, the final **e** is elided: **l'hôpital** [lopital]. These rules do not apply to words beginning with an **h aspiré**, so **un havre** (*a port, haven*) and **Le Havre** are pronounced [un∣ avre] and [lë ∣ avre], with a slight break, indicated here by ∣, between the article and the first vowel of the word. Despite its name, the "aspirated" **h** is not pronounced. In the following recording, the first six words begin with a silent **h**, the other six with an aspirate. Listen carefully to the word preceding the **h**-word:

a. **une heure**	d. **l'hébergement**	g. **Les Hauts**	j. **un haricot**
b. **un hôtel**	e. **très heureux**	h. **la haine**	k. **le hasard**
c. **elle habite**	f. **un homme**	i. **la halle**	l. **le hockey**

Determining which category an **h**-word belongs to is difficult (although many foreign words imported into French, such as **un hold-up** and **le hip-hop**, are categorised as **h aspiré**). The wordlists have to be learned, so we suggest that you pay close attention to the pronunciation in our recording and, if necessary, make your own list. Start by visiting a site such as www.espacefrancais.com/le-h-aspire-et-le-h-muet/.

The French **r** can be hard for learners to pronounce because there is no equivalent sound in English. It is pronounced at the back of the throat, with the tip of the tongue against the bottom teeth. To approximate the sound, imagine you are trying to clear your throat before speaking.

a. **rouge**	d. **réseau**	g. **en retard**
b. **garage**	e. **merci**	h. **manger**
c. **trente**	f. **très**	i. **régulièrement**

Of course, the **r** is not pronounced at the end of a word (listen again to **au revoir**).

◆ VOWELS

French has two types of vowel sounds, oral and nasal, whereas almost all English vowels are oral. And while English makes a clear distinction between long and short sounds (think *rich* and *reach*), French vowels fall somewhere in between: **riche** is neither as short as *rich* nor as long as *reach*. Here are the first four basic vowel sounds:

a. **avoir**	d. **expo**	g. **mardi**	j. **orange**
b. **acheter**	e. **merci**	h. **ici**	k. **projet**
c. **salle**	f. **cher**	i. **ski**	l. **voler**

The pronunciation of **e** changes depending on whether the letter carries an accent (see below, Diacritics) or if it is followed by another letter. In the above examples, you will notice that the final **e** is silent.

The **u** sound poses a problem for English-speakers because there is no exact equivalent. To produce it, say [ou] while moving your lips to pronounce [ee]. This sound is important because there are several pairs of similar words, like **vu** and **vous**, that can be easily confused, so practise carefully. Listen to the **u** in the first group of words, compare them with the second group, and then practise aloud in word pairs:

a. **tu**	d. **dessus**	g. **tout**	j. **dessous**
b. **vu**	e. **du**	h. **vous**	k. **doux**
c. **pu**	f. **rue**	i. **poux**[1]	l. **roux**[2]

[1] *flea* [2] *auburn*

Other vowels are nasalised, which means they are pronounced by letting air escape through the nose as well as the mouth. (You can try blocking one of your nostrils with a finger!). Nasalisation is particularly evident when a vowel sound (either a single vowel or combinations such **ei** and **ai**) is followed by the consonants **n** or **m**, which become silent.

a. lin[1]	d. en	g. on	j. importer
b. vin	e. encore	h. son	k. main
c. pain	f. Jean	i. pardon	l. frein[2]

[1] *linen* [2] *brake*

Vowels can be combined to produce the following sounds: **ai** → [open "e"]; **au** → [o]; **eu** → [euh]; and **ou** → [oo]. Listen and repeat:

a. lait	d. aussi	g. deux	j. vous
b. mais	e. autre	h. peu	k. beaucoup
c. français	f. gauche	i. cheveu	l. pouvez

The vowel **e**, without an acute accent (see below), at the end of a word is usually silent: for instance **une pile**, *a battery*, is [oon peel]. However, when added to the end of a masculine adjective to make it feminine, the **e** causes the final consonant to be pronounced. Listen to the difference with these pairs of adjectives:

a. grand → grande	d. vert → verte	g. important → importante
b. français → française	e. brun → brune	h. prochain → prochaine
c. petit → petite	f. haut → haute	i. amusant → amusante

One unusual vowel in French is the ligature, when **o** and **e** are written as a single character: **œ**. This combination is generally pronounced [eu]. Listen to the following words:

a. un œil	d. une sœur
b. un œuf	e. un cœur
c. un bœuf	f. un nœud

In fact, the pronunciation will depend on a couple of other factors, including the etymology of the word (Greek or Latin). But for our purposes, the above rule is sufficient.

◆ DIACRITICS

There are three main accents, or diacritics, that can be placed on vowels: ´ (acute), ` (grave) and ^ (circumflex). In some cases, they simply provide a visual indication of grammatical function, without changing the pronunciation: for example, **a** and **à** (respectively, the third person singular of **avoir** and a preposition meaning *to* or *at*). Likewise, the grave accent shows the difference between the conjunction **ou**, *or*, and the adverb/pronoun **où**, *where*.

In other cases, a diacritic alters the pronunciation. The letter **e** is important because it is the only vowel that can take all three accents. The "bare" **e** is either mute, usually at the end of a word (**balle**), or unstressed (**merci**). With an acute accent, **é** is pronounced a little like [/ay/], though not as long. Listen to the difference between each pair of words:

a. **occupe → occupé**	c. **souffle → soufflé**
b. **désire → désiré**	d. **allume → allumé**

The grave accent, **è**, produces an open sound, like the *e* in the English word *pet*. It is often, but not always, placed over the letter **e** when the next syllable is mute:

a. **père**	e. **pièce**
b. **mère**	f. **espèce**
c. **très**	g. **achètes**
d. **quatrième***	h. **problème**

* the – **ième** ending added to a cardinal number creates the ordinal, like *-th* in English.

The only other vowels taking the grave accent are **à** and **ù** (the latter used only in **où**, *where*), and there is no change in pronunciation.

The circumflex, **^**, is the only accent that can be used with all five vowels. It serves several functions. For example, it signals that a word is of Latin origin and that one or more letters, usually an **s**, have been removed. (Interestingly, the **s** is generally present in the English equivalent: **une forêt**, *a forest*). It also helps to distinguish between homophones such as **sur / sûr** (*on / sure*) and **du / dû** (*of / owed*). However, the only vowels that actually change pronunciation with a circumflex (and, even then, only subtly,) are **a**, **e** and **o**. Listen to these pairs:

a. **prêt → pré**	c. **tâche → tache**	e. **côte → cote**
b. **hôte → hotte**	d. **pâtes → pattes**	

For the purposes of this course, it is more important to recognise the differences between the written words than the slight differences in sounds.

In addition to the three accents we have just seen, there are two other diacritics that should be learned because they can change the pronunciation of the vowel or consonant they are applied to.

The **tréma**, or diaresis, indicates that two vowels must be pronounced separately rather than as a diphthong. The most common of these are **Noël**, *Christmas* [noh-el] and **maïs**, *corn* [my-ees] (rather than **mais**, *but*, which is pronounced [may]).

With other word pairs (for example, **chat** and **château**), the differences are slight and need not concern us for the time being.

Finally, we have **la cédille**, or cedilla – a hook-like mark beneath the letter **c** that changes the pronunciation to an [s]. It is used only if the **c** occurs before the vowels **a**, **o** and **u**. This is because **e** and **i** always produce the [s] sound when preceded by **c**. Listen to these pairs of related words, while looking at the spelling:

a. **France → français**	d. **recevoir → reçu**
b. **commerce → commerçant**	e. **lancer → lançons**
c. **glace → glaçon**	f. **grincer → grinçant**

◆ CONNECTING THE SOUNDS: LINKAGE AND LIAISON

Linkage (**enchaînement**) is when the final consonant of a word is run into the initial vowel (or **h**) of the following one. Liaison is similar to linkage but involves the pronunciation of an otherwise silent final consonant. In both cases, the aim is to make sentences flow smoothly. The basic rules are simple:

– The final **n** on the masculine indefinite article **un** is sounded if the following word starts with a vowel: **un ami**. The same rule applies to **une** because the final **e** is silent (see above): **une amie**.
– The final **s** on the plural definite articles **ils** and **elles** becomes a [z]: **elles achètent**. The same applies to the pronouns **nous** and **vous**: **nous avons**, **vous allez**.
– The final **s** on a plural adjective is liaised with its noun: **les grands enfants**.
– The same rule applies to a final **x**: **beaux arts**.
– A final **t** or **d** is liaised, both being pronounced [t]: **petit ami**, **grand artiste**.
Liaison is not permitted in some cases:
– with the conjunction **et**: **un café et un thé**
– between a singular noun and the following word: **un enfant intéressant**
– with an **h aspiré** (see above)
– with proper names: **Robert est intelligent**
(In the initial modules of this course, we show all these links using an underscore.)
Listen and repeat:

a. **elles achètent**	e. **trois euros**	i. **des héros**	m. **ils ont une voiture**
b. **nous avons**	f. **plus occupé**	j. **un grand artiste**	n. **elles ont une voiture**
c. **beaux arts**	g. **deux hôtels**	k. **un petit ami**	o. **Robert est intelligent**
d. **avant-hier**	h. **tout à l'heure**	l. **un enfant intéressant**	p. **un café et un thé**

In some cases, liaison (but not linkage) is used in formal register only, or by careful speakers, to show they are well-educated. For instance, in a phrase like **ils ont une**

voiture, the first link (**ils_ont**) is obligatory but the second (**ont_une**) is optional. Basically, everyday spoken French uses the obligatory liaisons only. Listening to the public radio, for example, newscasters will stick to the basic rules but a member of the Académie française discussing her latest novel will be liaising away, nineteen to the dozen. The more fluent your French becomes, the more comfortable you will feel when linking words together.

◆ STRESS

French is a syllable-timed language, meaning that all the syllables in a word or sentence are given more or less the same importance. As a result, vowel sounds are not reduced or weakened. By contrast, English is a stress-timed language: syllables are emphasised at regular intervals and those that are unstressed are pronounced less clearly. For example, *comfortable* is usually pronounced [kumftëbël], (three syllables are pronounced instead of four, while the "o" in the second syllable and the "a" in the third have the same sound). By contrast, the French equivalent, **confortable**, marks all four of its syllables and the vowel sounds are clear. Listen to these words and notice how clearly the syllables are pronounced:

a. **une conférence**	e. **une exposition**	i. **malheureusement**
b. **un informaticien**	f. **l'hébergement**	j. **une téléspectatrice**
c. **confortable**	g. **un renseignement**	k. **le surlendemain**
d. **une messagerie**	h. **énormément**	l. **un réfrigérateur**

As a rule, the last syllable of a French word is accentuated slightly more than the others, but not at all to the same degree as English. Although short vowels may be "squeezed" by the syllable stress in a sentence, the sounds are still quite clear. Listen to the following sentences, without thinking too much about the meaning (which is provided in a separate table underneath):

a. **Comment vas-tu ?**	f. **Je fais du ski chaque année en décembre.**
b. **Je suis très occupée.**	g. **Nous n'avons pas pensé à cela.**
c. **Combien est-ce que ça coûte ?**	h. **Les appartements coûtent les yeux de la tête.**
d. **J'ai fait la grasse matinée.**	i. **Pour quelle date souhaitez-vous réserver ?**
e. **Ce n'est pas grave.**	j. **Je prendrai des pommes de terre, des oignons et quelques poireaux.**

Now mask the text and listen again.

a. *How are you?*	f. *I go skiing every year in December.*
b. *I'm very busy.*	g. *We hadn't thought of that.*
c. *How much does it cost?*	h. *The flats cost an arm and a leg.*
d. *I slept in.*	i. *What date do you want to book for?*
e. *It's not important.*	j. *I'll take some potatoes, some onions and a couple of leeks.*

◆ INTERFERENCE

A great many English words come from French, and some are even identical. That is both an advantage and a drawback. The danger lies in mistaking the meaning, the pronunciation or both. Whenever you come across one of these homographs, always check the pronunciation before saying it aloud. A good dictionary will help. Read these words, then listen carefully to the recording.

a. **un cousin**	d. **un moment**	g. **une station**	j. **un train**
b. **grave**	e. **dîner**	h. **un costume**	k. **une suggestion**
c. **baskets**	f. **laid**	i. **un journal**	l. **le pain**

Another problem is "franglais", or seemingly English words that have been adopted by French speakers but that have a different meaning (see Module 18).

◆ PUNCTUATION

Finally, a word on punctuation. The aim of this course is to get you speaking and reading French rather than writing it. However, you are bound to notice a few differences in the way that punctuation marks are written. In particular, French leaves a space before "strong" punctuation marks such as the question and exclamation marks (**Quel est votre nom ?**/*What's your name?*; **Attendez-moi !**/*Wait for me!*). The same applies to semi-colons and colons. If you intend to write in French, we suggest you change the language settings on your word processor. But if you forget, you will still be understood. *Of course!*/**Bien entendu !**

I.
MEETING AND GREETING

II.
MAKING CONVERSATION

III.
TELLING STORIES

IV.
ENJOYING FREE TIME

I

MEETING

AND

GREETING

1.
INTRODUCTIONS

PRISE DE CONTACT

AIMS	NOTIONS
• INTRODUCING YOURSELF	• MASCULINE AND FEMININE GENDERS
• SAYING HELLO AND GOODBYE	• *ÊTRE* (TO BE) AND *AVOIR* (TO HAVE)
• THANKING SOMEONE	• *TU* AND *VOUS*
	• NEGATIVE

INTRODUCTIONS

– Hello *(good day)*, I'm Léon. And you?

– My name is *(I me call)* Virginie. Pleased [to meet you].

– I'm here at the Sorbonne for the climate conference *(on the climate)*.

– Me too.

– Are you *(you are)* French, Virginie? You have a slight *(small)* accent.

– No, I'm Swiss. But I live in *(at)* Lyon.

– Lyon is a beautiful city.

– Yes, very nice. And you? Are you *(you are)* from Paris?

– No, not at all. I'm not French. I'm Belgian!

– Hi, Virginie. How are you?

– Hi, Jean. Very well, thanks. And you?

– Fine. But I'm late for the conference.

– Then so am I *(me too)*! Goodbye, Léon.

– But wait for me!

– Bonjour, je suis Léon. Et vous ?

– Je m'appelle Virginie. Enchantée.

– Je suis ici à la Sorbonne pour la conférence sur le climat.

– Moi aussi.

– Vous êtes française, Virginie ? Vous avez un petit accent.

– Non, je suis suisse. Mais j'habite à Lyon.

– C'est une belle ville, Lyon.

– Oui, très sympa. Et vous ? Vous êtes de Paris ?

– Non, pas du tout. Je ne suis pas français. Je suis belge !

– Salut, Virginie. Tu vas bien ?

– Salut, Jean. Très bien, merci. Et toi ?

– Ça va. Mais je suis en retard pour la conférence.

– Alors, moi aussi ! Au revoir, Léon.

– Mais, attendez-moi !

■ UNDERSTANDING THE DIALOGUE

WORDS AND PHRASES

→ **Bonjour** literally means *good day* (**bon** + **jour**) but is used more broadly to mean *good morning*, *good afternoon* or simply *hello*. **Salut** is a familiar greeting used by young people or between good friends. To say *goodbye*, we use **au revoir**.

→ **enchanté**, literally "enchanted", is used in everyday French to mean *Pleased to meet you*. In this conversation, the person using the expression is female, so the word has to "agree" with her gender. For this, we add another **-e** to the word ending: **Enchantée**. This does not change the pronunciation. We'll tell you more about agreement later.

→ **sympa** is an abbreviation of the adjective **sympathique**, which translates a variety of English adjectives, such as *pleasant*, *kind* and *friendly*. The nearest equivalent is *nice*, also an all-purpose adjective.

→ **Français / français**: As in English, nouns of nationality take an initial capital: **Les Français sont sympas**, *French people are nice*. By contrast, we use a small letter for adjectives of nationality: **Il est français**, *He's French*.

CULTURE NOTES

Although this book concentrates on the language spoken in France, French is an official language in 28 other nations across the world, from Algeria to the Seychelles. It is also used by a number of international organisations, including the United Nations, the OECD and the International Olympic Committee. So when you hear someone speaking French, it may be worth asking whether they were born in Bordeaux, Belgium or Burundi!

Lyon (sometimes written *Lyons* in English), in east-central France, is the county's third-largest city. A UNESCO World Heritage Site, it is also famed for its claim to the title of Food Capital of the World.

La Sorbonne is a prestigious university founded in Paris in the 13th century by Robert de Sorbon. Although the main building is still located in the once-bohemian Latin Quarter (so-called because Latin was the only language used for teaching at the university in the Middle Ages), there are actually 14 Sorbonne-affiliated faculties and institutes dotted all over Paris.

◆ GRAMMAR

GENDER

All French nouns are either masculine or feminine. Identifying the right gender can sometimes be problematic, but here are some basic rules:

- Logically, all nouns referring to men (**homme**, *man*; **frère**, *brother*; **père**, *father*, **mari**, *husband*, etc.) are masculine, and those designating women (**femme**, *women/ wife*, **sœur**, *sister*; **mère**, *mother*, etc.) are feminine;
- Nouns ending in **-é** (**café**, *coffee / café*), **-age** (**ménage**, *household*), **-isme** (**tourisme**, *tourism*), **-eau** (**manteau**, *coat*), **-in** (**vin**, *wine*) and **-ment** (**gouverne-ment**, *government*) are generally masculine;
- Nouns ending in **-be** (**robe**, *dress*), **-té** (**beauté**, *beauty*), **-erie** (**boulangerie**, *bakery*), **-tion** (**nation**, *nation*), **-ssion** (**émission**, *TV / radio programme*) are generally feminine. (There are, however, a number of exceptions.)

The accompanying articles also agree: **le** and **un** (*the* and *a*) are masculine, **la** and **une** are feminine: **un accent**, *an accent*; **une conference**, *a conference / lecture*; **la ville**, *the city*; **le climat**, *the climat*. However, if the first letter of the noun is a vowel, the second letter of the definite article is elided: **l'accent**. That's why it is so important to learn the gender of a French noun, along with its meaning!

There is no equivalent of the neutral pronoun *it* in French.

SUBJECT PRONOUNS

Here are the subject forms of French personal pronouns:

je	*I*	**nous**	*we*
tu	*you* (familiar)	**vous**	*you* (formal/plural)
il	*he /it*	**ils**	*they*
elle	*she / it*		

Since French does not have a neutral pronoun, **il** and **elle** can mean *it*. Note that **je**, *I*, does not take an initial capital. Remember also that the final **s** is not voiced, so **il** and **ils** are pronounced identically, as are **elle** and **elles**. However, because the accompanying verb will be in either the single or the plural, depending on the context, there is almost no chance of confusion.

ÊTRE AND *AVOIR* - "TO BE" AND "TO HAVE"

These are two of the most important verbs in French, because they are both main (or lexical) verbs and auxiliaries – as in English. They are also irregular:

être, *to be*			
je suis	*I am*	**nous sommes**	*we are*
tu es	*you are* (familiar)	**vous êtes**	*you are*
il / elle est	*he / she / it is*	**ils sont**	*they are*

avoir, *to have*			
j'ai	*I have*	**nous avons**	*we have*
tu as	*you have* (familiar)	**vous avez**	*you have*
il / elle a	*he / she / it has*	**ils ont**	*they have*

* Pronunciation note: take care not to confuse **ils sont** (*they are*) – pronounced with a soft "s", [eelssohn] – and **ils ont** (*they have*), pronounced with a "z": [eelzohn]. Note that infinitives in French are single words; there is no equivalent of the infinitive particle *to*.

TU AND VOUS

French has two words for *you*: **tu** and **vous**, each with a corresponding verb form. Basically, **tu** is used when addressing family, friends and young people, while **vous** is more formal; it's also the plural form of *you*. So, when talking with your son or daughter, for instance, you say **Comment vas-tu ?**, *How are you?*, but if you address a stranger – or more than one person – the correct form is **Comment allez-vous ?**. There are subtle differences but the basic rule is: **tu** = familiar; **vous** =formal, plural.

THE NEGATIVE

The negative form uses two words: **ne** immediately before the word and **pas** immediately after it: **Je suis française → Je ne suis pas française**. Don't use one without the other!

THE INTERROGATIVE

There are several ways of asking a question. The simplest is to raise the intonation at the end of the sentence. Thus the declarative **Vous êtes française**, *You are French*, can be made into the question *Are you French?* simply by lifting the intonation on **française**: **Vous êtes française ?** We'll look at the other possibilities later on.

● VOCABULARY

avoir *to have*
attendre *to wait*
être *to be*
s'appeler *to be called, to be named*
habiter *to live*

un accent *an accent*
le climat *the climate*
une conférence *a conference*
une ville *a town, a city*

suisse *Swiss* (adjective)
belge *Belgian* (adjective)
français *French* (adjective)

oui *yes*
non *no*
bien *well, good*
en retard *late* (think "tardy")
sympa *nice, good*

Au revoir *Goodbye*
Bonjour *Good morning, Good afternoon, Hello*
Ça va *I'm fine*
Enchanté *(m.)* **Enchantée** *(f.) Pleased to meet you*
Merci *Thank you, Thanks*
Moi aussi *Me too*
Pas du tout *Not at all*
Salut *Hi*

That's the end of your first lesson. We're taking things slowly and progressively, but you can already construct simple sentences and ask basic questions. You could even attend a climate conference! **Allons-y** ("Let's go on").

EXERCISES

1. CONJUGATE THE VERBS *AVOIR* AND *ÊTRE*

a. Je .... *(être)* français et ma femme .... *(être)* belge.

b. Virginie .... *(avoir)* un petit accent.

c. Ils .... *(être)* en retard pour la conférence.

d. Vous .... *(être)* très sympa.

e. Elles .... *(avoir)* un frère et il .... *(avoir)* deux sœurs.

2. PUT THESE SENTENCES INTO THE NEGATIVE FORM

a. Alain est français. ....

b. Ils sont en retard. ....

c. Virginie a deux sœurs. ....

d. Lyon est une belle ville. ....

e. Nous sommes à la Sorbonne. ....

f. Je suis belge. ....

3. WHAT GENDER ARE THESE NOUNS? ADD THE DEFINITE AND THE INDEFINITE ARTICLES FOR EACH OF THEM

a. émission	_ _	_ _	f. conférence	_ _	_ _
b. ville	_ _	_ _	g. robe	_ _	_ _
c. manteau	_ _	_ _	h. vin	_ _	_ _
d. boulangerie	_ _	_ _	i. père	_ _	_ _
e. café	_ _	_ _	j. nation	_ _	_ _

4. TRANSLATE THESE SENTENCES INTO FRENCH

03

When you have finished, listen to the recording then check your written answers:

a. Hi Jean, how are you? – Very well, thanks.

b. Are you Belgian? – Not at all. I'm Swiss.

c. Lyon is a beautiful city.

d. She's late. – Me too.

e. Goodbye. – Wait for me!

2.
GETTING TO KNOW YOU

FAIRE CONNAISSANCE

AIMS	NOTIONS

- ASK SIMPLE QUESTIONS
- GIVE INFORMATION ABOUT YOUR JOB

- PLURAL NOUNS
- POSITION AND AGREEMENT OF ADJECTIVES
- GENDER (CONTINUED)
- INTERROGATIVE (CONTINUED)

— What do you do for a living *(like work)*, Lucien?

— I'm [a] teacher in a primary school *(school primary)* in Marseille.

— How many students *(pupils)* do you have in your class?

— I have two classes of 30 students at the moment because one of my colleagues is ill.

— It's a very difficult profession *(profession very difficult)*, isn't it?

— Not really. The children are sweet *(adorable)* and my colleagues are nice. You know, all my family is into teaching: my father is [a] French teacher, my sister teaches *(the)* English and *(the)* maths in a secondary school and my older brother is [a] head master *(director of school)*.

— Are you married?

— Yes, and I have two children: a son [who is] *(of)* six *(years)* and a daughter [who is] *(of)* four *(years)*.

— Is your wife [a] teacher, too *(also)*?

— No, she is [a] manager of a small travel agency. And you, what do you do, Sophie?

— I'm [a] computer scientist, specialised in networks.

— Very interesting. I have a cousin who is [a] computer scientist. What company do you work for?

— I don't work for a company: I'm [a] freelancer *(independent)*.

— You're lucky!

– Qu'est-ce que vous faites comme travail, Lucien ?

– Je suis professeur dans une école primaire à Marseille.

– Vous avez combien d'élèves dans votre classe ?

– J'ai deux classes de trente élèves en ce moment parce qu'un de mes collègues est malade.

– C'est une profession très difficile, non ?

– Pas vraiment. Les enfants sont adorables et mes collègues sont gentils. Vous savez, toute ma famille est dans l'enseignement : mon père est professeur de français, ma sœur enseigne l'anglais et les maths dans un lycée et mon frère aîné est directeur d'école.

– Est-ce que vous êtes marié ?

– Oui, et j'ai deux enfants : un fils de six ans et une fille de quatre ans.

– Est-ce que votre femme est professeur aussi ?

– Non, elle est directrice d'une petite agence de voyages. Et vous, que faites-vous, Sophie?

– Je suis informaticienne, spécialisée dans les réseaux.

– Très intéressant. J'ai un cousin qui est informaticien. Vous travaillez pour quelle société ?

– Je ne travaille pas pour une société : je suis indépendante.

– Vous avez de la chance !

■ UNDERSTANDING THE DIALOGUE

WORDS AND PHRASES

→ **combien** means both *how much* and *how many*: French makes no distinction between individual and collective nouns in this context: **combien d'élèves**, *how many students*, **combien de temps**, *how much time.*

→ **malade** (from which we get the English word *malady* as well as the prefix *mal-*, used in words like *maladjusted* and *malfunction*) is an adjective meaning *sick* or *ill*. **Mon fils est malade**, *My son is ill*. The word can also be used as a noun to mean *an invalid* or *a sick person*. Many French words derived from Latin are used in English, as we will see.

→ **le travail** means *the work*: **Le travail est essentiel**, *Work is essential*, while **un emploi** is *a job*, for which one is paid. (The government-funded employment agency in France is called **Pôle emploi**.) The two words sometimes overlap, and we will meet them again later on in this course.

→ **oui**, *yes*, and **non**, *no*, are quite sufficient in themselves: there is no equivalent of *yes I do* or *no she isn't*, for example. But with an informal question, formed raising the intonation at the end of a statement, it is possible to add **non** to emphasise the interrogative form: **C'est difficile, non ?**, *It's difficult isn't it?*

→ **avoir de la chance**: *to be lucky* (literally "to have the luck"). Several French expressions using the verb **avoir**, *to have*, are translated into English with *to be*.

→ **Je suis professeur, elle est informaticienne**, *I am a teacher, she is a computer engineer*: The indefinite article is not used immediately before a person's occupation.

→ **une fille** can be either *a daughter* or *a girl* : **Ma fille s'appelle Sophie**, *My daughter is called Sophie*. **Il enseigne dans une école de filles**, *He teaches in a girls' school*. In most cases, you can determine the meaning from the context. Likewise, **une femme** can mean *a woman* or *a wife*: **Sophie est ma femme**, *Sophie is my wife*. **Un de mes collègues est une femme**, *One of my colleagues is a woman*.

CULTURE NOTES

The French school system is divided into four levels: **l'école maternelle** ("maternal" or *nursery school*), **l'école primaire** (*primary school*), **le collège** (roughly equivalent to the middle school in the UK system) and **le lycée** (*secondary school*). Education is compulsory between the ages of 6 and 16, but most children start school well before the minimum age.

 **GRAMMAR**

FAIRE, TO DO/MAKE

Another important – and irregular verb – is **faire**, which means both *to do* and *to make*:

je fais	*I do/make*	nous faisons	*we do/make*
tu fais	*you do/make* (familiar)	vous faites	*you do/make* (formal, plural)
il/elle fait	*he/she/it does/makes*	ils/elles font	*they make*

Unlike English, French has no continuous verb forms, so **je fais** means *I do* (or *make*) as well as *I am doing* (*making*). For the pronunciation, remember that the final consonant is silent.

PLURAL NOUNS

The usual way to form the plural is by adding a final – and silent – **s** to the noun: **un collègue**, **deux collègues**, etc. Singular nouns ending in **s** are unchanged in the plural: **un fils**, **deux fils**; *one son, two sons*. That same rule applies to nouns ending in **x** and **z**: **un nez**, **deux nez** (*nose*); **une voix**, **deux voix** (*voice*). There are a few slightly irregular forms, which we shall see later on.

POSITION AND AGREEMENT OF ADJECTIVES

Adjectives generally follow the noun they qualify (although some come before it) and always agree in both gender and number. For the gender, we generally add a final **e** to the masculine form to create the feminine: **un frère aîné**, *an older brother*, **une sœur aînée**, *an older sister*. For adjectives ending in **l**, **n**, and **s**, the consonant is doubled before adding the **e**: **Il est gentil, Elle est gentille**, *He is nice, She is nice*. However, the masculine form of certain adjectives ends in an **e** – for instance, **difficile**, *difficult*. In this case, they do not change in the singular: **un travail difficile, une profession difficile**.

To form the plural of an adjective, simply add a final **s**: **Le collègue est malade** → **Les collègues sont malades**, *The colleagues are ill* (remember that the **s** is silent in both cases).

These rules mean that the same adjective can have four forms, even though the pronunciation is almost identical:

gentil	masculine singular	un fils gentil	a nice son
gentille	feminine singular	une sœur gentille	a nice sister
gentils	masculine plural	des enfants gentils	nice children
gentilles	feminine plural	des familles gentilles	nice families

GENDER (CONTINUED)

Several nouns, especially those referring to occupations, have both a masculine and a feminine form:
– in many cases, adding a final **e** to the masculine noun is sufficient: **un avocat** → **une avocate** (a lawyer). If the noun already ends in **e**, simply change the definite or
– indefinite article: **un/le journaliste** → **une/la journaliste** (a journalist)
– the **-ien** ending is changed by adding **-ne**: **l'/un informaticien** → **l'/une informaticienne**
– masculine nouns ending in **-eur** have one of three feminine endings: **-euse**: **un serveur** → **une serveuse** (a waiter), **-ice**: **le/un directeur** → **la/une directrice** (a director or manager), **-esse**: **le/prince** → **la/une princesse** (prince/princess)
Since French is a living language, words and usage are constantly evolving. Moreover, gender is a sensitive issue, so don't be surprised to find two forms for the same noun: **une maire** and **une mairesse** for a mayoress, for example.

DEFINITE ARTICLES

In many ways, the four definite articles – **le** (masculine), **la** (feminine), **l'** (used before masculine or feminine nouns starting with a vowel) and **les** (plural masculine or feminine) – are used in the same way as in English: to introduce a definite statement like the ones in this module: **Les enfants sont adorables**, The children (i.e. that I teach) are lovely. But they are also used before nouns in a general sense: **Elle enseigne l'anglais et les maths**, She teaches English and maths. **Il est spécialisé dans les réseaux**, He's specialised in networks (i.e. networks in general). This is a very important point to remember, as we'll see in the next module.

THE INTERROGATIVE (CONTINUED)

We know how to ask a question by raising the intonation at the end of a declarative sentence (see Module 1). Another simple interrogative form consists in adding **est-ce que** (literally "is it that", pronounced [esske]) before the noun or pronoun: **Sophie est mariée** → **Est-ce que Sophie est mariée ?**, Sophie is married → Is Sophie married? The final **e** of **que** is elided if the following word begins with a vowel: **Est-ce qu'elle est mariée ?**

●VOCABULARY

avoir de la chance *to be lucky*
enseigner *to teach*
faire *to make, to do*
savoir *to know*
travailler *to work*

une agence de voyages *a travel agency*
la chance *luck*
une classe *a class*
un(e) collègue *a colleague*
un(e) cousin(e) *a cousin*
un directeur / une directrice *a director, a manager*
une école *a school*
une école primaire *a primary school*
une famille *a family*
une femme *a wife, a woman*
une fille *a daugher, a girl*
un fils *a son* (le final "s" is voiced: [fees])
un(e) informaticien(ne) *a computer scientist, analyst, engineer, etc.*
un moment *a moment*
le travail *work*
un professeur *a teacher*
un réseau *a network* (the plural takes a silent **x**: **réseaux**)
une société *a company*

adorable *sweet, lovely*
aîné(e) (adj.) *older / elder*
difficile *difficult*
gentil(le) *nice, kind*

indépendant(e) *independent, freelance* (note the spelling)
malade *ill, sick*
marié(e) *married*

combien *how much/how many*
parce que *because*
trente *thirty*
très *very*
vraiment *really, truly*
en ce moment *at the moment*

EXERCISES

1. CONJUGATE THE VERB *FAIRE*

a. Nous (*faire*) l'enseignement en français. →

b. Je (*faire*) une conférence à Marseille. →

c. Qu'est-ce qu'elle (*faire*) comme travail ? →

d. Qu'est-ce que vous (*faire*) dans votre classe ? →

2. CHANGE THESE MASCULINE NOUNS TO THE FEMININE, AND VICE VERSA

a. un serveur _ _ _ _ _ _ _ _ _ _

b. une journaliste _ _ _ _ _ _ _ _ _ _

c. un avocat _ _ _ _ _ _ _ _ _ _

d. un directeur _ _ _ _ _ _ _ _ _ _

e. une informaticienne _ _ _ _ _ _ _ _ _ _

3. PUT THE ADJECTIVES INTO THE CORRECT FORM

a. Les familles sont (*gentil*).

b. L'école est très (*petit*).

c. Mes collègues sont (*malade*).

d. L'informaticien est (*spécialisé*) dans les réseaux.

e. Sophie travaille dans une (*petit*) agence de voyages.

04

4. TRANSLATE THESE SENTENCES INTO FRENCH

a. He teaches maths in a primary school. →

b. Are you married, Sophie? – Yes, and I have a son. →

c. What kind of work do you do? →

d. How many children do you have in your class at the moment? →

e. He is the manager of a small travel agency in Lyon. →

3.
IN BRITTANY

EN BRETAGNE

<table>
<tr><td>AIMS</td><td>NOTIONS</td></tr>
</table>

- ASK ABOUT DISTANCE / LOCATION
- GIVE DIRECTIONS
- EXPLAIN WHAT YOU WANT TO DO

- *DE*
- PARTITIVE ARTICLES
- INTERROGATIVE ADJECTIVES
- INTERROGATIVE FORM (CONTINUED)
- *ALLER, VOULOIR, POUVOIR*

VISITING BRITTANY

– Good morning sir. What can I do for you?

– I'm spending several days here in Brittany with my family and we want to go to the Mont Saint Michel by bike. Can you give me some advice(s)?

– But of course. It *(that)* is an excellent idea. At what hotel or *(what)* guest house *(room)* are you?

– We're not at a *(the)* hotel. We are with *(at the home of)* friends in Rennes.

– But it's much too far! It is *(there is)* more than 80 kilometres *(49.5 miles)*. Look [at] this map. You see?

– Indeed! Sorry, I don't know the region. I am from Nice.

– Ah, I understand. Do you have *(have you)* a car?

– No [we don't].

– No problem. You can leave tonight by coach and spend the night at La Rive. It's *(at)* 2 kilometres from the Mont. Here *(Hold)*, take these brochures and this map.

– Thank you, that's very kind of you *(you are very kind)*.

– Do you have [any] other questions?

– Yes: do you know at good restaurant near here?

– Try *Chez Yannick*: they have pancakes, good meat and cider. Do you want the address?

– [Yes] please.

— Bonjour monsieur. Qu'est-ce que je peux faire pour vous ?

— Je passe quelques jours ici en Bretagne avec ma famille et nous voulons aller au Mont Saint Michel à vélo. Pouvez-vous me donner quelques conseils ?

— Mais bien sûr. C'est une excellente idée. À quel hôtel ou quelle chambre d'hôte êtes-vous ?

— Nous ne sommes pas à l'hôtel. Nous sommes chez des amis à Rennes.

— Mais c'est beaucoup trop loin ! Il y a plus de quatre-vingts kilomètres ! Regardez ce plan. Vous voyez ?

— En effet ! Désolé, je ne connais pas la région. Je suis de Nice.

— Ah, je comprends. Avez-vous une voiture ?

— Non.

— Pas de problème. Vous pouvez partir ce soir en car et passer la nuit à La Rive. C'est à deux kilomètres du Mont. Tenez, prenez ces brochures et cette carte.

— Merci, vous êtes très gentille.

— Avez-vous d'autres questions ?

— Oui : est-ce que vous connaissez un bon restaurant près d'ici ?

— Essayez *Chez Yannick* : ils ont des crêpes, de la bonne viande et du cidre. Voulez-vous l'adresse ?

— S'il vous plaît.

UNDERSTANDING THE DIALOGUE
WORDS AND PHRASES

→ **passer**, *to pass*, means *to spend* when used with expressions of time: **Nous passons quelques jours à Nice chaque année**, *We spend a few days in Nice every year*.

→ **à vélo, en car**: In English, we use *by* with an action verb to describe a means of transport (*by bus*, etc.), except for *on foot*. In French, we usually use **en** (**en car**, *by coach*, **en voiture**, *by car*, etc.), but there are also some exceptions, notably **à pied**, *on foot* and **à vélo**, *by bike*.

→ **conseil**, *advice*, is an uncountable noun in English but not in French: **un conseil**, *a piece of advice*, **des conseils**, *some advice*.

→ **chez** is a very useful word. From the Latin *casa*, **chez** basically means *house* or *home*: **Je suis chez Rémi**, *I'm at Rémi's [house]*. It is generally followed by either a personal noun – many restaurants are named after their owners: **Chez Jean, Chez Georges**, etc. – or a pronoun: **chez nous**, *at our place*.

→ **beaucoup de** means *much, many, a lot of* (as with **combien**, French makes no distinction between individual and collective nouns in this context): **Elle n'a pas beaucoup de temps**, *She doesn't have much time*; **Je n'ai pas beaucoup d'élèves dans ma classe**, *I don't have many students in my class*. The word is also used frequently in the expression **Merci beaucoup**, *Thanks very much / a lot*.

→ **Tenez** is the imperative form of **tenir**, *to hold* and is used when giving or showing something to someone. It can be translated by *here, take this*, etc. **Avez-vous une carte ? – Tenez**; *Do you have a map? – Here you are*. (The familiar form is **Tiens !**)

→ **s'il vous plaît**, literally "if you please", simply means *please*. **Voulez-vous un plan ? – Oui, s'il vous plaît**, *Do you want a map, – Yes please*. **Oui** can be dropped, because the assent is understood: **Voulez-vous une crêpe ? – S'il vous plaît**, *Do you want a pancake? – Please*.

CULTURE NOTES

France is the world's top travel destination, and tourism – **le tourisme** – accounts for some 7 per cent of gross domestic product. From rugged Brittany – **la Bretagne** – in the north to the glamorous sun-drenched Riviera – **la Côte d'Azur**, or "azure coast" – on the shores of the Mediterranean, the country has some of the most beautiful and varied scenery in the world. One of the most visited landmarks is **le Mont Saint Michel**, a tiny island topped by a mediaeval monastery and nestled in a bay on the Normandy / Brittany coast.

◆ GRAMMAR

THE THIRD INTERROGATIVE

We know how to ask a simple question by raising the intonation at the end of a declarative sentence (Module 1) and using **est-ce que** at the beginning of the question (Module 2). There is a third possibility, which consists in inverting the pronoun and the main verb: **Vous avez une voiture** → **Avez-vous une voiture?** (*You have a car* → *Do you have a car?*). This is more formal than the other two constructions, although it is commonly used with the auxiliaries **être** (*to be*) and **avoir** (*to have*). So, to ask someone if they come from Nice, for example, you have three choices:
1) **Vous êtes de Nice ?** 2) **Est-ce que vous êtes de Nice ?** 3) **Êtes-vous de Nice ?** The meaning is the same but the register is different: (1) spoken, (2) informal, (3) formal. (See the note on **vouloir**.)

DE

We have already learned the preposition **de**, which can mean *from* (**Vous êtes de Paris**, *You're from Paris.*) and *of* (**Il est professeur de français**, *He's a teacher of French*, i.e. *a French teacher*). Do not confuse **de** with one of the partitive articles (see below).

DU, DE LA, DE L', DES

These partitive articles express an unspecified quantity of a noun: **du** with the masculine, **de la** with the feminine and **des** with the plural. They perform the same function as *some* in English but in many cases are not translated: **Nous avons du cidre, de la viande et des crêpes**, *We have cider, meat and pancakes.* If the noun begins with a vowel, we use **de l'** in the singular, regardless of the gender: **Il a de l'argent**, *He has [some] money.* The same articles are used with all three forms of the interrogative:
Avez-vous des enfants ?, *Do you have any children?*
Est-que tu as de la famille en Bretagne ?, *Do you have any family in Brittany?*
Yannick a du travail ?, *Does Yannick have any work?*
Unlike English, French makes no difference between *some* and *any* in this context: **Est-ce que vous avez des amis à Rennes ?**, *Do you have some / any friends in Rennes?*

QUEL, QUELLE, QUELS, QUELLES

These interrogative adjectives are the equivalent of *which* or *what*: **Pour quelle société est-ce qu'elle travaille ?**, *What company does she work for?*; **À quel hôtel êtes-vous ?**, *What hotel are you in?*; **Quels restaurants sont ouverts le dimanche ?**, *Which restaurants are open on Sunday?*; **Quelles cartes voulez-vous ?**,

What maps do you want? All four words are pronounced the same way, except before a vowel (**quels accents ?, quelles écoles ?**, etc.) More on this later.

THREE IMPORTANT IRREGULAR VERBS: *ALLER, VOULOIR, POUVOIR*

Here are three of the most useful verbs in French: **aller**, *to go*, **vouloir**, *to want* and **pouvoir**, *can/to be able to*. All three are irregular:

• aller: **je vais; tu vas; il/elle va; nous allons; vous allez; ils/elles vont**, *I go; you go* (familiar); *he/she/it goes; we go; you go* (formal, plural); *they go*

The negative and interrogative forms are the same as for other verbs: **Je ne vais pas à Rennes ce soir**, *I'm not going to Rennes this evening.* **Est-ce qu'ils vont au Mont Saint Michel ?**, *Are they going to the Mont Saint Michel?* However, as we saw in the first module, **aller** is also used – instead of *to be* – to talk about how you feel: **Je vais bien**, *I'm well.* (The verb is also used as an auxiliary, as we will see later.)

• vouloir: **je veux; tu veux; il/elle veut; nous voulons; vous voulez; ils/elles veulent**, *I want; you want* (familiar); *he/she/it wants; we want; you want* (formal, plural); *they want*

Although **est-ce que** can be used to ask a question with **vouloir** (**est-ce que vous voulez… ?**), the inverted form is very common, even in informal speech: **Voulez-vous / Veux-tu le nom du restaurant ?**, *Do you want the name of the restaurant?*

• pouvoir: **je peux; tu peux; il/elle peut; nous pouvons; vous pouvez; ils/elles peuvent**, *I can; you can* (familiar), etc.

Any verb that follows **pouvoir** is always in the infinitive: **Est-ce que vous pouvez me donner un conseil ?**, *Can you give me some advice* (lit. "an advice")?, **Nous pouvons partir ce soir**, *We can leave this evening.* **Désolé, je ne peux pas vous aider**, *I'm sorry, I can't help you.*

PERSONAL PRONOUNS *LE, LA, LES* BEFORE THE VERB

Note the difference in construction between French and English:
Il veut le faire, *He wants to do it.*
Je ne la connais pas, *I don't know her / it.*
Où sont les vélos? – Nous les avons, *Where are the bikes? – We've got them.*
The pronoun comes before the verb, not after it. Remember also that there are no neutral nouns in French, so **le** and **la** can mean *he, she* AND *it*, depending on the gender of the noun you are referring to.

●VOCABULARY

aller *to go*
comprendre *to understand*
connaître *to know*
donner *to give*
partir *to leave*
passer *to spend* (time)
pouvoir *can, to be able to*
prendre *to take*
regarder *to look at*
vouloir *to want*

une adresse *an address* (note the difference in spelling)
l'aide *help* (think "aid")
un(e) ami(e) *a friend* (male/female)
un hôtel *a hotel*
une idée *an idea*
un car *a coach* (not to be confused with **une voiture**, see below)
une carte *a map*
une chambre *a bedroom*
le cidre *cider*
un conseil *a piece of / some advice*
une crêpe *a pancake*
une famille *a family*
un guide *a guidebook, a guide*

une nuit *a night*
une question *a question*
une région *a region*
un restaurant *a restaurant*
la viande *meat*
une voiture *a car* (not to be confused with **un car**, see above)

autre / d'autre(s) *other(s)*
beaucoup (de) *a lot (of), much, many*
chez *at the home of*
quelque *some* (plu. **quelques**)

Bien sûr *Of course.*
En effet *Indeed* (lit. "in effect")
Merci pour tout *Thanks for everything*
Pas de problème *No problem*
S'il vous plaît *Please / Yes please*
Tenez ! *Here / There you are.*

By now, you know that the **tu** form of a verb is familiar and that **vous** is either formal or plural, so we will stop pointing this out in the verb tables.

EXERCISES

1. CONJUGATE THE VERB IN PARENTHESES

a. Nous .... (*pouvoir*) aller à Rennes en car.

b. Je .... (*aller*) chez mon ami Georges ce soir.

c. Jean-Pierre et Amélie .... (*vouloir*) venir avec nous.

d. Elle .... (*pouvoir*) nous donner l'adresse d'un bon restaurant.

e. Ils .... (*vouloir*) des crêpes et du cidre.

2. CHANGE EACH SENTENCE INTO A QUESTION USING THE SECOND AND THIRD FORMS OF THE INTERROGATIVE (SEE GRAMMAR)

a. Il est de Nice.

b. Elles connaissent bien la région.

c. Vous prenez le bus pour aller au Mont Saint Michel.

d. Nous sommes en retard.

e. Ils font de la bonne viande dans ce restaurant.

3. NOW PUT THE AFFIRMATIVE SENTENCES INTO THE NEGATIVE

a. .... / b. .... / c. .... / d. .... / e. ....

4. PUT THE WORD IN PARENTHESES IN THE CORRECT FORM

a. À .... (*quel*) chambre d'hôte êtes-vous ?

b. .... (*Quel*) est l'adresse de la sœur de Philippe ?

c. .... (*Quel*) restaurants sont ouverts le week-end ?

d. .... (*Quel*) émissions aimez-vous à la télévision ?

e. Nous avons .... (*de*) café, ... (*de*) viande et .... (*de*) crêpes

5. TRANSLATE THESE SENTENCES INTO FRENCH

05

a. Are you from Nice?* – No, I'm from Paris.

b. The hotel is two kilometres from the school.

c. Take this map. – Thank you very much for your help.

d. Can you give* me some advice? – Of course.

e. We don't have much time. – You can leave by bus this evening.

* (2 forms possible)

4.
HOME AND FAMILY

LA MAISON ET LA FAMILLE

AIMS

- TALK ABOUT FAMILY RELATIONS
- PRESENT THE LAYOUT OF THE HOME
- ASK ABOUT LOCATIONS

NOTIONS

- PRESENT TENSE OF *-ER* VERBS
- POSITION OF ADJECTIVES
- POSSESSIVE ADJECTIVES
- IMMEDIATE FUTURE FORM OF VERBS

AT HOME [HOUSE]

(At Margaux's house in Boulogne on Sea)

– This evening, my brother Olivier and his friend Alice are eating at our place *(our home)*, with their children. They have a/one daughter *(girl)* and a/one son *(boy)*. They come to dinner every Wednesday *(all the Wednesdays)* and we go to their place *(their home)* once *(one time)* a *(by)* month.

– Do you have [any] sisters, Margaux?

– Yes, I have two. The eldest, Mégane, is in Germany. My other sister is called Ariane and she lives in Strasbourg. It's quite far, but we talk regularly by phone or messaging. My parents also live in Alsace: my mother is [an] accountant and my father is the mayor of their village.

– What are you cooking this evening?

– I'm making *(preparing)* a tomato salad, a pork roast and a chocolate cake. Alice loves desserts but she doesn't like fresh fruit(s).

– Can I help with *(to do)* anything *(something)*?

– You can lay *(put)* the table if you want.

– Where is the dining room?

– This evening we're eating in the living room. Go [and] get *(look for)* the cutlery in the kitchen. The forks, the knives and the spoons are in the drawers next to the fridge, and the plates and glasses are in the red cupboard.

– I can't *(don't)* find the glasses. Where are they?

– In that case they're still in the dish washer, behind the door.

– There [we are]: everything is ready.

– Thanks for your help.

(Later)

– But where are Olivier and Alice? It's already 8.30. I'm very hungry, and you too I suppose.

– I hope they're not lost. Or perhaps *(that)* Olivier is still in the office?

– I'm going to call him. Pass me my mobile please. Wait a minute. I'm stupid! Today is *(we are)* Tuesday, not Wednesday …

(Chez Margaux, à Boulogne-sur-Mer)

– Ce soir, mon frère Olivier et son amie Alice mangent chez nous, avec leurs enfants. Ils ont une fille et un garçon. Ils viennent dîner tous les mercredis et nous allons chez eux une fois par mois.

– Avez-vous des sœurs, Margaux ?

– Oui, j'en ai deux. L'aînée, Mégane, est en Allemagne. Mon autre sœur s'appelle Ariane et elle habite à Strasbourg. C'est assez loin, mais nous nous parlons régulièrement par téléphone ou messagerie. Mes parents aussi habitent en Alsace : ma mère est comptable et mon père est le maire de leur village.

– Qu'est-ce que vous cuisinez ce soir ?

– Je prépare une salade de tomates, un rôti de porc et un gâteau au chocolat : Alice adore les desserts mais elle n'aime pas les fruits frais.

– Est-ce que je peux vous aider à faire quelque chose ?

– Vous pouvez mettre la table si vous voulez.

– Où est la salle à manger ?

– Ce soir nous allons manger dans le salon. Allez chercher les couverts à la cuisine. Les fourchettes, les couteaux et les cuillères sont dans les tiroirs à côté du frigo, et les assiettes et les verres sont dans le placard rouge.

– Je ne trouve pas les verres. Où sont-ils ?

– Dans ce cas, ils sont toujours dans le lave-vaisselle, derrière la porte.

– Voilà : tout est prêt.

– Merci pour votre aide.

(Plus tard)

– Mais où sont Olivier et Alice ? Il est déjà huit heures et demie. J'ai très faim, et vous aussi je suppose.

– J'espère qu'ils ne sont pas perdus. Ou peut-être qu'Olivier est toujours au bureau ?

– Je vais l'appeler. Passez-moi mon portable s'il vous plait. Attendez une minute. Je suis bête ! Aujourd'hui nous sommes mardi, pas mercredi…

UNDERSTANDING THE DIALOGUE
WORDS AND PHRASES

→ **La famille**, *the family*, generally comprises **la mère**, *the mother* and **le père**, *the father*, as well one or more children, **un enfant / des enfants**: **le fils**, *the son* (note the pronunciation: [feess]) and **la fille**, *the daughter* (seen in Module 2). Other members may include **le frère**, *the brother* and **la sœur**, *the sister* (see the Pronunciation section at the beginning of this course), **l'oncle**, *the uncle*, **la tante**, *the aunt*, and **le cousin / la cousine**, *the male cousin / female cousin*.

→ Days of the week: **lundi**, *Monday*, **mardi**, *Tuesday*, **mercredi**, *Wednesday*, **jeudi**, *Thursday*, **vendredi**, *Friday*, **samedi**, *Saturday*, **dimanche**, *Sunday*

All seven nouns are masculine, and none of them take an initial capital letter. And to make life easy for us, French has borrowed our word le **week-end** (but added a hyphen).

→ **eux**, *them*, is a disjunctive pronoun. For the time being, just memorise **chez nous** (*our place*) and **chez eux** (*their place*). We will go into greater detail later on in the course.

→ **avoir faim**: in English, we say we *are hungry*, but the French say they "have hunger" (**la faim**). Likewise, *to be thirsty* is **avoir soif** ("have thirst"). There are several other cases in which expressions with *to be* + adjective are translated by **avoir** + noun. We'll see these later on.

→ Like **de** (Module 3), the preposition **à** has several meanings: *at* (**Je suis à la Sorbonne**, *I'm at the Sorbonne*), *in* (**Elle travaille à Strasbourg**, *She works in Strasbourg*) and also, if used with a verb of motion, *to*: **Nous allons à Rennes**, *We're going to Rennes*.

→ **maire, mère, mer**: like every language, French has many homophones (words with the same pronunciation but different spellings). Here are three: **le maire**, *the mayor*, **la mère**, *the mother*, and **la mer**, *the sea*.

→ **un couvert**, the participle of the verb **couvrir**, *to cover*, means *a place setting at a table*. It consists of **un couteau**, *a knife* (note the irregular plural: **couteaux**), **une fourchette**, *a fork*, **une cuillère** (or **cuiller**), *a spoon*, and **une serviette**, *a serviette* or *napkin*. You might also find **une cuillère à café**, *a teaspoon* (literally "coffee spoon"), as well as **le sel**, *salt*, **le poivre**, *pepper*, and **la moutarde**, *mustard*.

→ **toujours** translates two English words: *always* (if the action happens continually) or *still* (if it is continuing). **Jean est toujours en retard**, *John is always late*; **Les verres sont toujours dans le lave-vaisselle**, *The glasses are still in the dishwasher*.

→ **bête** is used as an adjective meaning anything from *stupid* to *silly*, depending on the context and the speaker.

CULTURE NOTES

Regional identities are very strong in France, each region having its own distinctive personality. People will still identify themselves as **un Breton** (*a Breton*), **un Auvergnat** (a person from the **Auvergne**) or **un Provençal** (**Provence**).
Alsace, in eastern France, is a case in point. Bordered by the Vosges mountains (**les Vosges**, pron. [voej]) to the west and the river Rhine (**le Rhin**, pron. [ran]) to the east, it is part of the region known as **le Grand Est** ("the great east"). Alsace has strong cultural ties with its immediate neighbour. Indeed, in terms of architecture, culture, religion (Protestantism) and food, the region is very different from the rest of France. It also has its own Germanic language, **l'alsacien** or **Elsässisch**, used alongside French on highway signage and street name signs and still spoken by some Alsatians (**Alsaciens**).

GRAMMAR
VERBS ENDING IN -ER

There are three groups of verbs, classified by their endings. The first –and largest – group consists of regular verbs ending in **-er**. In this lesson, we have seen 15 of the most common ones. The present indicative tense is conjugated like this:

je trouve	*I find*	**nous trouvons**	*we find*
tu trouves	*you find* (familiar)	**vous trouvez**	*you find*
il/elle trouve	*he/she/it finds*	**ils/elles trouvent**	*they find*

The negative forms are:
je ne trouve pas; tu ne trouves pas; il/elle ne trouve pas; nous ne trouvons pas; vous ne trouvez pas; ils/elles ne trouvent pas, *I don't (can't) find*, etc.

And the interrogative forms, using **est-ce que**, are:
Est-ce que **je trouve; tu trouves; il/elle trouve; nous trouvons; vous trouvez; ils/elles trouvent ?**, *Do/Can I; you; he/she; we; you; they find?*

There is only one irregular verb in this group (**aller**, *to go*, see Module 3) but, in some cases, the verb stems can change form. Since these exceptions do not affect the pronunciation, we'll see them later on.

POSITION OF ADJECTIVES

Adjectives describing colours, shapes, nationalities, etc. come immediately after the noun they describe: **le placard rouge**, *the red cupboard*; **des fruits frais**, *fresh fruit*; **une profession difficile**, *a difficult profession*. However, some common adjectives are placed in front of the noun: **un petit verre**, *a small glass*, **une belle ville**, *a beautiful town*, **un bon restaurant**, *a good restaurant*. We will give more examples in the upcoming lessons.

POSSESSIVE ADJECTIVES

We have already come across these words in earlier modules. Now it's time to learn them by heart:

mon / ma / mes	my	notre / nos	our
ton / ta / tes	your	votre / vos	your
son / sa / ses	his / her / its	leur / leurs	their

• Possessive adjectives always come before the noun they describe, agreeing with it in both gender and number: **Voici ma femme, mon frère et mes parents**, *Here's my wife, my brother and my parents*. Unlike in English, though, possessive adjectives do not agree with the "owner" of the noun. Consequently, **Ses enfants habitent en Bretagne mais sa sœur est en Alsace** means *His/her children live in Brittany but his/her sister is in Alsace*. Both adjectives (**ses, sa**) agree with their nouns (masculine plural; feminine singular) but the owner can be male or female. This takes a bit of getting used to at first but soon becomes second nature, providing you learn your noun genders.
• If a feminine singular noun (or an adjective) begins with a vowel, however, we use the masculine possessive to make it easier to pronounce: **son assiette**, *his/her plate*; **ton aide**, *your help*; **mon autre sœur**, *my other sister*. This rule applies only to the three singular forms: **mon, ton** and **son**.

ALLER TO EXPRESS THE IMMEDIATE FUTURE

Like English, French uses the verb *to go*, **aller**, in order to express the immediate future. **Nous allons manger à huit heures**, *We're going to eat at eight o'clock*. **Je vais appeler ma sœur**, *I'm going to call my sister*. Remember, however, that there is no progressive form in French (**nous mangeons**, *we eat / we are eating*).

INDEFINITE ARTICLE: "A" AND "ONE"

The indefinite article **un** is also the word for *one*, so **un frère** can mean *a brother* or *one brother*. The same applies to the feminine **une**: **une sœur**, *a / one sister*.

● VOCABULARY

adorer *to adore*
aider *to help* (cognate: *to aid*)
aimer *to like, to love*
appeler *to call* (transitive verb)
avoir faim *to be hungry*
avoir soif *to be thirsty*
chercher *to look for*
cuisiner *to cook*
dîner *to dine, to have dinner*
habiter *to live* [in a place]
manger *to eat*
mettre *to put*
mettre la table *to lay the table*
parler *to speak*
passer *to pass* (when referring to time, *to spend*)
peut-être *maybe, possibly* (formed from the 3rd person of **pouvoir** see Module 3)
préparer *to prepare*
supposer *to suppose*
trouver *to find*

à côté de *next to, beside*
bête *silly, stupid*
déjà *already*
derrière *behind*
frais *fresh*
perdu *lost*
régulièrement *regularly*
rôti *roast*

l'aîné(e) (noun) *the eldest*
l'Allemagne *Germany*
le porc *pork* (Remember that the final **-c** as well as the plural **-s** are not pronounced.)

un (téléphone) portable *a mobile (phone).* (Sometimes called **un mobile**)
un bureau *an office*
un(e) comptable *an accountant* (male/female)
un couteau (pl. **couteaux**) *a knife*
un couvert *a place setting* [table]
une cuillère *a spoon* (sometimes spelled **une cuiller**)
une cuisine *a kitchen*
un dessert *a dessert* (the double **s** is sybillant)
une fourchette *a fork*
un frère *a brother*
un frigo *a fridge* (short form of **un réfrigérateur**, *a refrigerator*)
un gâteau *a cake*
un lave-vaisselle *a dishwasher*
un maire *a mayor* (the title applies to both men and women)
une mère *a mother*
une messagerie *messaging service*
un mois *a month*
un père *a father*
une porte *a door*
une salle *a room*
une salle à manger *a dining room*
un salon *a living room*
un tiroir *a drawer*
une sœur *a sister*
une tomate *a tomato*

Attendez une minute *Wait a minute*
Dans ce cas *In that case*
Merci pour votre aide *Thanks for your help*
Voilà *There you are*

EXERCISES

1. CONJUGATE THESE VERBS IN THE AFFIRMATIVE

a. Jean et sa femme .... (*habiter*) à Strasbourg.

b. Nous .... (*chercher*) la salle de conférence.

c. Qu'est-ce que tu .... (*préparer*) pour le dîner de ce soir ?

d. Vous .... (*cuisiner*) vraiment très bien, madame !

e. Je .... (*manger*) tout, et ma femme .... (*aime*) beaucoup les desserts.

2. PUT THESE VERBS INTO THE NEGATIVE FORM

a. Je trouve les verres dans le placard. →

b. Le lave-vaisselle est derrière la porte. →

c. Ma sœur et son fils habitent en Alsace. →

d. Nous aidons mon frère au bureau. →

e. Vous parlez très bien le français. →

3. CHOOSE THE CORRECT POSSESSIVE ADJECTIVE

a. (*Notre - Nos*) enfants sont en Alsace avec (*mon - ma - mes*) père.

b. Appelez (*son - sa - ses*) frère : il est très sympa.

c. Passe-moi (*ton - ta - tes*) assiette, s'il te plaît.

d. J'adore (*votre - vos*) gâteaux, ils sont vraiment bons.

e. (*Leur - Leurs*) amis sont à Rennes, où (*leur - leurs*) fils est professeur.

4. TRANSLATE THESE SENTENCES INTO FRENCH

06

a. The knives, forks and spoons are still in the dishwasher. →

b. My sister works at the Sorbonne in Paris but she's going to Rennes. →

c. I'm hungry and I'm thirsty. – Me too! →

d. Go and get the plates from the cupboard in the living room. →

e. Can I help with anything? – No, thanks. Everything is ready. →

> You'll notice that we are building up your vocabulary from lesson to lesson rather than giving you a long list of all the words your need to discuss a particular topic. That's how you learn a language naturally!

5.
WHERE IS...?

OÙ EST... ?

AIMS	NOTIONS

- ASK SIMPLE QUESTIONS
- GIVE INFORMATION ABOUT YOUR JOB

- DIRECT OBJECT PRONOUNS
- QUESTIONS WITH *COMBIEN DE*
- *N'EST-CE PAS ?*
- *IL Y A* AND *OU/OÙ*

THINGS TO DO

(In the street)

— Excuse me, can you help me? Do you know where the Orsay Museum is?

— Yes, it's opposite the Louvre and near the National Assembly. You can go there on *(to)* foot, but it's a bit far. — It's better to take the metro.

— No, I prefer [to] walk. The weather is fine *(it makes handsome)*, for once!

— OK. Turn *(to)* left and go as far as the church on the corner of *(the)* Bonaparte street. Turn *(to)* right and continue straight on for *(during)* five or six hundred metres. Next, cross the crossroads but don't take the first road on [the] *(to)* left …

— Fine…. where is the metro station?

(In the café)

— Your friends like *(the)* modern art, don't they? There's an exhibition at the Quinze-Vingt *(fifteen-twenty)* gallery but for two days only. Tomorrow it opens at ten o'clock *(hours)* but closes for lunch between noon and two o'clock *(hours)*. Then, it opens again *(to new)* for three or four hours in the afternoon.

— How much [do] the tickets cost?

— There are several possibilities: if you buy them on the spot *(place)*, they cost 22 euros, but you can buy them online for 17. There are even reduced rates for young [people] from 18 to 25 *(years)*.

— How much does that cost *(It's how much)*?

— I don't know the price.

— Do you know if you *(one)* can pay by smartphone?

— I'm not sure, but I suppose you can *(that yes)*. In any case, the exhibition is very interesting: everyone is talking about it and I really want *(have great envy)* to go *(there)*.

— We're interested too *(we too, it interests us)*.

— So how many tickets [do] I buy?

(Dans la rue)

— Excusez-moi, pouvez-vous m'aider ? Savez-vous où est le musée d'Orsay ?

— Oui, il est en face du Louvre et près de l'Assemblée nationale. Vous pouvez y aller à pied, mais c'est un peu loin. Il vaut mieux prendre le métro.

— Non, je préfère marcher. Il fait beau, pour une fois !

— D'accord. Prenez à gauche ici et allez jusqu'à l'église à l'angle de la rue Bonaparte. Tournez à droite et continuez tout droit pendant cinq ou six cents mètres. Ensuite, traversez le carrefour mais ne prenez pas la première rue à gauche…

— Bon…. où est la station de métro ?

(Au café)

— Tes amis aiment l'art moderne, n'est-ce pas ? Il y a une exposition à la Galerie Quinze-Vingt mais pendant deux jours seulement. Demain elle n'ouvre pas avant dix heures et ferme pour le déjeuner entre midi et deux heures. Puis, elle ouvre à nouveau pendant trois ou quatre heures dans l'après-midi.

— Combien coûtent les billets ?

— Il y a plusieurs possibilités : si tu les achètes sur place, ils coûtent vingt-deux euros mais tu peux les acheter en ligne pour dix-sept. Il y a même des tarifs réduits pour les jeunes de dix-huit à vingt-cinq ans.

— C'est combien ?

— Je ne connais pas le prix.

— Et est-ce que tu sais si on peut payer par smartphone ?

— Je ne suis pas sûr, mais je suppose que oui. En tout cas, l'expo est très intéressante : tout le monde en parle et j'ai très envie d'y aller.

— Nous aussi, ça nous intéresse.

— Alors, j'achète combien de billets ?

UNDERSTANDING THE DIALOGUE

WORDS AND PHRASES

→ When giving directions with verbs like **aller** (*to go*) and **tourner** (*to turn*), remember to add the preposition **à** to **gauche** (*left*) and **droite** (*right*): **Tournez à gauche et ensuite à droite**, *Turn left and then right.* (You can also use the verb **prendre**, *to take*, which we will see in detail in the next module.) Other useful expressions are **jusqu'à**, *up to/as far as*: **Allez jusqu'à l'église**, *Go as far as the church*; **en face de**, *opposite*; **près de**, *near*; and **tout droit**, *straight ahead* (don't confuse **droit** and **droite**): **Continuez tout droit: le musée est en face de l'école, sur votre droite,** *Continue straight ahead: the museum is opposite the school, on your right.*

→ **une station**, *a station*, is used for **le métro** (short for **le métropolitain**), the underground railway system operating in Paris and several other major cities, including Lyon and Marseille. The noun **le métro** can refer to both the system (**le métro parisien**, *the Paris metro*) and a particular station: **le métro Jourdain**, *the Jourdain metro station*. A station on an overground railway system is called **une gare**. (Note the term **arrêt de bus**, *bus stop*.).

→ **beau** means *handsome, good-looking,* etc. (and is the root of English words like *beautiful* and *beauty*). The idiomatic expression **il fait beau** describes fine weather. **Il fait beau aujourd'hui,** *The weather is fine today* or, colloquially, *Nice weather today.*

→ **peu** is a useful word. As a noun (**un peu**, followed by **de**), it means *a little, not much*: **Avez-vous un peu de temps ?** *Do you have a little time?* **Parlez-vous français ? – Un peu,** *Do you speak French? – A little.* **Peu** is also an adverb (and therefore without an article): **J'ai peu de temps ce matin**, *I have little time this morning.* **Elle mange très peu,** *She eats very little.*

→ **tout le monde**, *everyone, everybody*. The expression, literally "all the world", is used with a singular verb, as in English: **Tout le monde a faim**, *Everybody is hungry.*

→ Cardinal numbers from one to seventy:

1 un/une	11 onze	21 vingt et un	40 quarante
2 deux	12 douze	22 vingt-deux	50 cinquante
3 trois	13 treize	23 vingt-trois	60 soixante
4 quatre	14 quatorze	24 vingt-quatre	70 soixante-dix
5 cinq	15 quinze	25 vingt-cinq	
6 six	16 seize	26 vingt-six	
7 sept	17 dix-sept	27 vingt-sept	
8 huit	18 dix-huit	28 vingt-huit	
9 neuf	19 dix-neuf	29 vingt-neuf	
10 dix	20 vingt	30 trente	

– Remember that **un** is used with masculine nouns and **une** with feminine ones.

– As in English, numbers above 20 are formed with the "tens" unit (20, 30, 40, etc) followed directly, and connected with a hyphen, by the numbers from 1 to 9. The only exceptions are for 21, 31, 41, 51 and 61, which add **et** (**vingt et un, trente et un**, etc.), with no hyphen.

– The numbers from 71 to 99 are slightly more complicated, so we'll save them for another module.

– Practice is vital for learning numbers. Try flipping quickly through this book, reading the page numbers out loud. Go from front to back, then back to front.

CULTURE NOTES

Paris (pronounced "[paree]") is the capital of France. The city itself, **la ville de Paris**, is quite small in comparison with the likes of London or New York: altogether, its twenty districts, known as **arrondissements** (literally: "roundings") have a total population of around 2.3 million. But the metropolitan area, known as **la Métropole du Grand Paris**, is home to some 7 million people.

Among its many attractions, Paris has some of the world's greatest museums, notably **le musée du Louvre**, home to **La Joconde** (*"The Mona Lisa"*), **la Vénus de Milo** and many other world-class artworks. A more recent, but equally popular, attraction is **le musée d'Orsay** (*the Orsay museum*), a converted 19th century railway station housing the finest collection of Impressionist and post-Impressionist art in the world. (The noun **un musée**, *a museum*, is also used to describe an art gallery open to the public; **une galerie** is a private gallery or a room in a public gallery.)

L'Assemblée nationale, *the National Assembly*, is the lower house of France's parliament, located on the left bank of the River Seine.

GRAMMAR
DIRECT OBJECT PRONOUNS

Direct objects are people or things that "receive" an action (for example, *Tell me your name*). A direct pronoun can replace a noun, and thus avoid repetition, if the identity of the "receiver" is clear. So if you ask someone **Pouvez-vous m'aider?**, *Can you help me?*, it is obvious that you are the person asking for help. Here are all the direct object pronouns:

me (m' before a vowel)	*me*	nous	*us*
te (t' before a vowel)	*you*	vous	*you*
le (l' before a vowel)	*him/it*	les	*them*
la (l' before a vowel)	*her/it*		

Unlike English, the pronoun generally comes before the verb:
Je le connais, *I know him* (or *it*).
Nous ne la comprenons pas, *We don't understand her* (or *it*)
Pouvez-vous nous aider ?, *Can you help us?*
Où est-ce que tu les achètes ?, *Where do you buy them?*
The only slight complication occurs if the verb following the pronoun starts with a vowel, because the final vowel of **me / te / le / la** is elided. For example, the direct object of the question **Pouvez-vous l'aider ?** could be either a masculine or a feminine noun (*Can you help him/her?*). In most cases, though, the context makes the meaning clear. We'll see later how to avoid ambiguity.

FORMING QUESTIONS WITH *COMBIEN (DE)*

The adverb **combien**, first seen in Module 1, means *how much / how many*. It is usually placed at the beginning or end of the question: **Combien voulez-vous ?**, *How much/many do you want?* or **Tu veux combien ?**, *How much/many do you want?* If **combien** is followed by a direct object, we need the preposition **de** (**d'** before a vowel): **Combien de verres sont dans le placard ?**, *How many glasses are in the cupboard?* If using a verb, place it directly after **combien: Combien coûtent les billets ?**, *How much do the tickets cost?*, but if the demonstrative pronoun **ça** is used, the verb comes after it: **Combien ça coûte ?**, *How much does it cost?* (You might also hear **Ça fait combien ?**, which means the same thing but is very idiomatic.)

THE QUESTION TAG *N'EST-CE PAS ?*

N'est-ce pas is an inversion of **ce n'est pas**, *it is not*. It serves the same function as the question tag in English (*isn't she, doesn't he,* etc.) but is much easier to use because it is invariable. For example, **Elle parle anglais, n'est-ce pas ?**, *She speaks English doesn't she?* **Ton frère est professeur, n'est-ce pas ?**, *Your brother is a teacher, isn't he?* In everyday French, **n'est-ce pas** always comes at the end of the question and is pronounced with a rising intonation. There are other, more formal, ways to use **n'est-ce pas**, but we will not bother with them.

▲ CONJUGATIONS

SAVOIR

Another important – and irregular – verb is **savoir**, *to know*:

je sais	*I know*	nous savons	*we know*
tu sais	*you know* (informal)	vous savez	*you know*
il/elle sait	*he/she/it knows*	ils/elles savent	*they know*

The negative form is regular: **Je ne sais pas**, *I don't know*, **Nous ne savons pas**, *We do not know*, etc. As for the interrogative, the third form (inversion) is commonly used: **Savez-vous où je peux trouver un restaurant ?**, *Do you know where I can find a restaurant?* (You can, of course, use the other two forms: **Vous savez où... ? / Est-ce que vous savez... ?**).

In addition to **savoir**, French has another verb for *to know*: **connaître** (see Module 3). Broadly, the first one applies to things, the second to people:

– **Je sais que le métro Saint Michel n'est pas loin**, *I know that the St Michel metro station isn't far*

– **Il ne connaît pas mon père**, *He doesn't know my father*.

The two notions are a bit more complex, however, and overlap in certain cases. We will learn more as we move forward.

IL Y A

This very common and useful expression (literally "it there has") means *there is* or *there are*. It is usually followed by a noun, a number or an indefinite pronoun. **Il y a trente élèves dans la classe**, *There are 30 students in the class*. **Il y a une exposition intéressante au musée d'Orsay**, *There's an interesting exhibition at the Orsay Museum*. The negative is **il n'y a pas**: **Il n'y a pas de verres dans le placard**, *There aren't any glasses in the cupboard*. The simplest way to form the interrogative is with **est-ce que**, eliding the final e of que: **Est-ce qu'il y a une station de métro près d'ici ?**, *Is there a metro station near here?* We'll look at another meaning of **il y a** later on.

OU AND *OÙ*

Don't confuse these two words, which are pronounced the same. **Ou**, without an accent on the **u**, means *or*: **quel hôtel ou quelle chambre d'hôte** (*which hotel or guest house*), whereas **où**, with an accent, means *where*: **Où est votre voiture ?**, *Where is your car?*

⬡ EXERCISES

1. REPLACE THE SUBJECT PRONOUN WITH THE EQUIVALENT DIRECT OBJECT PRONOUN

a. Pouvez-vous (*je*) aider ? →

b. Nous ne (*ils*) connaissons pas. →

c. Est-ce que Marie aime son travail ? – Elle (*le*) adore ! →

d. Est-ce que tu (*elle*) achètes, cette carte ? →

e. Je (*tu*) attends au musée d'Orsay. →

2. CONJUGATE THESE VERBS IN THE AFFIRMATIVE OR NEGATIVE, AS INDICATED

a. Nous (*savoir*, negative) si Jean vient ce soir. →

b. (*Continuer*, affirmative) tout droit puis (*tourner*, affirmative) à gauche. →

c. Ils (*aller*, affirmative) à pied, mais c'est très loin. →

d. Les billets pour l'expo (*coûter*, affirmative) vingt euros. →

e. Est-ce tu (*savoir*, affirmative) si la galerie ouvre à deux heures ? – Non, je (*savoir*, negative). →

3. FILL IN THE MISSING WORDS

a. Prenez la première rue _ _ droite. L'église est à l'_ _ _ _ _ de la rue Jacob.

b. Vos amis aiment l'art moderne, n'est- _ _ _ _ _ _ _.?

c. _ _ _ _ le monde aime l'art moderne.

d. _ _ _ _ _ _ _ coûtent les billets ? – Ils coutent vingt euros.

e. Le musée est un peu loin. Il vaut _ _ _ _ _ prendre le métro.

🔊 4. TRANSLATE THESE NUMBERS, THEN SAY THEM ALOUD

a. 15 _ _ _ _ _   d. 33 _ _ _ _ _ _ _ _   g. 12 _ _ _

b. 22 _ _ _ _ _ _ _ _   e. 70 _ _ _ _ _ _   h. 21 _ _ _ _ _ _ _ _

c. 45 _ _ _ _ _ _ _ _   f. 61 _ _ _ _ _ _ _ _ _   i. 17 _ _ _ _ _

● VOCABULARY

acheter *to buy*
avoir envie *to want*
continuer *to continue*
coûter *to cost*
fermer *to close*
intéresser *to interest*
marcher *to walk*
ouvrir *to open*
payer *to pay*
préférer *to prefer*
supposer *to suppose*
tourner *to turn*
traverser *to cross*
voir *to see*

un angle *a corner*
un arrêt (de bus) *a (bus) stop*
l'Assemblée nationale *the National Assembly* (lower house of parliament)
un billet *a ticket* (train, admission, lottery, etc.)
un carrefour *a crossroads*
le déjeuner *lunch*
une église *a church*
une exposition (familiar: **une expo**) *an exhibition*
un jour *a day*
un mètre *a/one metre* (3.2 ft)
le métro *the metro system* (Paris, Lyon, Marseille); also used for a metro station
un musée *a museum, an art gallery*
un pied *a foot*
un prix *a price* (but also *a prize*: **le Prix Nobel**, *the Nobel prize*)

une station *a station* (metro, etc.)
un tarif *a fee, price, fare*
un tarif réduit *a reduced price*

après *after*
avant *before*
cent *a/one hundred*
combien *how much / how many*
demain *tomorrow*
droite *right*
gauche *left*
en ligne *online*
en face de *opposite*
jusqu'à *as far as, until* (distance)
loin *far*
midi *noon*
l'après-midi *afternoon*
pendant *during, for* (period of time)
près de *near*
puis *then*
seulement *only*
tout droit *straight on*
beau *handsome, beautiful, good-looking*
intéressant *interesting*
sûr *sure*
y *there*

il vaut mieux *it's better to* + verb
il fait beau *the weather is fine*
pour une fois *for once*
sur place *on the spot* (literally: "on place")
tout le monde *everybody, everyone*

5. TRANSLATE THESE SENTENCES INTO FRENCH*

a. He doesn't understand her. Can you (*familiar form*) help him?

b. I like these tomatoes. Where do you buy them?

c. How much are the tickets? – They cost twenty seven euros.

d. Do you know (*two interrogative forms possible*) where I can find a restaurant?

e. It's better to take the metro. The Orsay Museum is quite far.

* Unless otherwise specified, use the formal **vous** to translate *you*.

To help you expand your vocabulary, we have chosen several verbs that resemble their English counterparts (**continuer, coûter, payer**, etc.). But, as we shall see, there are many French words that have different meanings from a similar-sounding word in English. These so-called false cognates are commonly known as **faux-amis** (*false friends*).

The close connection between the two languages and the global dominance of English have given rise to one of the most divisive issues in French: the whole-sale adoption of English words, such as **le smartphone** and **le week-end**. Another bone of linguistic contention is **le franglais**, words and expressions that look like English but would not be recognised as such by a native speaker – for instance **un pressing** (*a dry-cleaner's*) or **un relooking** (*a makeover*). We'll talk more about this topic later.

6.
WHAT TIME IS IT?

QUELLE HEURE EST-IL ?

AIMS	NOTIONS

- ASK AND TELL THE TIME
- CHOOSE ÍTEMS ON A MENU
- EXPLAIN CHOICES

- USING THE IMPERSONAL FORM OF VERBS
- EMPHATIC PRONOUNS
- SECOND CONJUGATION: VERBS ENDING IN *-IR*

LET'S HAVE LUNCH!

– What time is it now, Anne-Marie?

– I think that it's nearly one o'clock *(hour)*. Indeed, it's ten to one *(one hour less ten)*.

– I'm starving *(dying of hunger)*! Let's go [and] and get something to eat *(eat something)*.

– I have an appointment with a customer [at] around 2.15 or 2.30, so we *(one)* have *(the)* time for a quick lunch *(lunch quickly)* together, if you want.

– With pleasure. Do you know a place in the neighbourhood?

– Let me think *(reflect)*. Yes, there is a nice bistro in front of the station. What's more, it's not expensive. Come with me.

– Let's *(there)* go right away!

(In the bistro)

– A table for two? This way *(by here)* please. Here [is] the menu *(card)*, and there is the menu of the day, on the wall, with hot and cold dishes.

– What are you going to choose, Michel?

– I try not to eat too much because I don't want to put on weight *(fatten)*. That is why, in a *(the)* restaurant, I always choose a fish or a salad rather than [some] meat and, at home, I try not to fill my plate. But I don't always succeed!

– You're kidding? You, you don't need to lose weight *(to thin)*! I do *(me, yes)*.

(Later)

– Aren't you finishing your dish? It is going [to] get cold.

– No, I have eaten too much …but a I want a caramel cream to finish the meal.

– Good idea. Me too. This restaurant is excellent; I am going to leave a review *(advice)* on [the] Internet …and I am coming back [for] lunch [the day] after tomorrow!

DÉJEUNONS !

— Quelle heure est-il maintenant, Anne-Marie ?

— Je pense qu'il est presque une heure. En effet, il est une heure moins dix.

— Je meurs de faim ! Allons manger quelque chose.

— J'ai un rendez-vous avec un client vers deux heures et quart ou deux heures et demie donc on a le temps de déjeuner rapidement ensemble, si tu veux.

— Avec plaisir. Est-ce que tu connais un endroit dans le quartier ?

— Laisse-moi réfléchir. Oui, il y a un bon bistrot devant la gare. En plus, il n'est pas cher. Viens avec moi.

— Allons-y tout de suite !

(Au bistrot)

— Une table pour deux ? Par ici s'il vous plaît. Voici la carte, et voilà le menu du jour, au mur, avec des plats chauds et froids.

— Qu'est-ce tu vas choisir, Michel ?

— J'essaie de ne pas trop manger car je ne veux pas grossir. C'est pourquoi, au restaurant, je choisis toujours un poisson ou une salade plutôt que de la viande, et, chez moi, j'essaie de ne pas remplir mon assiette. Mais je ne réussis pas toujours !

— Tu plaisantes ? Toi, tu n'as pas besoin de maigrir ! Moi, si.

(Plus tard)

— Tu ne finis pas ton plat ? Il va refroidir.

— Non, j'ai trop mangé… mais j'ai envie d'une crème caramel pour finir le repas.

— Bonne idée. Moi aussi. Ce restaurant est excellent ; je vais laisser un avis sur Internet … et je reviens déjeuner après-demain !

UNDERSTANDING THE DIALOGUE
WORDS AND PHRASES

→ **une heure**, an/one hour (remember the rule for the indefinite article, Module 4). But with a definite article, **l'heure** means the time: **Quelle heure est-il ?** What time is it? (or, more familiarly, **Il est quelle heure ?**). The response starts with **Il est...** (It is...). When giving the time, **heure(s)** is used after the full hour, like o'clock: **Il est cinq heures**, It's five o'clock. However, unlike English (It's five), **heure(s)** is never omitted. When the time is after the hour, simply add the number of minutes: **Il est huit heures vingt**, It's 8.20; **Il est trois heures cinquante**, It's 3.50.

Although there is no word for past the hour in this context, it's possible to give the number of minutes to the following hour using **moins**, less: So, 3.50 can also be expressed as: **Il est quatre heures moins dix**. For quarter and half-hours, we use **et quart** (quarter past), **et demie** (half past) and **moins le quart** (quarter to). **Il est dix heures et quart**, It's 10.15; **Il est neuf heures et demie**, It's 9.30; **Il est deux heures moins le quart**, It's 1.45 (literally "two hours less the quarter").

French has no equivalent for am or pm so, if necessary, specify **du matin, de l'après-midi**, or **du soir**: **Il est huit heures du matin** (8 am), **Il est quatre heures de l'après-midi** (4 pm), **Il est onze heures du soir**, (It's 11 pm). Lastly, we have already learned **le temps**, which, unlike **l'heure**, refers to the passage of time (**passer le temps**, spend time, etc.) not to a specific moment.

→ **mourir**, to die, is an irregular verb. The present tense is commonly used in the expression **Je meurs de faim**, I'm starving (literally "I'm dying of hunger").

→ **un quartier**, a quarter, is used, as in English, to refer to a neighbourhood. The descriptive term **de quartier** means local, neighbourhood: **un bar de quartier**, a local bar.

→ **un besoin** means a need, so **avoir besoin** means to need (literally "to have need"). Like **avoir envie**, to want, the two words are always used together, along with **de** if followed by a direct object: **Nous avons besoin de vos conseils**, We need your advice.

→ **car** is a coordinating conjunction meaning because, for. Synonymous with **parce que**, it is often used in longer sentences. Do not confuse it with **un car**, a coach (Module 3)!

→ **plaisanter**, to joke, shares the same etymology as pleasing, and the noun **une plaisanterie**, a joke, is a calque for a pleasantry. The exclamation **Tu plaisantes !** (or, more formally, **Vous plaisantez !**) is equivalent to You're kidding me/You're joking!

→ **après**, after, is used in many compound nouns, such as **l'après-midi**, the afternoon, **l'après-rasage**, aftershave, **après-vente**, aftersales. **Après-demain** means *the day after tomorrow* (no need to translate *the* or *day*): **Il revient après-demain,** *He's coming back the day after tomorrow.*

CULTURE NOTES

Food and the culinary arts have always been an important part of French culture. Everyday conversation often centres on eating and drinking and each region has its own specialities (for instance, seafood in Brittany, cassoulet in the southwest, and sauerkraut in Alsace). The simplest type of restaurant – apart from **les cafés**, which generally serve sandwiches, salads and snacks – is **un bistrot** (note the final **-t**). Traditionally, **bistrots** serve simple and reasonably priced meals. In recent years, however, young chefs have joined in a movement called **la bistronomie** (a compound of **le bistrot** and **la gastronomie**, *fine dining*), which involves serving inventive cuisine in unfussy surroundings.

◆ GRAMMAR
THE IMPERSONAL FORM *ON*

The impersonal pronoun **on** is loosely related to its English counterpart *one* (**On peut payer par smartphone,** *One can pay by smartphone*) but is much more common because it is used widely in informal speech instead of **nous: Nous avons le temps de déjeuner ensemble** → **On a le temps de déjeuner ensemble,** *We have time to get lunch together.* Although this type of construction is considered familiar, it is very useful and totally acceptable in everyday French. **On** can also replace **quelqu'un**, *someone*, or another indefinite subject like *they* (i.e. people in general): **On dit que son film est très intéressant,** *They say that his/her film is very interesting.*

VOICI AND *VOILÀ*

These two prepositions are commonly used to indicate the position of something or someone relative to the speaker. **Voici** refers to an object close by (it's a compound of **vois**, *see*, and **ici**, *here*), while **voilà** designates something farther away (**vois + là-bas**, *over there*): **Voici votre table, et voilà le menu:** *Here's your table, and there's the menu.* In practice, there is some overlap between the two (**Me voilà !**, *Here I am!*) but, for the time being, just remember the basic distinction: **voici** = *here*, **voilà** = *there*.

EMPHATIC PRONOUNS

The main emphatic pronouns, also called stressed pronouns, are **moi**, *me*; **toi**, *you*; **lui**, *him*; **elle**, *her*; **nous**, *us*; **vous**, *you*; **eux**, *them* (masculine); **elles**, *them* (feminine).

They are used in a variety of ways, usually for emphasis – hence their name.
The simplest form is the inclusory construction **Moi aussi**, *Me too*, seen in Module 1.
Thus, **Elle est en retard. – Lui aussi**, *She's late. – So's he.* **Vous êtes sur Twitter ?
Nous aussi !**, *You're on Twitter? So are we!*
Another common use of emphatic pronouns is with the imperative form. For the time being we will concentrate on the first person: **Attendez-moi**, *Wait for me.* **Passez-moi le téléphone s'il vous plaît**, *Hand me the phone, please.*
Finally, these pronouns are used when comparing and contrasting two people or things. For example, **Tu n'as pas besoin de maigrir**, *You don't need to slim*, can be made more emphatic by adding the pronoun: **Toi, tu n'as pas besoin de maigrir mais elle, si.** Which can be translated as *You don't need to slim, but she really does* (remember that French does not use auxiliaries in the same way that English uses *does, aren't*, etc.).

▲ CONJUGATION

SECOND GROUP: VERBS ENDING IN -*IR*

Verbs with the infinitive ending in **-ir** form the second group of regular verbs. Here are the principal forms of **choisir**, *to choose*, formed by dropping the infinitive ending:

je choisis	I choose	nous choisissons	we choose
tu choisis	you choose	vous choisissez	you choose
il/elle choisit	he/she/it chooses	ils/elles choisissent	they choose

Listen carefully to the difference between the single and the double "s": **choisissez**, [shwazissay]

The negative forms are:
je ne choisis pas; tu ne choisis pas; il/elle ne choisit pas; nous ne choisissons pas; vous ne choisissez pas; ils/elles ne choisissent pas, *I don't (can't) choose*, etc.

The interrogative forms, using **est-ce que**, are:
Est-ce que je choisis; tu choisis; il/elle choisit; nous choisissons; vous choisissez; ils/elles choisissent ?, *Do (Can) I choose?*, etc.

Notice that the **nous** and **vous** forms have an extra syllable: **choisissons** and **choisissez**. And remember that the final consonants are all silent.
A few verbs ending in **-ir** are not actually part of this group; they belong to the third and final group (see Module 12) because they are irregular. One of the most important of these is **venir**, *to come*: **je viens; tu viens; il/elle vient; nous venons; vous venez; ils/elles viennent**, *I come*, etc.

● VOCABULARY

avoir besoin *to need*
connaitre *to know*
choisir *to choose*
déjeuner *to (have) lunch*
essayer *to try*
finir *to finish*
grossir *to put on weight, to get fat*
laisser *to leave*
maigrir *to lose weight, to slim*
mourir *to die*
penser *to think*
plaisanter *to joke*
réfléchir *to reflect on, to think about*
refroidir *to go cold* (see below, **froid**)
remplir *to fill (up)*
réussir *to succeed*
revenir *to come back* (formed from **re–** and **venir**)
venir *to come*

un avis *an opinion*
une carte *an à la carte menu* (see also Module 3)
un client / une cliente *a client, a customer* (male/female)
une crème *a cream* (dairy or cosmetic)
une crème (au) caramel *a caramel custard*

une gare *a station* (railway, bus)
Internet *the internet* (no definite article, always an initial capital)
un menu *a fixed-price menu*
un mur *a wall*
un plat *a dish, a course* (meal)
un poisson *a fish*
un quartier *a neighbourhood, district*
un rendez-vous *a meeting*

après-demain *the day after tomorrow*
cher / chère *expensive*
froid(e) *cold* (see above, **refroidir**)
rapidement *quickly*
car *because*
devant *in front of*
ensemble *together*
maintenant *now*
plutôt que *rather than*
presque *nearly, almost*
tout de suite *straight away, right now*
vers *towards, around*
voici *here* (designates an object close to the speaker)
voilà *there* (designates an object distant from the speaker)

Par ici *This way* (literally "by here")
Avec plaisir *With pleasure*

Telling the time is a reflex. The best way to acquire that immediate response in a foreign language is to look at your watch, phone or clock regularly and read the time aloud. Simple, but effective!

EXERCISES

1. CONJUGATE THE VERBS IN PARENTHESES

a. Elle (*maigrir* : _ _ _ _ _ _ _) mais son mari (*grossir* : _ _ _ _ _ _) – il mange trop.

b. Steve essaie de parler correctement le français mais il ne (*réussir* : _ _ _ _ _ _ _) pas toujours.

c. Vous (*choisir* : _ _ _ _ _ _ _ _ _) toujours une crème caramel pour le dessert. – Mais toi aussi !

d. C'est un nouveau quartier que nous (*découvrir* : _ _ _ _ _ _ _ _ _ _) ensemble.

e. Finissez votre plat : il va (*refroidir* : _ _ _ _ _ _ _ _ _).

2. PUT THE VERBS INTO THE NEGATIVE OR INTERROGATIVE (*EST-CE QUE*) FORMS, AS INDICATED

a. Je (*remplir*, negative) mon assiette car je ne veux pas grossir. →

b. Vous (*finir*, interrogative) votre dessert ? J'ai très faim ! →

c. Le problème avec Anne-Marie et Michel est qu'ils (*réfléchir*, negative). →

d. Nous (*choisir*, negative) nos amis. Ils viennent vers nous. →

e. Ils (*revenir*, interrogative) demain ? →

3. *QUELLE HEURE EST-IL ?* WRITE THESE TIMES OUT IN FULL
08

a. 11.45   d. 9.40   g. 1.35

b. 6.10   e. 8.30   h. 2.50

c. 3.15   f. 4.25   i. 9.05

4. TRANSLATE THESE SENTENCES INTO FRENCH*
08

a. Here is your table and there is the menu, on the wall. →

b. What are you going to choose? – Let me think. →

c. We (*two possibilities*) don't have time to eat together. I have a meeting. →

d. Do they know a good place in the neighbourhood? →

e. Let's go right away. – No, let's come back the day after tomorrow. →

* Unless otherwise specified, use the formal **vous** to translate you.

7.
AN APPOINTMENT

UN RENDEZ-VOUS

AIMS	NOTIONS

AIMS

- CONSOLIDATE YOUR KNOWLEDGE
- EXPRESS TIME USING THE 24 HOUR CLOCK
- LEARN TO SPELL

NOTIONS

- EXPRESS AN OBLIGATION
- DEFINE A TIME PERIOD
- DESCRIBE THINGS AND ACTIONS

YOU'RE EARLY.

– I have [an] appointment with Mr Desprat at 3pm *(15 hours)*.

– Okay. What is your name?

– My name is Juvigny, Romain Juvigny.

– Can you spell it please?

– Of course: J-U-V-I-G-N-Y

– But you're early: it's 2.30pm *(14 hours 30)*. Sit [down] in the waiting room over there. I'll inform *(warn)* Mr Desprat. There is a coffee machine in front of the lift and [some] cups on the table next to [it]. You have [some] sugar and [some] spoons in one of the drawers under the desk. Help *(serve)* yourself *(you)*. It's free.

– Thank you very much. You're very kind. … Um, excuse me: I think that the machine is not working / doesn't work.

– You have [to] turn it on *(light it)*. Press *(on)* the green button, at the bottom left.

(Later)

– Miss, I have been waiting *(I wait)* for three quarters of [an] hour. I have to leave at 4pm *(16 hours)* at the latest because I have another meeting.

– I'm sorry *(regret)*, but Mr Desprat is very busy at the moment. He's currently on the telephone with a colleague in Belgium and he has to finish an urgent dossier before 15.45. Can you wait *(still)* 10 minutes [more]? I know he really wants to meet you.

– Well, OK. Ten minutes or so, but no more. In any case, your boss is late.

– Oh no, sir, it's his watch that is not on time *(at the hour)*.

– J'ai rendez-vous avec Monsieur Desprat à quinze heures.

– D'accord. Quel est votre nom ?

– Je m'appelle Juvigny, Romain Juvigny.

– Pouvez-vous l'épeler s'il vous plaît ?

– Bien sûr : J-U-V-I-G-N-Y

– Mais vous êtes en avance : il est quatorze heures trente. Asseyez-vous dans la salle d'attente là-bas. Je vais prévenir Monsieur Desprat. Il y a une machine à café devant l'ascenseur et des tasses sur la table à côté. Vous avez du sucre et des cuillères dans un des tiroirs sous le bureau. Servez-vous. C'est gratuit.

– Merci bien. Vous êtes très gentille. … Euh, excusez-moi : je pense que la machine ne marche pas.

– Vous devez l'allumer. Appuyez sur le bouton vert, en bas à droite.

(Plus tard)

– Mademoiselle : j'attends depuis trois quarts d'heure. Je dois partir à seize heures au plus tard car j'ai un autre rendez-vous.

– Je regrette, mais Monsieur Desprat est très occupé en ce moment. Il est actuellement au téléphone avec un collègue en Belgique et il doit terminer un dossier urgent avant quinze heures quarante-cinq. Pouvez-vous attendre encore dix minutes ? Je sais qu'il a très envie de vous rencontrer.

– Bon, d'accord. Une dizaine de minutes, mais pas plus. En tout cas, votre patron est en retard.

– Ah non, monsieur, c'est sa montre qui n'est pas à l'heure.

■ UNDERSTANDING THE DIALOGUE

WORDS AND PHRASES

→ Here are the 26 letters of the alphabet*:

A	a	J	zhee	S	es
B	bay	K	ka	T	tay
C	say	L	el	U	ü
D	day	M	em	V	vay
E	eu	N	en	W	doobl-vay
F	ef	O	o	X	iks
G	zhay	P	pay	Y	ee grek
H	ash	Q	kü	Z	zed
I	ee	R	air		

* See the introduction for information on pronunciation, as well as on accents (é, è, for example), diacritical marks (ë) and the ligature (œ).

– In this module, pay special attention to the **u** sound, which has no equivalent in English. One simple way to pronounce this vowel is to purse your lips to say [ou], then, without moving them, say [ee]. The sound should be nasal. (In our figurative pronunciation, we represent it as /[ü]/). Listen carefully to the recording to identify the difference between **sur** and **sous**.

– Take care not to confuse the letters **g** /[zhay]/ and **j** /[zhee]/.

– The letters **w** and **k** are found chiefly in loan words. The former is usually pronounced as a semivowel, like in English (**un week-end, le web**) but, very occasionally – despite being called *double-v* – as a fricative "v" (**un wagon**). The latter has the same pronunciation as in English.

→ **allumer** means *to light* (a fire, a cigarette, etc.). But it also means to *switch/turn on*: **Allumez la lumière avant d'entrer dans la chambre**, *Turn on the light before going into the bedroom*. An electrical switch is called **un interrupteur** (because it interrupts the flow of electric current).

→ **marcher**, *to walk* (see Module 5), is the origin of the English verb *to march*. But, when applied to a machine or a system, it also means *to work*: **Comment marche cette machine ?**, *How does this machine work?* In familiar French, **Ça marche !** is often the affirmative answer to a request or a suggestion: **Je veux partir demain matin. – Ça marche !**, *I want to leave tomorrow morning. – That's fine!*

→ The 24-hour clock is used not only in formal contexts such as travel timetables, business hours and TV schedules, but also when talking to friends or colleagues about appointments, plans and other everyday events.

It is very simple to use: simply state the hour, from 1 to 24, followed by **heure(s)** then the number of minutes: **neuf heures dix** = *9.10 am*; **vingt-deux heures quarante-cinq** = *11.45 pm*, etc. You do not need to add **du matin, de l'après-midi** or **du soir**.

Note that *noon* and *midnight* can be expressed either as **douze heures** and **vingt-quatre heures**, respectively, or as **midi** and **minuit**.

The system can take some getting used to (for example, not confusing **16 h 00** with 6 o'clock!) but it is ultimately very logical. So if the clock on your cellphone is set to a 12-hour cycle, switch it immediately to the 24-hour mode and start practising!

→ **dizaine**, *approximately ten*. The suffix **-aine** can be added to multiples of ten, as well as to fifteen, to give an approximate number: **Il faut attendre une vingtaine de minutes**, *You have to wait about 20 minutes*. **Il y a une trentaine d'élèves dans la classe**, *There are about 30 students in the class*. Lastly, when talking about time, **une quinzaine** can mean a *fortnight* (French measures 15 days, compared with 14 nights in English).

CULTURE NOTES

Like many western countries, France is increasingly becoming a 24-hour economy. Big cities such as Paris and Lyon resemble London or New York when it comes to time-poverty. Nevertheless, in smaller towns, the pace can be more relaxed, with many shops closing for several hours at lunchtime.

From a business perspective, things have changed considerably in the past decades. Officially, *the working week* (**la semaine de travail**) is still 35 hours (cut from 39hrs at the turn of the last century), although companies have an increasing amount of flexibility to negotiate longer work periods. The official holiday entitlement is still five weeks. Being *on time* (**à l'heure**) for business appointments is very important, but socially there is greater leeway.

Discovering these cultural differences is one of the pleasures of learning a language.

◆ GRAMMAR

DEPUIS

Depuis (literally "from then") translates both *for* and *since*, regardless of whether we are referring to a specific date or period of time. It is used with the present tense if the action being described began in the past and continues into the present, **Mon oncle habite à Rouen depuis 2005**, *My uncle has lived in Rouen since 2005*. **Il travaille comme informaticien depuis dix ans**, *He has worked as a computer analyst for ten years*.

There is a different rule for the negative form, which we will see when we learn the past tense.

MORE PREPOSITIONS AND ADVERBS

In this module, we have learned **sous**, *under / beneath*: **Les boutons sont sous le bureau**, *The buttons are under the desk.* Let's revise all the prepositions we have learned so far:

à	to / at	par	by
avant	before	**pendant**	during
après	after	**pour**	for
chez	at/to the home of	**près de**	near
depuis	since /for	**sous**	under
derrière	behind	**dans**	in
devant	in front of	**sur**	on
en	in	**vers**	towards
jusqu'au / à la	until / up to		

Two more useful words are the adverbs **là-bas**, *over there* – **Où est la salle d'attente ? –Là-bas, près de l'ascenseur.** *Where is the waiting room? – Over there, next to the lift* – and **en bas**, *at the bottom.* **Le bouton est en bas**, *The button is at the bottom.*

▲ CONJUGATION

DEVOIR

Another very useful – and irregular – verb, **devoir** means *must* or *to have to* (French makes no distinction between the two forms). Here is the present tense:

je dois	I must	**nous devons**	we must
tu dois	you must	**vous devez**	you must
il/elle doit	he / she / it must	**ils/elles doivent**	they must

The negative forms are:

je ne dois pas	I must not	nous ne devons pas	we must not
tu ne dois pas	you must not	vous ne devez pas	you must not
il/elle ne doit pas	he/she/it must not	ils/elles ne doivent pas	they must not

And the interrogative forms, using **est-ce que**, are:

Est-ce que je dois... ?	Must I...?	Est-ce que nous devons... ?	Must we...?
Est-ce que tu dois... ?	Must you...?	Est-ce que vous devez... ?	Must you...?
Est-ce qu'il/elle doit... ?	Must he/she/it...?	Est-ce qu'ils/ elles doivent... ?	Must they...?

Like two other important irregular verbs, **pouvoir** (can) and **vouloir** (to want), **devoir** can be followed by an infinitive without a preposition: **Tu dois partir dans une heure**, You have to leave in an hour. **Vous ne devez pas sortir après vingt-trois heures**, You mustn't go out after 11 pm. **Est-ce que je dois appuyer sur ce bouton ?**, Do I have to press this button?

There are many more shades of meaning – for instance, **devoir** can imply a supposition or a probability – but we will see these later on.

● EXERCISES

1. CONJUGATE THE VERB *DEVOIR* IN THE PRESENT INDICATIVE

a. Nous .... partir dans une heure au plus tard.

b. Je .... finir ce dossier avant de rencontrer le client.

c. Désolé, mais tu .... attendre encore une dizaine de minutes.

d. Vous .... appuyer sur le bouton pour allumer la machine.

e. Ils .... parler avec un collègue avant de répondre.

2. PUT *DEVOIR* INTO THE NEGATIVE OR THE INTERROGATIVE WITH *EST-CE QUE...*

a. Tu *(negative)* arriver en avance pour le rendez-vous. →

b. Je *(interrogative)* allumer la machine ? →

c. Vous *(negative)* manger trop de viande si vous ne voulez pas grossir. →

d. Tu *(interrogative)* acheter les billets en ligne ? →

3. CHOOSE THE CORRECT PREPOSITION

a. La machine est *(under)* la table. →

b. Attendez-nous *(in front of)* la galerie. →

c. La salle d'attente est *(behind)* l'ascenseur. →

d. Est-ce que je dois marcher *(up to)* carrefour ? →

e. Je l'attends *(for)* une heure et demie. →

f. Marie travaille comme informaticienne *(for)* quinze ans. →

4. TRANSLATE THESE SENTENCES INTO FRENCH

09

a. Can you spell your name please? – R.O.M.A.I.N. T.A.R.D.Y →

b. Turn on the lights before going into the kitchen. →

c. There are about thirty people in front of the museum. →

d. We have to leave at five o'clock* at the latest. →

e. Mr Desprats wants to meet you. – He's very kind but I have to leave. →

* Use two different ways to give the time

VOCABULARY

appuyer *to push, to press*
arriver *to arrive*
épeler *to spell*
être occupé(e) *to be busy*
  (masculine/feminine)
marcher *to walk, to work* (machine,
  etc.)
prévenir *to warn, to inform*
regretter *to regret*
rencontrer *to meet*
s'asseoir *to sit (down)*
servir *to serve*
terminer *to finish* (think "terminate")

à côté (de) *alongside, next to*
à droite *on/to the right*
à l'heure *on time*
avant *before* (time)
depuis *since / for*
devant *in front of*
en avance *early, ahead of schedule*
en bas *at the bottom*
gratuit *free*
là-bas *over there* (note the grave
  accent on the **à**)
sous *under*

la Belgique *Belgium*
un bouton *a button* (machine,
  clothes, etc.)
un(e) collègue *a colleague*
une dizaine *ten or so*
un dossier *a dossier, a file*
une machine à café *a coffee
  machine*
une montre *a watch*
un patron *a boss*

Asseyez-vous *Sit down*
au plus tard *at the latest*
Je regrette… *I'm sorry*
Servez-vous *Help yourself/
  youselves*

Regular revision is vitally important when you start learning a language. Don't hesitate to go back to a previous module if you have forgotten or are not sure about something.

II

MAKING

CONVERSATION

8.
THIS WEEKEND

CE WEEK-END

AIMS	NOTIONS

- TALK ABOUT PLANS
- DISCUSS THE WEATHER
- LEARN NUMBERS FROM 70 UPWARDS

- OTHER NEGATIVE FORMS
- VERBS ENDING IN *-OIR*
- PARTITIVE ARTICLE CHANGE

WHAT HAVE YOU BEEN UP TO?

– Sit down, Suzie. These chairs are really comfortable. Do you want a cigarette?

– No thanks, I don't smoke any more *(not smoke more)*.

– Well have *(take)* a coffee.

– I don't drink *(of)* coffee after lunch: it prevents me from sleeping *(to sleep)*.

– Is that true? Maybe you want a tea?

– I don't take *(of)* tea, either. I don't like the taste. I don't want anything *(nothing)*, thank you.

– You're really tiresome. Tell me, what are you up to *(do you become)* at the moment?

– I'm very busy this week, as usual. This afternoon, I have a sports class; that's why I'm wearing these trainers. And this weekend I really must go down *(in the)* south to see my grandparents. My grandfather is *(has)* more than 75 *(years)* and my grandmother is *(has)* nearly 82 *(years)*. They no longer travel *(not travel more)* and, in any case, they never come to Paris and they don't have *(receive)* many visitors. So I try to see them at least two or three times a *(by)* year. But it's not easy because they live in the country and there are no more direct trains. I'm obliged to rent a car at Nice station *(station of Nice)* and do more than 95 kilometres. But I can't disappoint them.

– What is the weather there at the moment? *(Some)* Rain? *(Some)* Clouds?

– Not at all! It's summer and it is *(makes)* fine and hot, with lots of sun. It never rains in the Midi – or very rarely.

— Assieds-toi, Suzie. Ces chaises sont très confortables. Veux-tu une cigarette ?

— Non merci, je ne fume plus.

— Alors prends un café.

— Je ne bois pas de café après le déjeuner : ça m'empêche de dormir.

— C'est vrai ? Tu veux un thé, peut-être ?

— Je ne prends pas de thé non plus. Je n'aime pas le goût. Je ne veux rien, merci.

— Tu es vraiment pénible ! Dis-mois, qu'est-ce que tu deviens en ce moment ?

— Je suis très occupée cette semaine, comme d'habitude. Cet après-midi, j'ai un cours de sport ; c'est pour ça que je porte ces baskets. Et ce week-end je dois absolument descendre dans le sud pour voir mes grands-parents. Mon grand-père a plus de soixante-quinze ans, et ma grand-mère a presque quatre-vingt-deux ans. Ils ne voyagent plus et, de toute façon, ils ne viennent jamais à Paris et ils ne reçoivent pas beaucoup de visiteurs. Alors j'essaie de les voir au moins deux ou trois fois par an. Mais ce n'est pas facile parce qu'ils habitent à la campagne et il n'y a plus de trains directs. Je suis obligée de louer une voiture à la gare de Nice et faire plus de quatre-vingt-quinze kilomètres. Mais je ne peux pas les décevoir.

— Quel temps fait-il là-bas en ce moment ? De la pluie ? Des nuages ?

— Pas du tout ! C'est l'été et il fait beau et chaud, avec beaucoup de soleil. Il ne pleut jamais dans le Midi — ou très rarement.

■ UNDERSTANDING THE DIALOGUE
WORDS AND PHRASES

→ In Module 5, we learned the numbers from 1 to 69. Today we will continue counting, from 70 to 99. For this, you'll need to do a bit of arithmetic: 70 is treated as 60 plus 10 = **soixante-dix**, so the next nine numbers are 60+11 (**soixante et onze**), 60+12 (**soixante-douze**), etc.

70	soixante-dix	75	soixante-quinze
71	soixante et onze	76	soixante-seize
72	soixante-douze	77	soixante-dix-sept
73	soixante-treize	78	soixante-dix-huit
74	soixante-quatorze	79	soixante-dix-neuf

Eighty is four twenties, or **quatre-vingts**:

80	quatre-vingts	85	quatre-vingt-cinq
81	quatre-vingt-un	86	quatre-vingt-six
82	quatre-vingt-deux	87	quatre-vingt-sept
83	quatre-vingt-trois	88	quatre-vingt-huit
84	quatre-vingt-quatre	89	quatre-vingt-neuf

When we reach 90, we revert to the same system as for 70:

90	quatre-vingt-dix	95	quatre-vingt-quinze
91	quatre-vingt-onze	96	quatre-vingt-seize
92	quatre-vingt-douze	97	quatre-vingt-dix-sept
93	quatre-vingt-treize	98	quatre-vingt-dix-huit
94	quatre-vingt-quatorze	99	quatre-vingt-dix-neuf

100 is **cent** – and we start over again (**cent-un, cent-deux**, etc.).
Belgium and Switzerland have slightly different – and arguably more logical – systems. Both use **septante** for 70 (thus **septante et un** for 71, etc.) and **nonante** for 90 (**nonante et un**, etc.). In addition, Switzerland often uses **huitante** for 80. (Remember that English once had a similar construction, evidenced in Abraham Lincoln's Gettysburg Address, which begins *Fourscore and seven years ago...*). But even if you use the French system in Belgium (or vice versa) you will almost certainly be understood.

The use of hyphens and the terminal **–s** on **vingt** is quite complex, so for the time being you should concentrate on learning the numbers and acquiring the automatic reflex of seeing and saying them aloud.

Lastly, there is only one word for 0 in French: **zéro**, which translates both *zero* and *nought* as well as the *oh* used in phone numbers. Moreover, one reason why learning the numbering system is so important is that phone numbers are read and pronounced in pairs, so, for instance, 17 is not "one seven" but **dix-sept**. We'll see this in more detail later on.

→ The weather, **le temps**, is a topic of conversation in most languages, and French is no exception. We have already seen that the verb **faire** is used instead of *to be* (**Il fait beau**, *It's fine*, Module 5). Here are some more common phrases: **Quel temps fait-il ?** *What's the weather like?* (using **est-ce que** rather than the inversion would make the sentence too long). **Il fait mauvais**, *The weather is bad*. **Il fait chaud / froid**, *It's hot / cold*. **Il pleut**, *It's raining* (or *It rains*, depending on the context).

To describe the type of weather we use a noun, instead of an adjective as in English, and **il y a**: **Il y a du soleil / du vent / de la pluie / des nuages**, etc. *It's sunny /windy / rainy, / cloudy*, etc.

Remember that **le temps** means both *the weather* and *the time*, but the context will make the meaning clear. Lastly, you might want to check *the weather forecast*. The official term is **le bulletin météorologique** but almost everyone uses the abbreviated form **la météo**: **Quelle est la météo pour demain ?**, *What's the weather forecast for tomorrow?*

→ **devenir** means *to become* and is conjugated like **venir** (Module 5): But the idiomatic expression **Qu'est-ce que vous devenez / tu deviens ?** (literally "What are you becoming?") is the equivalent of *How are you getting on?* or *What have you been up to?*: **Qu'est-ce que tu deviens, mon ami ? – Je travaille à Marseille**, *What have you been up to, my friend? – I'm working in Marseille*.

→ **non plus** (literally "no more") is the equivalent of *either/neither*. **Je n'aime pas le café, et je ne bois pas de thé non plus**, *I don't like coffee and I don't drink tea either*. **Non plus** can also be used with emphatic pronouns: **Je n'aime pas le thé. – Moi non plus**, *I don't like tea. – Neither do I / Me neither*. In this context, it's the negative form of **Moi aussi**.

CULTURE NOTES

The noun **midi**, as we know, means *noon*, the middle of the day. But **le Midi** refers expressly to the region of southern France comprising the Mediterranean coastline, from the Italian to the Spanish borders, and its hinterland. It includes glamorous seaside resorts such as Nice and Cannes but also spectacularly beautiful mountainous regions (**les Alpes de Haute Provence**), the olive groves and lavender fields of **la Provence** and the sunny plains of **le Languedoc**.

Culturally, **le Midi** is a mixture of French, Italian and Catalan influences. Traditionally, the gateway to the southern region is the Roman-founded town of **Valence**, hence the expression **À Valence le Midi commence**, *The Midi begins at Valence* although other towns in the region also lay claim to that title!

The north-south divide in France – sometimes referred to humorously as the butter/olive oil partition – is a historical reality reflected in an age-old language divide: people who lived in northern France originally spoke Gallo-Roman while those in the south used Roman-inspired Latin. The differences were epitomised in the two words for "*yes*": **oïl** in the north, **oc** in the south – hence **Languedoc**.

But why **le Midi** rather than **le sud**? The word comes from the Latin for midday, when the sun is at its highest and, seen from the northern hemisphere, appears in the south*. In modern French, **le sud** refers to the southern half of the country in general whereas **le Midi** is a specific region.

* One of the main railway stations in Belgium's capital is **la Gare du Midi**, known in English as *Brussels-South station*.

◆ GRAMMAR
OTHER NEGATIVE FORMS

We know how to negate verbs using **ne... pas**. We can also replace **pas** by one of several adverbs to alter the meaning of the sentence. But, unlike English, we always use the double negative:

– **ne... plus**, *no longer*, *any more*:

Je ne l'aime plus, *I don't love him/her/it any more*.

Ils n'habitent plus à cette adresse, *They no longer live at this address*.

– **ne... jamais**, *never*, *ever*:

Tu ne me téléphones jamais ! *You never phone me!*

Je ne vais jamais au travail en voiture, *I never drive to work* (go to work by car)

– **ne... rien**, *nothing*:

Qu'est ce qu'il veut, ton frère ? – Il ne veut rien, *What does your brother want? – He doesn't want anything*.

Le chinois est trop difficile ! Je ne comprends rien, *Chinese is too difficult! I don't understand anything*.

There are several more constructions using **ne** and an adverb, but these three are the most commonly used.

DEMONSTRATIVE ADJECTIVES

These adjectives are used to point out (or "demonstrate") something or somebody. They agree in number and, in most cases, gender. They are **ce** (masculine singular), **cette** (feminine singular), and **ces** (masculine and feminine plural). Additionally, if a masculine singular noun begins with a vowel or an **h-**, **ce** become **cet** (and sounds exactly the same as **cette**). Unlike English, French demonstrative adjectives do not indicate the speaker's position relative to the object or person being "demonstrated" (*this vs that, these vs those*).

Cette chaise n'est pas très confortable, *This/That chair isn't very comfortable.*
Qu'est-ce que tu fais ce week-end? *What are you doing this weekend?*
Ces cours sont très intéressants, *These lessons are very interesting.*
Ce magasin est fermé cet après-midi, *This / that shop is closed this afternoon.*
(Be careful not to confuse **cette / cet** with **c'est**)

DU OR *DE*? PARTITIVE ARTICLE CHANGE

Definite articles do not change if a sentence is put into the negative. For example: **J'aime le café**, *I like coffee*, becomes **Je n'aime pas le café**. But if we use one of the partitive articles (**du, de la, d'** or **des**) to express an indefinite quantity, they change to **de** (instead of **du** and **de la**) or **d'** (instead of **de l'**) in a negative sentence. For example:
Il achète du pain → **Il n'achète pas de pain**, *He's buying (some) bread* → *He's not buying (any) bread.*
Je bois de l'eau → **Je ne bois pas d'eau**, *I drink (some) water* → *I don't drink (any) water.*
Remember: if no quantity is expressed, use **de / d'** in negative sentences.

PARTICIPLE AGREEMENT

We know that adjectives agree with the gender of the noun they are associated with. The same rule therefore applies to participle adjectives. For instance, a man who is busy or obliged to do something will say: **Je suis occupé** and **Je suis obligé** whereas a woman will say **Je suis occupée** and **Je suis obligée**. In this case, there is no difference in pronunciation. We'll learn more about agreement shortly when we work on the past tense.

▲ CONJUGATIONS

VERBS ENDING IN -OIR

These belong to the third group, made up of mostly irregular verbs and divided into three subgroups whose endings are **-oir**, **-ir** and **-re**.

The **-oir** subgroup comprises some of the most frequently used verbs in French, including four we already know: **avoir** (Module 1), **vouloir** and **pouvoir** (Module 3), **savoir** (Module 5) and **devoir** (Module 7).

Another important verb in this subgroup, used extensively in everyday conversation, is **voir**, *to see*.

je vois	*I see*	nous voyons	*we see*
tu vois	*you see*	vous voyez	*you see*
il/elle voit	*he/she/it sees*	ils/elles voient	*they see*

The negative is formed, as usual, with **ne... pas** and the interrogative with **est-ce que** or by inversion: **Je ne vois pas**; **Est-ce que tu vois.../Vois-tu ?**

A handful of verbs ending in – **cevoir** – notably **recevoir**, *to receive*, and **décevoir**, *to disappoint* – follow the same pattern:

je reçois	*I receive*	nous recevons	*we receive*
tu reçois	*you receive*	vous recevez	*you receive*
il/elle reçoit	*he/she/it receives*	ils/elles reçoivent	*they receive*

(Note how the **v** of the stem is dropped for the first three persons but returns for **nous**, **vous** and **ils/elles**.)

Lastly, **pleuvoir**, *to rain*, is also irregular but it is an impersonal verb (i.e. used only in the infinitive and the third person): **Il va pleuvoir demain**, *It's going to rain*, **Il ne pleut pas aujourd'hui**, *It isn't raining today*.

▲ EXERCISES

1. CONJUGATE THESE VERBS IN THE CORRECT FORM

a. Nous (*recevoir*, negative: …………………………) beaucoup de visiteurs en été.

b. Est-ce que vous (*voir* …………………………..) ce que je veux dire ?

c. Est-ce qu'il (*pleuvoir*…………………………...) à Nantes, Barbara ?

d. Mes grands-parents (*vouloir*, negative: …………………………...) venir me voir dans le Midi.

e. Tu me (*décevoir*…………………………...) beaucoup !

● VOCABULARY

boire *to drink*
dormir *to sleep*
décevoir *to disappoint*
descendre *to descend, to go down*
devenir *to become*
empêcher *to prevent*
fumer *to smoke*
pleuvoir *to rain*
louer *to rent*
recevoir *to receive, to get*
voyager *to travel* (see **agence de voyages**, Module 2)

la campagne *the country(side)*
une grande-mère *a grandmother*
un grand-parent *a grandparent*
un grand-père *a grandfather*
le Midi *the south of France, the Midi*
un nuage *a cloud*
la pluie *the rain*
un train *a train*
un visiteur *a visitor*

absolument *absolutely*
comme d'habitude *as usual*
confortable *comfortable* (notice the "n")
de toute façon *in any case*
non plus *either/neither*
pénible *tiresome, difficult*
rarement *rarely*

Assieds-toi *Sit down* (informal)
Je suis très occupé(e) *I'm very busy*
Quel temps fait-il ? *What's the weather like?*
Qu'est-ce que tu deviens ? *What's happening with you?*

2. TRANSLATE THESE SIMPLE SENTENCES USING *NE... JAMAIS, NE...PLUS* **OR** *NE...RIEN*

10

a. I don't love them anymore. →

b. We never drive to work. →

c. You (*familiar*) don't understand anything. →

d. My grandparents never come to Paris. →

e. I don't smoke any more. →

3. WRITE THESE NUMBERS IN FULL* THEN READ THEM ALOUD

10

a. 77..

b. 89 ....

c. 93 ....

d. 74...

e. 80...

f. 71...

g. 92 ....

h. 78...

i. 85...

j. 91...

k. 99...

l. 88...

* Use the French system

4. TRANSLATE THESE SENTENCES INTO FRENCH

10

a. Simon is very busy at the moment. – As usual! →

b. What's the weather like in Marseille this week? – It's fine and very hot. →

c. I don't drink coffee in the afternoon. – Me neither. It prevents me from sleeping. →

d. There are no longer any direct trains. – Is that true? →

e. What's happening with you? – I really must rent a car and go down south this weekend. →

Don't forget to flip quickly through this book on a regular basis and read the page numbers aloud!

9.
HOLIDAYS

LES VACANCES

AIMS	NOTIONS

- ASK ABOUT POSSIBILITIES
- EXPRESS PREFERENCES
- GIVE DATES (DAYS, MONTHS)

- QUESTION WORDS
- CONDITIONAL (FIRST NOTIONS)
- AGREEMENT OF ADJECTIVES

AT THE TRAVEL AGENT

– Can I *(inform you)* give you some information?

– I would like to take a holiday *(some holidays)* because I'm very tired.

– When would you like to leave? And what would you like to do?

– I don't have any firm plans *(precise projects)*. Do you have any suggestions?

– There's a lot of choice: skiing in the Alps, [a] beach on the Riviera, a cruise ... take a look *(throw an eye)* at this catalogue. When are you free, *(at)* what period?

– I would really like to leave during the second fortnight *(of)* in May.

– Why in May? Why not in June or July?

– Because there are a lot of long weekends *(bridges)* in May and I would like to take advantage of them!

– I get you *(heard)*. But you know, it's more expensive. How do you want to leave *(You want to leave how)*? By *(in)* train? By *(in)* plane?

– By *(in)* train if it's possible. I'm afraid of planes *(the plane)*. What *(of what)* are you thinking [of]?

– I have a stay in Corsica at the hotel Bonaparte in Calvi, flight and accommodation included *(understood)*, with some excursions. It's a very beautiful spot. But that's right *(it's true)*, you don't want to fly. If not, you could spend a week in a small seaside resort.

– How much does that cost? I hope that it's not too expensive?

– No, only 400 euros, travel included.

– You're right: it's cheap. And what are the dates?

– From Monday 20 to Friday 24 May. Is that okay with you *(it goes you)*?

– It suits me perfectly. I'm very happy. I'm going to pack *(make my suitcases)*!

— Est-ce que je peux vous renseigner ?

— Je voudrais prendre des vacances parce que je suis très fatiguée.

— Quand voudriez-vous partir ? Et que voudriez-vous faire ?

— Je n'ai pas de projets précis. Avez-vous des suggestions ?

— Il y a beaucoup de choix : du ski dans les Alpes, de la plage sur la Côte d'Azur, une croisière… jetez un œil à ce catalogue. Quand êtes-vous libre, à quelle période ?

— J'aimerais beaucoup partir pendant la première quinzaine de mai.

— Pourquoi en mai ? Pourquoi pas en juin ou juillet ?

— Parce qu'il y a beaucoup de ponts en mai et je voudrais en profiter !

— Entendu. Mais vous savez, c'est plus cher. Vous voulez partir comment ? En train ? En avion ?

— En train si c'est possible. J'ai peur de l'avion. À quoi pensez-vous ?

— J'ai un séjour en Corse à l'hôtel Bonaparte à Calvi, vol et hébergement compris, avec quelques excursions. C'est un très bel endroit. Mais c'est vrai, vous ne voulez pas prendre l'avion. Sinon, vous pourriez passer une semaine dans une petite station balnéaire.

— Combien ça coûte ? J'espère que ce n'est pas trop cher ?

— Non, seulement quatre cents euros, voyage compris.

— Vous avez raison : c'est bon marché. Et quelles sont les dates ?

— Du lundi vingt au vendredi vingt-quatre mai. Ça vous va ?

— Ça me va parfaitement. Je suis très heureuse. Je vais faire mes valises !

■ UNDERSTANDING THE DIALOGUE
WORDS AND PHRASES

→ Months of the year: despite the final **s**, **un mois** (pl. **les mois**), *a month*, is singular (**moi** means *me*). Like the days of the week (Module 4), the month names all begin with a small letter.

janvier	January	juillet	July
février	February	août	August
mars	March	septembre	September
avril	April	octobre	October
mai	May	novembre	November
juin	June	décembre	December

The French nouns have the same roots as their English counterparts, so they should be easy to remember. The adjective *monthly* is **mensuel(le)**.

→ **renseigner** means *to provide information* (it shares the same root as **enseigner**, *to teach*, Module 2). **Pouvez-vous me renseigner s'il vous plait ?**, *Can you give me some information, please?*. In a public building, the sign **RENSEIGNEMENTS** denotes the information desk. You may also come across the verb if asked to fill in a form giving personal information: **Renseignez cette fiche, s'il vous plait**, *Fill out this form, please.*

→ **libre** means *free* in the sense of "not occupied" (compared with **gratuit**, *free of charge*, seen in Module 7). You might ask a taxi driver **Êtes-vous libre ?**, *Are you free?* The sign **Entrée libre** on a shopfront means *Feel free to browse* (literally "Entrance free").

→ **entendu** is the past participle of **entendre**, *to hear*. You can use it to acknowledge that you have heard and agree with someone. **Nous partons à dix heures. – Entendu.** *We're leaving at 10am. – Right.* Likewise, **compris** is the past participle of **comprendre**, *to understand*. It is used as an adjective to mean *included*, particularly on menus (**Service compris**, *Service included*) and package deal offers (**Tout compris**, *All inclusive*).

→ **un œil**, *an eye* (pron. [ahn_euy]) is irregular in the plural: **les yeux** [layzyeu]. The expression **jeter un œil** (or sometimes **un coup d'œil**) means *to take a look at, to glance at*. The only other common nouns with an irregular plural are **mesdames**, **mesdemoiselles** and **messieurs** (*ladies, misses, gentlemen*). This is logical because the singular possessive adjectives that form part of the words, **mon-** and

ma-, become **mes-** in the plural. (The three words are often used to commence a speech, just like *Ladies* and *Gentlemen*).

→ **peur**, *fear*, and **raison**, *reason*, are two more of the nouns used in expressions with **avoir** rather than *to be* (Module 4): **J'ai très peur,** *I'm very scared.* **Tu as raison, ce n'est pas cher,** *You're right, it's not expensive.*

→ **bon marché** (literally "good market") is an adjective meaning *inexpensive*: **Ce magasin de sport est vraiment bon marché,** *This sports shop is really inexpensive.* An alternative is to put **cher**, *expensive*, into the negative: **Ce magasin n'est pas cher.**

→ **Ça vous va ?** (familiar: **Ça te va ?**) is a common way of asking whether something is suitable: **L'hôtel coûte cent-cinquante euros la nuit. Ça te va ?** *The hotel costs 150 euros per night. Is that OK with you?* To answer, use **oui** or **non**, or, alternatively, the personal pronoun: **Ça me va / Ça nous va.**

CULTURE NOTES

Les vacances, *holidays*, are an important part of French life. Under current legislation, full-time workers are entitled to five weeks' annual paid holiday (the official term is **les congés payés**). This, together with a number of official days off, **les jours fériés** (1st November, 15th August), **les fêtes de fin d'année** (*the end-of-year holiday period*), **la Fête du travail** (*Labour Day*, 1st May), **la Fête Nationale** (*Bastille Day*, 14th July) and half a dozen other official holidays, makes France one of the most generous countries in terms of vacation entitlement. As for vocabulary, **les vacances** (generally plural) means a *vacation*, **un congé** is a *day off* or a *leave period*, and **une fête** (the original of our word a *feast*) is a *celebratory holiday*. (In addition, some Catholics still wish each other **Bonne fête** on their saint's day.)

Another particularity is **le pont** (literally, "the bridge"): if a public holiday falls, say, on a Tuesday or a Thursday, many people will take an extra day's holiday to make a long weekend – hence the "bridge". (Should the holiday fall on a Wednesday, some will take another day or two, turning **un pont** into **un viaduc**, *viaduct*!) Despite all this rest and merrymaking, however, France has one of the highest rates of labour productivity in the world.

◆ GRAMMAR

QUESTION WORDS

In English, most question words begin with *wh-*. The equivalent in French is **qu-** or **co-**. Let's take stock of what we know:

• QU-

– **qui**, *who(m)*, is used to ask questions about people: **Qui êtes-vous ?**, *Who are you?*; **Qui vois-tu ?**, *Who(m) do you see?* In a less formal register, the interrogative form with **est-ce que** is used: **Qui est-ce que tu vois ?** And, of course, you can simply raise your voice at the end of the question, putting **qui** at the end: **Vous êtes qui ?** (Remember that *whom* is rarely used in informal English.)

– **quand**, *when*, follows the same rule as **qui**: **Quand voulez-vous venir ?**, *When do you want to come?* **Quand est-ce que tu veux venir ?**, *Tu veux venir quand?*

– **que**, *what*, is used in questions about things or actions: **Que voulez-vous ?**, *What do you want?*, **Que vois-tu ?**, *What do you see?* With **est-ce que**, the question becomes a bit longer: **Qu'est-ce que vous voulez ?** (Remember that **que** becomes **qu'** in front of a vowel.)

However, **que** cannot be used after a preposition. So, for example, if we use it in a rising-intonation interrogative, it is replaced by **quoi**: **Vous voulez quoi ?** *What do you want?*

– **quoi** is used as an initial interrogative pronoun in certain circumstances, notably the expressions **Quoi de neuf ?**, *What's new?* and **Quoi faire ?**, *What should I / we do?* **Quoi** is also used in the compound **pourquoi**, *why* (lit. *for+what*): **Pourquoi voulez-vous partir en mai ?**, *Why do you want to go away in May?*

• CO-

– **comment**, *how*, introduces a question and can be followed by all three interrogative constructions: **Comment allez-vous ?**, *How are you?*, **Comment est-ce que je peux prendre rendez-vous ?** *How can I make an appointment?*, **Comment tu vas ?**, *How are you doing?*

– **combien** means *how much / how many*. We know (Module 5) we can use the inversion, **Combien coûtent les billets ?** and also the **est-ce que** form **Combien est-ce que tu peux payer ?**, *How much can you pay/afford?* For the rising-intonation form, however, the adverb shifts to the end of the question: **Tu peux payer combien ?**, **Les billets coûtent combien ?**

The sole exception to the **qu- / co-** rule is the conjunction **où**, *where*, which follows the same format as **que**: **Où habitez-vous ?**, *Where do you live?* **Où est que vous habitez ?**, **Tu habites où ?** (Remember that **où** is the only word in French with a grave accent on the **u**.)

MORE ABOUT ADJECTIVES

We know that adjectives generally come after the noun they qualify and always agree in number and gender. There are, however, numerous exceptions, some of which we have already learned. Below we review some of the basic rules:

• Formation

By convention, dictionaries and vocabulary lists give the masculine form of adjectives. To form the feminine, we generally add a terminal **-e** (**grand** → **grande**). If the masculine ends in a vowel (**joli**, *pretty*), then the feminine (**jolie**) is pronounced identically. But if the masculine ends in a silent consonant (**petit**), that consonant is pronounced when the **-e** is added (**petite**).

• Irregular adjectives

Here are some irregular forms (i.e. the masculine singular changes its ending in the feminine):

– The final consonant doubles:

-en and **-on**: **ancien** → **ancienne** (*former, ancient*); **bon** → **bonne** (*good*). (The same rule applies to **-an** but there are very few such adjectives.)

-el, **-eil** and **-il**: **naturel** (*natural*) → **naturelle**; **pareil** (*same*) → **pareille**; **gentil** (*kind*) → **gentille**

– **-f** and **-x** change, respectively, to **-ve** and **-se** (or **-sse**): **neuf** (*new*) → **neuve**; **heureux** (*happy*) → **heureuse**; **faux** (*false, wrong*) → **fausse**.

– **-er** changes to **-ère**: **dernier** (*last*) → **dernière**

– **-et** changes to **-ète**: **complet** (*full*) → **complète**

There are more of these exceptional forms, which we will point out as we go along.

• Plurals

Most plurals are formed by adding a (silent) **s** to the singular. However, if the singular already ends in an **s**, or an **x**, the ending does not change: **un projet précis** → **des projets précis**; **un homme heureux** → **des hommes heureux**.

• Position

Most adjectives are placed directly after the noun they qualify (**un projet précis, une chaise confortable, un rendez-vous important**, etc.). If an adverb of degree, such as **très**, *very*, is used in the sentence, it is placed before the adjective: **un rendez-vous très important**. However, some very common adjectives (including **petit, grand, beau/belle/bel**) come before the noun. We will see these exceptions in Module 15.

▲ CONJUGATION

THE CONDITIONAL

The conditional mood is important because it is used to express politeness, particularly when asking questions (*Could you tell me...?*) or expressing a preference (*I would like...*). As we have already seen, the two most important verbs in these contexts are **vouloir**, *to want*, and **pouvoir**, *to be able (to)*.

• **Vouloir**: Affirmative

je voudrais	I would like	nous voudrions	we would like
tu voudrais	you would like	vous voudriez	you would like
il/elle voudrait	he/she/it would like	ils/elles voudraient	they would like

• Negative:
je ne voudrais pas, *I would not like*, etc.

• Interrogative with **est-ce que...** :
Est-ce que je voudrais ... ?, *Would I want ...?*, etc.

• **Pouvoir**: Affirmative:

je pourrais	I could	nous pourrions	we could
tu pourrais	you could	vous pourriez	you could
il/elle pourrait	he/she/it could	ils/elles pourraient	they could

• Negative:
je ne pourrais pas, *I could not*, etc.

• Interrogative with **est-ce que...** :
Est-ce que je pourrais ... ?, *Could I ...?*, etc.
Here are some simple but useful phrases:
Nous voudrions une table pour deux s'il vous plait, *We would like a table for two, please.*
Je ne voudrais pas vous déranger, *I wouldn't want to bother you.*
Est-ce que je pourrais vous poser une question ?, *May I ask you a question?*
Nous ne pourrions pas accepter votre invitation, *We couldn't accept your invitation.*
(From now on, we will give you only the indicative form of the verb in table form, unless there are any major irregularities.)

VOCABULARY

avoir peur (de) *to be afraid (of)*
avoir raison *to be right*
entendre *to hear*
faire ses valises *to pack*
renseigner *to inform*
profiter *to take advantage of*

un avion *a plane*
le choix *choice* / **un choix** *a choice*
une croisière *a cruise*
une excursion *an excursion*
l'hébergement *accommodation*
un œil (plur. **les yeux**) *an eye*
une plage *a beach*
une période *a period* (time)
un pont *a bridge* (fam: *a long weekend*)
un projet *a plan, a project*
un séjour *a stay*
le ski *skiing* / **un ski** *a ski*
une station balnéaire *a seaside resort*
une suggestion *a suggestion*
une valise *a suitcase*
un vol *a flight*

bon marché *inexpensive*
compris *included*
heureux *happy*
libre *free* (i.e. unoccupied)
mai, etc. see list of months in *Understanding the dialogue*

Entendu *I understand, I get you*
Ça vous va ? *Is that suitable?*
Ça me va *That's fine by me.*
Combien est-ce que ça coûte ? *How much does it/that cost?*

We have started to give you formal rules for things such as adjectives and interrogatives, which you have already learned. That's the Assimil method: getting you to learn by using your natural powers of assimilation rather than by following sets of rules, tables and charts. **Bonne continuation !**

▲ EXERCISES

1. CONJUGATE *VOULOIR* / *POUVOIR* IN THE CONDITIONAL

a. Nous (*pouvoir* : ....) venir en mai si vous voulez.

b. Tu (*vouloir*, interrogative with *est-ce que*: ....) un verre de vin ?

c. Mon collègue (*pouvoir*, negative: ....) rencontrer votre client avant demain.

d. Vous (*vouloir*, interrogative with *est-ce que*: ....) voir la chambre d'hôtel ?

e. Vous (*pouvoir*, interrogative with *est-ce que*: ....) nous renseigner s'il vous plait ?

2. REPHRASE THESE QUESTIONS USING THE THIRD INTERROGATIVE (INVERSION)

a. Comment est-ce que nous pouvons prendre rendez-vous ?

b. Combien est-ce que tu peux payer ?

c. Où est-ce qu'ils habitent ?

d. Pourquoi est-ce qu'elle veut partir en mai ?

e. Quand est-ce que vous voulez venir ?

3. MAKE THESE ADJECTIVES AGREE WITH THEIR NOUNS

a. des villages _ _ _ _ _ (français)

b. la semaine _ _ _ _ _ _ _ _ _ (dernier)

c. deux amies_ _ _ _ _ _ _ _ _(gentil)

d. une semaine _ _ _ _ _ (complet)

e. une femme _ _ _ _ _ _ _ _ _ (seul)

f. des croisières _ _ _ _ _ _ _ (cher)

g. une montre _ _ _ _ _ (neuf)

h. une église _ _ _ _ _ (ancien)

i. des enfants _ _ _ _ _ (heureux)

j. trois mois _ _ _ _ _ (complet)

4. TRANSLATE THESE SENTENCES INTO FRENCH

11

a. The hotel is full in June, July and August, and it closes from November to March. →

b. What are you thinking about?* – The long weekends in the second fortnight of May. →

c. How can we make an appointment? (use **est-ce que**) →

d. She's right, it's cheap: a stay in Corsica for five hundred euros. →

e. How much does it cost?** – 250 euros. – That's fine by me. →

* Formal

** Two possibilities

10.
RELAXING

SE REPOSER

AIMS	NOTIONS

- **DESCRIBE A REGULAR ROUTINE**
- **CONTRADICT AN ASSERTION**

- **PRONOMINAL VERBS**
- **MAKING ADVERBS FROM ADJECTIVES**
- **USING *ON* INSTEAD OF *NOUS***

ARE YOU BORED?

— My wife is on [a] business trip in Switzerland all *(the)* week.

— You must *(yourself)* be bored all alone at home *(in the house)*!

— On [the] contrary, I'm *(myself)* enjoying [myself] hugely. It's very relaxing, you know.

— What *(how)*, you're *(yourself)* relaxing? You're having a lie-in *(do the fat morning)*, or what?

— On [the] contrary, I *(myself)* get up very early, around half past six. First, I look quickly [at] my emails and my schedule *(agenda)*. Next, I *(myself)* wash and *(myself)* shave peacefully while *(in)* listening to the radio. I *(myself)* dress simply: I put [on] a [pair of] jeans rather than a suit. Afterwards, I don't *(myself)* hurry. I make *(myself prepare)* a good, healthy breakfast *(little lunch)* with yoghurt and fruit*(s)*.

— I'm jealous because I rarely have time to *(myself)* rest like you. I have to *(myself)* look after *(occupy)* my children, who always *(themselves)* wake up early *(at good hour)*, even [at] the weekend. [In] the evening, I *(myself)* rarely go to bed before midnight and I'm exhausted!

— I'm very lucky, I know. I begin the day gently. I work hard *(seriously)* until lunchtime, around noon or half past twelve. I *(myself)* make a snack and I check again *(anew)* my emails for half an hour. Then I *(myself)* sit in front of the TV and, if there's a documentary or an entertaining series, I watch it. The problem is that I *(myself)* get bored easily, and sometimes I *(myself)* fall asleep completely after [at the end of] a quarter of an hour. When I *(myself)* wake up, the programme is usually over. But, well, I *(myself)* enjoy [myself].

— And your wife? What does she think about all that? Do you argue *(you dispute)*?

— Certainly not. We *(one)* never *(ourselves)* argue, especially when she's not there *(absent)*! We *(one ourselves)* talk by SMS around 11pm and then I *(myself)* go to bed. I *(myself)* go to sleep easily because my days are so exhausting!

— Ma femme est en voyage d'affaires en Suisse toute la semaine.

— Tu dois t'ennuyer tout seul à la maison !

— Au contraire, je m'amuse énormément. C'est très reposant, tu sais.

— Comment, tu te reposes ? Tu fais la grasse matinée, ou quoi ?

— Au contraire, je me lève très tôt, aux alentours de six heures et demie. D'abord, je regarde rapidement mes mails et mon agenda. Ensuite, je me lave et me rase tranquillement en écoutant la radio. Je m'habille simplement : je mets un jean plutôt qu'un costume. Après, je ne me dépêche pas. Je me prépare un bon petit déjeuner sain avec du yaourt et des fruits.

— Je suis jalouse parce que j'ai rarement le temps de me reposer comme toi. Je dois m'occuper de mes enfants, qui se réveillent toujours de bonne heure, même le week-end. Le soir, je me couche rarement avant minuit et je suis épuisée !

— J'ai beaucoup de chance, je sais. Je commence la journée doucement. Je travaille sérieusement jusqu'à l'heure de déjeuner, vers midi ou midi et demi. Je me fais un casse-croûte et je vérifie à nouveau mes courriels pendant une demi-heure. Puis je m'assois devant la télé et, s'il y a un documentaire ou une série amusante, je le regarde. Le problème est que je m'ennuie facilement, et parfois je m'endors complètement au bout d'un quart d'heure. Quand je me réveille, l'émission est généralement terminée. Mais, bon, je m'amuse.

— Et ta femme ? Qu'est-ce qu'elle pense de tout ça ? Est-ce que vous vous disputez ?

— Certainement pas. On ne se dispute jamais, surtout quand elle est absente ! On se parle par texto vers vingt-deux heures et ensuite je me couche. Je m'endors facilement parce que mes journées sont tellement épuisantes !

■ UNDERSTANDING THE DIALOGUE
WORDS AND PHRASES

→ The feminine singular noun **la matinée**, *the morning*, has basically the same meaning as **le matin**. The difference is that the latter denotes a precise time period (i.e. morning vs. afternoon or evening) whereas the former refers to duration or length of time ("during the morning"). So we say **Le matin, je bois toujours du café**, *I always drink coffee in the morning*, but **Je travaille toute la matinée**, *I work the whole morning*. The idiomatic expression **faire la grasse matinée** (literally "to do the fat morning") means *to sleep in* or have *a lazy morning*.

The same shift from a masculine noun to a feminine one ending in **–ée** can be found in other time-related words; **le jour** → **la journée**; **le soir** → **la soirée**; **l'an** → **l'année**.

→ The interjection **...ou quoi ?** at the end of a sentence is used in exactly the same way as or *what?* in English: **Tu viens, ou quoi ?**, *Are you coming, or what?* And, as in English, it is familiar.

→ The masculine plural noun **les alentours** means *the surroundings* (from the verb **entourer**, *to surround*): **Les alentours de Bordeaux sont très jolis**, *The surroundings of Bordeaux are very pretty*. By extension, the time-related expression **aux alentours de** means *around*: **Ma femme arrive aux alentours de vingt heures ce soir**, *My wife is arriving around 8pm this evening*.

→ **une croûte** means *a crust* (remember that a circumflex indicates a missing "s") and is used in the familiar expression **casser une croûte**, *to grab a bite* (literally "break a crust"). The masculine noun **un casse-croûte**, often advertised on the specials board in a café, is equivalent to *a snack*.

→ **le bout** (the "t" is silent) means *the end*, *the tip* (whence the English word *butt*). The expression **au bout de** therefore means *at the end of* (**au bout de la rue**, *at the end of the street*) and, by extension, *at the end of a period*, or simply *after* (**au bout d'une demi-heure**, *after half an hour*).

CULTURE NOTES

The media landscape in France has changed enormously in the past two decades. Arguably, the main sources of information and entertainment today are **les réseaux sociaux** (sing. **un réseau social**, *a social network*) and the internet (**Internet**, with a capital "I" and no definite article), not to mention **les messageries** (fem.), *messaging apps*. People who spend a lot of time online are known as **les internautes** (*web users*, *"netizens"*, etc.). Fortunately (or unfortunately) for our purposes, much of the web-related vocabulary in French comes directly from English, not just **le web** but also **un blog, un community manager** and the verb **tweeter**. But home-grown words do eventually edge some of them out (for instance, **un ordinateur** for *a computer* or **naviguer** for *to surf*).

◆ GRAMMAR
PRONOMINAL VERBS

A verb is pronominal if it is accompanied by a reflexive pronoun (equivalent to *myself*, *herself*, etc. in English). Pronominal verbs are formed by adding the pronoun **se** before the infinitive. They fall into three main categories: reflexive (the subject and object of the verb are the same), reciprocal (the verb has two subjects, each doing the action to the other), and idiomatic (the pronoun relates to neither the subject nor the object). They are all conjugated like a normal verb, preceded by a reflexive pronoun: **me**, *myself*; **te**, *yourself*; **se**, *himself/herself/itself*; **nous**, *ourselves*; **vous**, *yourselves*; **se**, *themselves*.

The **e** is elided if the verb begins with a vowel or an **h**: **s'endormir**, *to fall asleep*; **s'habiller**, *to get dressed*.

Reflexive verbs are much more common in French than in English, which takes for granted that the speaker performs the action on himself or herself. That is why **se** is rarely translated. Take, for example, **se réveiller**, *to wake up*:

je me réveille	*I wake up*	nous nous réveillons	*we wake up*
tu te réveilles	*you wake up*	vous vous réveillez	*you wake up*
il se réveille	*he/she/ it wakes up*	ils se réveillent	*they wake up*

The negative is formed with **ne** before the pronoun and **pas** after the verb: **il ne se réveille pas**.

The interrogative follows the same basic patterns as for non-reflexive verbs: (i) **Tu te réveilles ?** (ii) **Est-ce que tu te réveilles ?** (iii) **Te réveilles-tu ?** The inversion is quite formal, so we shall concentrate of the first two forms for the purposes of this course.

Reciprocal verbs are constructed in exactly the same way. The only difference with the reflexive form is that the pronoun is translated: **Ils se parlent au téléphone**, *They talk to one another on the phone*. **Les deux sœurs ne se ressemblent pas**, *The two sisters are not like one another*.

Third-category verbs are idiomatic and have to be learned (for example, **s'amuser**, *to have fun*). However, they follow the same rules as the other two categories for the formation of the negative and interrogative.

Many verbs can be used in both the regular and the pronominal forms. For example, **Elle se réveille à neuf heures**, *She wakes up at 9 o'clock* and **Elle réveille ses en-**

fants à neuf heures, *She wakes her children up at 9 o'clock*. Always check to see whether there is a reflexive pronoun. And remember that many verbs that are pronominal in French are translated by a normal form in English.

FORMING ADVERBS FROM ADJECTIVES

Forming adverbs from adjectives is quite easy. In most cases, the suffix **-ment** is added to the feminine singular noun: **sérieux → sérieuse → sérieusement**; **doux → douce → doucement**; **complet → complète → complètement**.
If the adjective already ends in an **e**, just add the suffix: **facile → facilement**; **rare → rarement**.
However, if the adjective ends in **é, i** or **u**, the ending is added to the masculine form: **absolu → absolument**; **vrai → vraiment**.
We will learn one more rule about this kind of adverb in another module.

ON: THE INFORMAL "WE"

In everyday spoken French, the first person plural **nous** is often replaced by the pronoun **on** and the third person singular as we saw in Module 6. Thus, for example, **Nous regardons un film** becomes **On regarde un film**. There is absolutely no difference in meaning, simply in register, with **on** + verb being less formal than **nous**.
This substitution is frequently used for reflexive verbs, possibly to avoid the repetition **nous nous**: **nous nous parlons → on se parle; nous nous aimons → on s'aime**.
The same mechanism exists in English with the impersonal pronoun *one*, but the register is completely the opposite (think Queen Elizabeth saying "*One is pleased to meet you*"). Although purists look down on the familiar use of **on**, it is both useful and commonplace. (We will see later how **on** is used as an indefinite pronoun and also to avoid a passive construction.)

THE PRESENT PARTICIPLE

The present participle of a verb can be identified by the **-ant** ending (equivalent to *-ing* in English), which is added to the stem of the first person plural of **-er, -ir** and **-re** verbs: **nous mangeons → mangeant, nous finissons → finissant, nous vendons → vendant**.
Often preceded by the preposition **en – en mangeant**, *while eating*, etc. – the present participle is used less frequently than in English because it is not part of a tense formation: *I am eating* is translated by the present simple: **Je mange**.
Present participles are invariable unless they are used as adjectives: **amuser → amusant: une série amusante**.

●VOCABULARY

amuser *to amuse*
s'amuser *to have fun, to enjoy oneself*
casser *to break*
se coucher *to go to bed*
se dépêcher *to hurry (up)*
se disputer *to argue* (think: "a dispute")
s'endormir *to fall asleep*
s'ennuyer *to get bored*
s'habiller *to get dressed*
se laver *to wash*
se lever *to get up*
s'occuper (de) *to take care of, to look after*
se préparer *to prepare, to get something ready*
se raser *to shave*
se reposer *to rest*
se réveiller *to wake up*

épuisé(e) *exhausted*
jaloux/-se *jealous*

doucement *gently, quietly*
énormément *enormously, hugely*
épuisant *exhausting*
rapidement *quickly, rapidly*
rarement *rarely*
reposant *relaxing* (from **se reposer**)
serieusement *seriously*
simplement *simply*
tranquillement *without hurrying*

un calendrier *a calendar, a schedule*
un casse-croûte *a snack*

un costume *a suit*
le courrier *mail*
un documentaire *a documentary*
une émission *a programme* (TV, radio)
une messagerie *a messaging service or app*
un petit déjeuner *breakfast* ("a little lunch")
un pull *a pullover, a jumper*
une série *a series* (no final "s" in the singular)
un texto *a text, an SMS*
un voyage d'affaires *a business trip*
un yaourt *a yoghurt*

au bout de *at the end of, after*
au contraire *on the contrary*
aux alentours de *approximately, around*
de bonne heure *early* ("good hour")

faire la grasse matinée *to have a lie-in, to sleep late*

▲ EXERCISES

1. CONJUGATE THESE PRONOMINAL VERBS

a. Ils (*se réveiller*...............) à sept heures, puis ils (*se raser*...............) et (*s'habiller*...............) rapidement.

b. Mélanie et son frère (*se disputer*........) tout le temps.

c. Je (*se lever*.............) avant toi et je (*se coucher*.............) après.

d. Nous (*se dépêcher*.............) parce que nous (*s'occuper*..........) du petit déjeuner ce matin.

e. J'espère que vous (*se reposer*...........) et, surtout, que vous (*s'amuser*.............).

2. PUT THESE SENTENCES INTO THE NEGATIVE OR SECOND INTERROGATIVE

a. Est-ce que tu (*se raser*...........) avant de t'habiller, ou après ?

b. Nous (*se disputer*, negative ....) ; nous parlons très fort, c'est tout !

c. Il n'est pas tard donc vous (*se dépêcher*, negative.............).

d. Est-ce que vous pouvez vous (*s'occuper*.............) du petit déjeuner s'il vous plait ?

e. Je suis fatigué parce que je (*se coucher*, negative with *jamais*.............) avant minuit.

3. MAKE ADVERBS FROM THESE ADJECTIVES

a. Réveillez-le *doux* →

b. Je peux le faire *facile* →

c. Je vois la famille très *rare* →

d. Pouvez-vous le faire *vrai* ? →

e. Je comprends *complet* →

4. TRANSLATE INTO FRENCH

a. What do you think of all that?– I'm enjoying myself enormously.

b. He gets bored easily and sometimes he falls asleep before the end of the programme.

c. My friends are arriving at the station around ten o'clock. They're exhausted.

d. We never argue because we rarely talk to each other.*

e. She has to look after her daughter, who always wakes up early.

* Use **on**

11.
SHOPPING

FAIRE DES ACHATS

AIMS	NOTIONS

- TALK ABOUT CLOTHING
- ASK ABOUT SIZES
- RECOMMEND

- DEMONSTRATIVE PRONOUNS
- MORE ABOUT ADJECTIVES

I HAVE NOTHING TO WEAR.

— I hate *(to do)* shopping but I'm going to a wedding this Saturday and I have nothing to wear *(me put)*.

— What? You have nothing to wear *(carry)*? That makes me *(to)* laugh! Look in this big wardrobe: it's full of clothes. You have *(some)* nice blouses, *(some)* big pullovers, *(some)* beautiful dresses …

— Yes, but nothing suits *(goes)* me! Look [at] my old skirts: this one is too short, that one is too long. As for my shoes, those that I have are all ugly, and…

— Okay, let's go. Luckily, I'm your good friend!

(In a clothes shop)

— Good morning, [are] you looking for something in *(of)* particular?

— I'm looking [for] a pretty [pair of] trousers to go with my new linen jacket *(in linen)*. I really like this one in the [shop] window *(pleases me well)*.

— What is your size? *(Of)* 36, I think. I have two models: this one in cotton and this one in wool. The wool one is certainly *(without doubt)* softer.

— [Do] you have other colours? Preferably light yellow *(of preference)*?

— No, I have it in grey, in blue, in black or in brown, like this. Everything except yellow!

— It doesn't matter *(not grave)*. Can I *(I can)* try the dark grey [one] please?

— Naturally. The fitting rooms are near the escalator *(rolling staircase)*

(Five minutes later)

— It's *(at)* the right *(good)* size. How much is it *(what is the price?)*

— The cotton one *(the one that is in cotton)* is on special offer *(promotion)*: it costs *(makes)* 370 euros. It's an excellent choice: it really suits you *(goes you very well)*. Anything else? A handbag? Or *(some)* shoes, perhaps? I have some pretty white pumps. Those that you're wearing are very comfortable, but these here are more elegant. What size are you? *(do you shoe)*. *(Of)* 37?

— No! I'm fed up with shops! Good bye.

— Je déteste faire du shopping mais je vais à un mariage ce samedi et je n'ai rien à me mettre.

— Quoi ? Tu n'as rien à porter ? Cela me fait rire ! Regarde dans cette grande garde-robe : c'est rempli de vêtements. Tu as de beaux chemisiers, de gros pulls, de belles robes…

— Oui, mais rien ne me va ! Regarde mes vieilles jupes : celle-ci est trop courte, celle-là est trop longue. Quant à mes chaussures, celles que j'ai sont toutes laides, et…

— D'accord, allons-y. Heureusement, je suis ton bon ami !

(Dans un magasin de vêtements)

— Bonjour, vous cherchez quelque chose de particulier ?

— Je cherche un joli pantalon pour aller avec ma nouvelle veste en lin. Celui dans la vitrine me plaît bien.

— Quelle est votre taille ? Du trente-six, je pense. J'ai deux nouveaux modèles : celui-ci en coton et celui-là en laine. Celui en laine est sans doute plus doux.

— Vous l'avez dans d'autres couleurs ? Jaune clair de préférence ?

— Non, je l'ai en gris, en bleu, en noir ou en marron, comme ceci. Tout sauf jaune !

— Ce n'est pas grave. Je peux essayer le gris foncé, s'il vous plaît ?

— Naturellement. Les cabines d'essayage sont près de l'escalier roulant.

(Cinq minutes plus tard)

— Il est à la bonne taille. Quel est le prix ?

— Celui qui est en coton est en promotion : il fait trois cent soixante-dix euros. C'est un excellent choix : il vous va vraiment bien.
Autre chose ? Un sac à main ? Ou des chaussures, peut-être ?
J'ai de beaux escarpins blancs. Ceux que vous portez sont très confortables, mais ceux-ci sont plus élégants. Quelle pointure faites-vous ? Vous chaussez du trente-sept ?

— Non ! J'en ai ras le bol des magasins ! Au revoir.

UNDERSTANDING THE DIALOGUE
WORDS AND PHRASES

→ **la taille,** *size,* refers to the overall dimensions of people and objects in general: **Quelle est la taille de la Tour Effeil ?,** *How big is the Eiffel Tower?* It is also used for clothes: **Quelle est votre taille ?,** *What size do you take?* For shoe sizes, however, we use **la pointure.** The verb **faire** is often used with both nouns. So instead of **Quelle est votre taille/pointure ?** you may be asked **Quelle taille/pointure faites-vous ?.** In a shoe shop, **un magasin de chaussures,** the verb **chausser,** *to shoe,* is used in the phrase **Vous chaussez du combien ?** "You shoe how much?", *What size do you take?* (Note that **la taille** also means *the waist,* so **le tour de taille** is your *waste size.*)

→ **porter,** *to carry,* also means *to wear:* **Elle porte une jupe bleue et un chemisier gris,** *She's wearing a blue skirt and a grey blouse.* The verb **mettre** is also used in the sense of *to put on.* **Mets un manteau, il fait froid,** *Put on a coat, it's cold.* Still on the topic of clothes, **aller,** *to go,* can take the meaning *to suit,* particularly with an adverb such as **bien,** *well.* **Cette robe te va super bien,** *That dress really does suit you.* So the expression **Rien ne me va** means *Nothing suits me.*

→ In addition to the clothes vocabulary in the dialogue, the following words will come in useful: **une chemise,** *a shirt,* (**une chemise de nuit,** *a nightdress*), **un costume,** *a man's suit,* **une chaussette,** *a sock,* **une cravate,** *a tie,* **un imperméable,** *a raincoat* (which is impermeable to water), **un manteau,** *a coat,* **une robe de chambre,** *a dressing gown,* and **un tailleur,** *a woman's suit* (also *a tailor*). When it comes to clothing, French is more logical than English because all the related nouns can be singular as well as plural. So *a pair of trousers* is simply **un pantalon.** Other "two-legged" garments follow the same rule: **un collant,** *a pair of tights,* **un jean,** *a pair of jeans,* **un short,** *a pair of shorts,* and **un pyjama,** *a pair of pyjamas.* Likewise, the general term for clothes, **les vêtements,** can be singularised: **un vêtement,** *an item of clothing.* How logical – and practical! Several other words for items of clothing are derived –and in some cases adapted – from English. They include **un pull** (or **un pullover**), *a jumper,* **un sweat** (pronounced [sweet]), *a sweatshirt* and **un tee-shirt** (or **teeshirt**), *a T-shirt.*

→ We saw **rouge,** *red,* in Module 4. Other common colours not mentioned in the module include **blanc** (fem. **blanche**), *white,* **orange,** *orange,* **rose,** *pink,* **vert** (fem. **verte**), *green,* and **violet** (fem. **violette**), *violet.* There are two words for *brown:* **brun** (which agrees with its noun: **brune, bruns, brunes**) and the invariable **marron** (**les yeux marron**). The latter is closer to chestnut brown, but the distinction between the two adjectives is sometimes hard to fathom, so it's easiest to memorise the adjective along with its noun.

→ The adjective **bon**, *good*, also means *correct, right*: **Est-ce le bon numéro de téléphone ?**, *Is this the right phone number?*

→ **ras le bol** (literally "rim of the bowl") is an idiomatic expression, generally used with **avoir**, always preceded by the preposition **en**, meaning that the person speaking cannot take the situation any more. The image is similar to the English expression *I've had it up to here.* **Elle en a ras le bol du shopping**, *She's fed up with shopping* or, idiomatically, *She's shopped out.* Remember that's it is hard to translate most idioms directly because so much depends on the context. For the time being, simply familiarise yourself with expressions like these because you are bound to hear them when talking with native speakers.

CULTURE NOTES

Napoleon Bonaparte once dismissed the English as **une nation de boutiquiers**, *a nation of shopkeepers*. But commerce and shopping thrive in the French-speaking world, too. As in many countries, the retail trade is split between **la grande distribution**, *mass retailing*, and **le petit commerce**, *small business*. The former sector comprises outlets known as **les grandes surfaces** (fem. "large surface areas"), a broad retail category that includes **les hypermarchés** (masc. *hypermarkets*), **les supermarchés** (masc., *supermarkets*), **les centres commerciaux** (masc. *shopping centres*), as well as **les grands magasins** (masc. *department stores*). Consumer habits are changing, however. In big cities such as Paris and Lyon, residents are increasingly attached to **les commerces de proximité** (masc.) *neighbourhood shops* (**le commerce** refers to *commerce* or *trade* in general, while **un commerce** means *a business* or *a store*). Meanwhile, technology is disrupting the mass retail sector, with the steady rise of **le commerce électronique** (often referred to by the loan term **l'e-commerce**, pronounced [ee-comairss]), or *online shopping*.

While the Anglosphere has adopted the word *boutique* (which in French means simply *a small shop*), the French have co-opted **le shopping**. However, the meaning is a little broader than the "regular" term **faire des achats**, *to purchase* or *to shop*; it contains the idea of browsing for goods as well as purchasing them. (An alternative expression is **faire les magasins**). The English term *to go window-shopping* is translated by the evocative **faire du lèche-vitrines**, i.e. to lick shop windows! (French-speaking Canadians use the more sober **le magasinage**). The term for *to go food shopping* is **faire les courses** (see Module 18).

◆ GRAMMAR

DEMONSTRATIVE PRONOUNS

These pronouns are used instead of a noun to indicate the thing or persons, whether singular or plural, being discussed (*the one, the ones*). We have already learned the most commonly used pair: **ce** and **ça** (the abbreviated form of **cela**, used in everyday conversation).

Let's take stock. Both pronouns are invariable and can be used with singular or plural nouns, as well as general statements (e.g. *This is a difficult topic.*).

• **Ce** is often used with **être** (and abbreviated to **c'est** in the singular) to mean *it* and *they* (as well as *this* and *that*)

C'est une excellente idée, *It's an excellent idea.*

Ce sont mes bons amis, *They are my good friends.*

• **Ça** generally means *this* or *that* and is used in preference to **cela** in everyday French:

Ça nous intéresse, *That interests us.*

Combien ça coûte ?, *How much does that cost?*

Ça/cela also replaces the demonstrative pronoun **ceci** in the spoken language, unless the speaker is indicating something close at hand, as in the dialogue: **Un manteau bleu, comme ceci**, *A blue coat, like this one.*

The other demonstrative pronouns are:

celui (m. sing.)	*the one*	**celle** (f. sing)	*the ones*
ceux (m. plu.)		**celles** (f. plu.)	

Like their English equivalents, they avoid repetition of a noun in the same sentence:

Regarde ces manteaux : celui que je porte est vieux, et ceux qui sont dans le placard sont laids, *Look at these coats: the one that I'm wearing is old, and the ones in the cupboard are ugly.*

Il y a deux types de robes : celle que je porte et celles que je veux porter, *There are two types of dresses: the one I'm wearing and the ones I want to wear.*

When used with **de**, demonstrative pronouns can indicate possession, just like the Saxon genitive does in English:

Ces chaussures sont celles de mon frère, *These shoes are my brother's ("those of my brother")*

Mon PC ne marche pas et celui de Romain est cassé, *My PC doesn't work and Romain's ("that of Romain") is broken.*

Lastly, the emphatic forms **celui-ci**, **celui-là**, **celle-ci**, **celle-là**, **ceux-ci** and **ceux-là** are used when indicating the position of the thing being referred to:

Quel est le prix des sandales ? – Ceux-ci sont très chers et ceux-là sont extrêmement chers, *How much do the sandals cost? – These ones are very expensive and those ones are extremely expensive.*

(**-ci** is, of course, an abbreviation of **ici**, *here*)

POSITION OF ADJECTIVES: "BAGS"

We learned in Module 4 that adjectives describing colours, shapes, nationalities, and so on come immediately after the noun they describe. But we have also seen that some adjectives come before their nouns. We can put these so-called attributive adjectives into the same "BAGS". In other words, an adjective comes before the noun if it describes Beauty (**beau, joli**), Age (**vieux, jeune**), Goodness or the opposite (**bon, mauvais**) or Size (**grand, petit**). Learn this little phrase to help you remember them:

Lacombe est un beau type, un vieux copain et un bon musicien qui vit dans une jolie maison située dans un petit village en France, *Lacombe is a handsome guy, an old chum and a good musician who lives in a pretty house located in a small village in France.*

Here's a partial list of the BAGS category, along with their feminine forms. The plurals are all regular:

beau*	belle	*good-looking / beautiful*
bon	bonne	*good*
excellent	excellente	*excellent*
gentil	gentille	*nice / kind*
grand	grande	*big*
gros	grosse	*fat / large*
jeune	jeune	*young*
joli	jolie	*nice*
long	longue	*long*
mauvais	mauvaise	*bad*
meilleur	meilleure	*better*
nouveau*	nouvelle	*new*
petit	petite	*small*
vieux*	vieille	*old*

* Remember that masculine adjectives ending in **-eau** (**beau, nouveau**, etc.) form their plural with an "x" instead of an "s" (**beaux, nouveaux**). Masculine singular adjectives ending in "s" or "x" (**gros, vieux**) do not change in the plural: **des gros pulls, des vieux vêtements.**

Three BAGS adjectives – **beau, vieux** and **nouveau** – have an irregular masculine form (**bel, vieil, nouvel**) if the singular noun they describe starts with a vowel. This is to make pronunciation easier: **un bel endroit** (a *lovely place*), **un vieil ordinateur** (*an old computer*), **un nouvel ami** (a *new [male] friend*). Do not confuse them with the feminine forms: **belle, vieille, nouvelle.** (Remember, too, that **h** is a half vowel, so we also say **un vieil homme,** *an old man,* **un nouvel hôtel,** etc.)

Lastly, the plural partitive article **des** (**J'ai des chaussures rouges,** *I've got red shoes*) changes to **de** before an attributive adjective: **Tu as de belles chaussures,** *You've got lovely shoes.*

▲ EXERCISES

1. REPLACE THE ENGLISH WORDS WITH THE CORRECT POSSESSIVE PRONOUN

a. (*these*) manteaux sont beaucoup trop petits pour elle.

b. J'adore les gâteaux au chocolat et (*those*) de ta mère sont délicieux.

c. Quelles chaussures préférez-vous : (*these ones*) ou (*those ones*) ?

d. Ma voiture ne marche pas et (*that*) de Romain est au garage.

e. (*these*) sont des tomates espagnoles, et (*these ones*) sont françaises.

2. PUT THE ADJECTIVES IN THE CORRECT PLACE, BEFORE OR AFTER THE NOUN

a. **vieux/vieille:** Elle habite dans une maison à la campagne. →

b. **bleu/e:** Je veux acheter une robe pour le mariage. →

c. **joli/e:** Vous avez un pantalon. – Merci ! →

d. **petit/e:** Nora travaille dans un magasin de vêtements à Lyon. →

e. **moderne:** Le Palais de Tokyo à Paris est spécialisé dans l'art. →

f. **gros/grosse:** Vous n'avez besoin que d'un pull. Il ne fait pas froid. →

3. MAKE THESE ADJECTIVES AGREE WITH THE NOUN

a. Un beau manteau → de* _ _ _ _ _ _ manteaux

b. Un vieux village → de _ _ _ _ _ villages

c. Un jeune informaticien → de _ _ _ _ _ informaticiens

d. Une gentille collègue → de _ _ _ _ _ _ _ _ collègue

e. Un mauvais film → de _ _ _ _ _ _ _ films

* Note that the partitive article is **de** (not **des**) because the adjective comes before the noun.

●VOCABULARY

aller *to go (with), to suit*
détester *to hate, detest*
essayer *to try on (for clothing)*
plaire *to please*
porter *to wear, to put*
regarder *to look*

une cabine d'essayage *a fitting room*
le coton *cotton* (note the single "**t**")
une couleur *a colour*
un escalier roulant/mécanique *an escalator**
une garde-robe *a wardrobe*
une jupe *a skirt*
la laine *wool*
le lin *linen* (cloth)
un magasin *a shop*
un mariage *a wedding, a marriage* (note the single "**r**")
un escarpin *a pump* (footwear)
un modèle *a model*
un pantalon *a pair of trousers*
un sac *a bag*
un sac à main *a handbag*
une sandale *a sandal*
le shopping see Culture Note
la taille *size, waist*
une veste *a jacket*
un vêtement *an item of clothing*
une vitrine *a shop window*
***un escalator** is also used in some stores

bleu(e) *blue*
gris(e) *grey*

jaune *yellow*
marron *(chestnut) brown*
noir(e) *black*
clair(e) *light* (for colours)
doux/douce *soft, gentle*
élégant(e) *elegant*
foncé(e) *dark* (for colours)
grave *serious, grave*
laid(e) *ugly*
plat(e) *flat*

en promotion *on special offer*
quant à *as for*

Ce n'est pas grave *It's not important*
J'en ai ras le bol ! *I'm fed up!*
Naturellement *Naturally, Of course*
Rien ne me va *Nothing suits me*

4. TRANSLATE INTO FRENCH

13

a. I'm looking for a new coat. – What size do you take? *

b. And some new shoes. – What size do you take? *

c. That one is an excellent choice. It suits you very well. **

d. Are you doing some shopping?* – No, I'm window-shopping.

e. She wants to buy a pair of trousers, a pair of jeans, a pair of tights, two nightshirts, a suit and three pairs of shorts.

* Two possibilities
** Use both the masculine and the feminine pronouns to make two sentences

12.
PHONE CONVERSATION

CONVERSATION AU TÉLÉPHONE

AIMS	NOTIONS

- USE THE TELEPHONE
- OFFER AND ACCEPT
- EXPRESS ENTHUSIASM

- RELATIVE PRONOUNS
- *-RE* VERBS
- *SAVOIR / CONNAÎTRE*

HOW IS YOUR BROTHER?

(On the phone)

– Hello, Michelle? [Can] you hear me?

– I hear you very badly. Speak louder *(more strong)* please.

– Wait: the signal is weak here. Stay where you are, I *(am)* going to go downstairs *(descend the staircase)*. [Can] do you hear me better now?

– Ah yes, I [can] hear you much better. So, how are you?

– I am *(going)* very well. I have loads *(full)* of work at the moment and I'm very happy. But I'm a bit worried about *(for)* my brother.

– The brother that I know, the doctor? I know that you are very close.

– No, the other [one], Maxime, who has lived *(lives)* in the Hauts-de-France for *(since)* five years. He [can't] find any work.

– What [is] he doing then *(so)*?

– Well, he reads a lot. He also writes articles for the newspaper and he [is] learning foreign languages: *(the)* Chinese, *(the)* Arabic.

– There are surely companies that [are] looking [for] people who speak *(the)* Chinese. Look *(hold)*, a man that I know works for a big foreign company. I can contact him if you want.

– That would be great! I will tell *(say it to)* my brother. Wait, don't hang up *(leave)*, I have another call and I must answer … Sorry, I'm going to leave you: it's the call that I have been *(am)* waiting for since this morning. I [am] selling my car and it's a buyer who [is] calling me.

– No problem, I understand. I [will] call you back later.

(Au téléphone)

— Allô, Michelle ? Tu m'entends ?

— Je t'entends très mal. Parle plus fort s'il te plaît.

— Attends : le signal est faible ici. Reste où tu es, je vais descendre l'escalier. Est-ce que tu m'entends mieux maintenant ?

— Ah oui, je t'entends beaucoup mieux. Alors, comment vas-tu ?

— Je vais très bien. J'ai plein de boulot actuellement et je suis très content. Mais je suis un peu inquiet pour mon frère.

— Le frère que je connais, le médecin ? Je sais que vous êtes très proches.

— Non, l'autre, Maxime, qui vit dans les Hauts-de-France depuis cinq ans. Il ne trouve pas de travail.

— Qu'est-ce qu'il fait, alors ?

— Eh bien, il lit beaucoup. Il écrit aussi des articles pour le journal et il apprend des langues étrangères : le chinois, l'arabe.

— Il y a sûrement des entreprises qui cherchent des gens qui parlent le chinois. Tiens, un homme que je connais travaille pour une société étrangère importante. Je peux le contacter si tu veux.

— Ça serait génial ! Je vais le dire à mon frère. Attends, ne quitte pas, j'ai un autre appel et je dois répondre ... Désolé, je vais te laisser : c'est le coup de fil que j'attends depuis ce matin. Je vends ma voiture et c'est un acheteur qui m'appelle.

— Pas de problème, je comprends. Je te rappelle tout à l'heure.

UNDERSTANDING THE DIALOGUE
WORDS AND PHRASES

→ **allô** comes from the English word *hello* and has the same meaning. But it is usually used only when answering or talking to someone on the phone. **Allô, est-ce que vous m'entendez ?**, *Hello, can you hear me?* You learned the usual forms of greeting (**Bonjour, Salut,** etc.) in Module 1.

→ **plein(e)** means *full*: **L'hôtel est plein,** *The hotel is full.* The expression **plein de** literally means *full of*, **Leur maison est pleine d'enfants,** *Their house is full of children.* Idiomatically, it is the equivalent (and origin) of *plenty of*: **J'ai plein d'idées,** *I've plenty of ideas.*

→ **boulot** is a familiar word meaning *work*. It can be either uncountable: **Maxime n'a pas assez de boulot,** *Maxime doesn't have enough work,* or countable: **Maxime a un nouveau boulot,** *Maxime has a new job.*

→ **actuellement** is a false cognate (see Module 5). It means *now* or at *present*. **Actuellement, mon frère vit à Lille,** *At present, my brother is living in Lille.* The plural noun **les actualités** means *the latest news*: **Ce site Internet présente les actualités internationales,** *This website presents the latest international news.* The English adverb *actually* is translated as **en fait.**

→ **quitter** means *to leave* (think of the English verb *to quit*): **Marie quitte la maison tous les jours à sept heures,** *Marie leaves the house every day at 7am.* When answering the phone, **Ne quittez pas / Ne quitte pas** (lit. "Don't leave") is the equivalent of *Hold the line, Hang on,* etc.

→ **le fil,** *the wire.* The expression **un coup de fil** (lit. "a blow of wire") is a familiar way to say **un appel téléphonique,** *a telephone call.* **Passe-moi un coup de fil,** *Give me a buzz.*

CULTURE NOTES

From an administrative viewpoint, "metropolitan" France (**la France metropolitaine**) comprises the European mainland and a number of adjacent islands, including Corsica (**la Corse**). The country is divided into 13 regions (**les régions**), subdivided into one hundred and one areas (**les départements**), which in turn are composed of **arrondissements** (see Module 5), **cantons** and **communes**. There are also five overseas regions (**les régions d'Outre-mer**) located in the Pacific Ocean and the Caribbean. The metropolitan **départements** are numbered from 01 to 95, followed by a three-digit code, while the five overseas regions have their own codes. Each **département** – many of which bear the name of a local river or mountain range – has an administrative headquarters, **une préfecture**, which is usually located in the largest town, called **le chef-lieu**, "chief place". The French often refer to the entire country as **la Métropole** and to the mainland part as **l'Héxagone** (*the hexagon*, the country's approximate geographical shape).

◆ GRAMMAR

RELATIVE PRONOUNS *QUI* AND *QUE*

Both these pronouns can refer to either people or things, **qui** as the subject of a sentence and **que** as a direct object. Used in a subordinate clause, they are equivalent to *who* (or *whom*), *which* and *that*.

L'homme qui travaille pour cette société belge s'appelle Jean Smet, *The man who works for that Belgian company is called Jean Smet.*

Unlike *who*, **qui** can be used with an impersonal noun:

Marseille est une ville qui a une longue histoire, *Marseille is a city that has a long history.*

You will note that **qui** is always followed by a verb because it refers to the subject. It is also used with a preposition (**à**, **de**, etc.) when referring to people:

La première personne à qui elle demande un conseil est son mari, *The first person who(m) she asks for advice is her husband.*

Que (which becomes **qu'** in front of a vowel) refers to the object, which can also be a person:

Marseille est la ville que j'aime le plus, *Marseille is the city that I like the most.*

Michel est l'homme qu'elle aime le plus, *Michel is the man that she loves the most.*

As the object of the sentence, **que** is always followed by the subject (**la ville qu'elle aime le plus**).

SAVOIR OR *CONNAÎTRE*?

We learned in Module 5 that there are two verbs that mean *to know*: **savoir** and **connaître**. We use **connaître** to mean that we know a place or person. The verb is usually followed by a noun:

Ils connaissent bien Paris, *They know Paris well.*

Je connais la raison de leur visite, *I know the reason for their visit.*

The derivative noun is **la connaissance**, which can either be abstract (*knowledge*) or concrete (*an acquaintance*) and can be used in the singular or the plural.

Mon frère aime bien faire de nouvelles connaissances, *My brother loves making new acquaintances / meeting new people.*

Je suis impressionné par ta connaissance du français, *I'm impressed by your knowledge of French.*

Savoir means to know how to do something or to be cognizant of something:

Que savez-vous de notre enterprise ?, *What do you know about our company?*

Nous savons que vous êtes inquiet, *We know that you are worried.*

It is usually followed by a clause or an infinitive, and can sometimes be translated by *can*: **Il sait parler le chinois,** *He knows how to speak Chinese* → *He can speak Chinese.* Unlike **la connaissance**, the derivative noun, **le savoir**, is always abstract and means *learning*.

▲ CONJUGATION

VERBS ENDING IN -RE

These verbs belong to the third group, along with those ending in **-ir** (without a present participle ending in **-issant**) and in **-oir**. To conjugate them, drop the **-re** ending and add the following:

vendre, *to sell*

je vends	I sell	nous vendons	we sell
tu vends	you sell	vous vendez	you sell
il/elle vend	he/she/it sells	ils/elles vendent	they sell

• Negative:

je ne vends pas, *I do not sell*, etc.

• Interrogative with **est-ce que...** :

Est-ce que je vends, *Do I sell...?*, etc.

Remember that the final **s** is silent, so the first, second and third persons are pronounced identically.

Many of these **-re** verbs are irregular, including a very common one, **dire,** *to say/to tell*. Here is the present form:

je dis	I say	nous disons	we say
tu dis	you say	vous dites	you say
il/elle dit	he/she/it says	ils/elles disent	they say

Another **-re** verb is **plaire,** *to please*, which we have already met in the expression of politeness **s'il vous/te plaît,** *please*.

From now on, we will give a single example for each verb form. If you are unsure about the spelling of the other forms, check the appendix.

●VOCABULARY

apprendre *to learn*
contacter *to contact*
écrire *to write*
entendre *to hear* (see Module 9)
laisser *to leave*
lire *to read*
rappeler *to call back*
rester *to stay*
vendre *to sell*

un acheteur *a buyer*
un appel *a call* (generally on the phone)
l'arabe *Arabic* (language – no initial capital)
un article *an article*
un/le boulot *a job, work*
le chinois *Chinese* (language – no initial capital)

mieux *better*
sûrement *surely*
actuellement *at the moment*
alors *then, so*
maintenant *now*
plein de *lots of*
tout à l'heure *later*

une entreprise *a company*
un escalier *a staircase*
les gens *people*
un journal *a newspaper*
une langue *a language* (also a tongue)
un médecin *a doctor*
un sujet *a subject*

une visite *a visit* (see **visiter**, Module 3)

content *happy*
étranger *foreign*
faible *weak*
fort *strong, loud*
génial *great, brilliant*
important *important, large*
inquiet *worried*
mal *badly*

Allô *Hello* (phone call only)
Tiens *Look, You know* (see Module 3)
Ne quitte/quittez pas *Hold the line*

▲ EXERCISES

1. CONJUGATE THE VERBS

a. Quelles langues étrangères (*apprendre* - inverted form: ....)-vous à l'école ?

b. Si vous (*dire*, negative: ....) combien ça coûte, je ne peux pas l'acheter.

c. Ils (*vendre*: ....) leur voiture parce qu'elle est vieille.

d. Est-ce tu (*lire*: ....) le chinois ?

e. Je (*connaitre*: ....) ton frère. Je (*savoir*: ....) où il habite.

2. COMPLETE THESE SENTENCES USING *QUI* OR *QUE*

a. Il y a beaucoup des gens _ _ _ cherchent du travail dans la région.

b. Ce sont les amis _ _ _ j'attends depuis ce matin.

c. New York est une ville _ _ _ ne dort jamais.

d. Mon fils, _ _ _ _ a vingt ans, est informaticien à Lille.

e. L'homme _ _ vit à Rennes écrit des livres _ _ _ j'aime beaucoup.

3. USE *SAVOIR* OR *CONNAITRE*, AS APPROPRIATE

a. Est-ce que tu .... Paris ? C'est une ville magnifique.

b. Je .... que vous êtes occupé mais j'ai besoin de vous parler.

c. Elle est très intelligente : elle .... parler le chinois et l'arabe.

d. Je .... que Maxime habite à Lille mais je ne .... pas l'adresse.

4. TRANSLATE INTO FRENCH

a. Hold the line please *(formal)*, I have another call. Sorry, I'm going to leave you.

b. Speak *(formal)* louder please. I can't [don't] hear you.

c. She's a bit worried about her brother. – The brother that/whom I know?

d. I know a company that is looking for people who speak Arabic.

e. No problem. He will call you *(informal)* back later if you like.

13.
TALKING ABOUT THE HOLIDAY

PARLER DES VACANCES

AIMS

- TALK ABOUT THE PAST
- MAKE COMPARISONS

NOTIONS

- PAST PARTICIPLE OF *-ER* VERBS
- *LE PASSÉ COMPOSÉ*
- COMPARATIVE ADJECTIVES

THE ISLE OF BEAUTY

(The travel agent is talking to Louise)

— So that's it? Your holidays are over?

— Yes, unfortunately. It's hard to go back to *(re-take)* work, but we are happy to get back to *(re-find)* our house.

— What did *(have)* you do, in the end *(finally)*?

— We *(have)* spent three weeks in Corsica.

— How was it *(it was how)*?

— Very nice, but complicated to organise! I reserved two months in advance because there is always a huge amount of people *(enormously of world)* in May. We *(have)* spent the first two weeks resting *(at calm)*. We found a very nice *(agreeable)* apartment almost on the beach.

— Did *(have)* you swim?

— I didn't *(haven't)* swim but we sailed *(done some sail)* and cycled *(some bike)*. After 15 days, we *(have)* rented a motorbike for a week to see the rest of the island. We *(have)* visited Ajaccio and the Bonaparte House, which I found fascinating, as well as Bastia. I didn't like *(haven't liked)* the Old Port but I loved the big square *(place)* in the middle of the town. It is as beautiful as the Place des Vosges in Paris.

— Did you visit *(have you visited)* the beautiful gardens, near the palace?

— No, we didn't think *(haven't thought)* of that. But for me, the most beautiful town by far is Bonifacio. It is smaller than Bastia and less big than Calvi.

— Everyone *(all the world)* enjoys *(appreciates)* that town, it's true.

— The only problem is that everything is so expensive — more expensive than a stay in the mountains.

— More expensive, perhaps, but more interesting and less far than a tropical island.

— So you know the Isle of Beauty well?

— Me? I never travel. I *(have)* visited Paris once but I didn't like the crowd.

(L'agent de voyages discute avec Louise)

— Alors, ça y est ? Vos vacances sont terminées ?

— Oui, malheureusement. C'est dur de reprendre le travail, mais nous sommes contents de retrouver notre maison.

— Qu'est-ce que vous avez fait, finalement ?

— Nous avons passé trois semaines en Corse.

— C'était comment ?

— Très chouette, mais compliqué à organiser ! J'ai réservé deux mois à l'avance parce qu'il y a toujours énormément de monde en mai. Nous avons passé les deux premières semaines au calme. Nous avons trouvé un appartement très agréable presque sur la plage.

— Avez-vous nagé ?

— Je n'ai pas nagé mais nous avons fait de la voile et du vélo. Après quinze jours, nous avons loué une moto pendant une semaine pour voir le reste de l'île. Nous avons visité Ajaccio et la Maison Bonaparte, que j'ai trouvée fascinante, ainsi que Bastia. Je n'ai pas aimé le Vieux-Port mais j'ai adoré la grande place au milieu de la ville. Elle est aussi belle que la Place des Vosges, à Paris.

— Avez-vous visité les beaux jardins, près du palais ?

— Non, nous n'avons pas pensé à cela. Mais, pour moi, la plus belle ville, de loin, est Bonifacio. Elle est plus petite que Bastia et moins grande que Calvi.

— Tout le monde apprécie cette ville, c'est vrai.

— Le seul problème est que tout est si cher — plus cher qu'un séjour à la montagne.

— Plus cher, peut-être, mais plus intéressant et moins loin qu'une île tropicale.

— Donc vous connaissez bien l'Île de Beauté ?

— Moi ? Je ne voyage jamais. J'ai visité une fois Paris mais je n'ai pas aimé la foule.

■ UNDERSTANDING THE DIALOGUE

WORDS AND PHRASES

→ **Ça y est**, literally "that there is", is a very common expression with multiple uses. It is most commonly used when completing an action: **Ça y est : j'ai terminé le travail !** *That's it, I've finished the job!* It also corresponds to *Done it!* or *Got it!*: **As-tu terminé ? – Oui, ça y est !** *Have you finished? – Yes, done it!*. See also the entry under Grammar.

→ **C'est comment ?** or, in the past, **C'était comment ?** is an idiomatic way of asking someone how they find or experience something: **C'est comment, Marseille ? – C'est une très belle ville**, *What's Marseille like? – It's a very beautiful city.* **C'était comment, ce restaurant ?** *What was the restaurant like?*.

→ **chouette** is a very idiomatic word – the noun, **une chouette** means *an owl!* – that basically means *nice* or *great*. It can be used as an (invariable) adjective: **C'est une île très chouette**, *It's a really nice island*; and also as an exclamation: **On va en Corse cette année. – Chouette !** *We're going to Corsica this year. – Great!*

→ **loin**, *far*, is used in several expressions that will be familiar to English-speakers. Two of these are **de loin**, *by far*, and **aller loin**, *to go far*. **Omar est de loin le meilleur joueur de l'équipe**, *Omar is by far the best player in the team.* **Nadia est très intelligente : elle va aller loin**, *Nadia is very smart: she'll go far.*

→ **faire**, *to do*, *to make* (see Module 2) is used with a noun to talk about practising certain sports or activities: **Je fais du ski chaque année en décembre**, *I go skiing every year in December.* **Tu veux faire de la voile ou du vélo ?**, *Do you want to go sailing or cycling?*. You'll find more of these expressions in the Vocabulary section.

→ **le monde** means *the world*. But it is also used to mean *people*: **Il y a beaucoup de monde dans les magasins aujourd'hui**, *There are a lot of people in the shops today*. (Remember that **tout le monde** means *everybody/everyone*, see Module 5.)

→ **cela**, the demonstrative pronoun, is the full form of **ça**, first seen in Module 5. It is more formal than the shorter form, which is used in everyday speech: **Nous n'avons pas pensé à cela** → **Nous n'avons pas pensé à ça**.

CULTURE NOTES

La Corse (*Corsica* both in English and the Corsican language) is an island 170 kilometres off the Mediterranean coast of France that comprises two **départements**: **Haute-Corse** and **Corse-du-Sud**. Known as **l'Île de beauté** "the ile of beauty", it is famed for dramatic scenery, mountainous terrain, beautiful sandy beaches and lush vegetation. Corsica has its own language (**le corse** – note the masculine gender) and a very strong cultural identity combining influences from all over the Mediterranean and beyond. Although a part of France since 1768 (and birthplace of Emperor **Napoléon Bonaparte**), Corsica has a strong separatist streak, summarised in its motto **Souvent conquise, jamais soumise** ("*Often conquered, never subdued*" or, in Corsican, **A spessu conquista mai sottumessa!**).

◆ GRAMMAR

PAST PARTICIPLE OF -*ER* VERBS

The past participle has several functions. While mainly used to form compound verbs, such as the **passé composé** (see below), it can also serve as an adjective. For verbs in the first group, the past participle is formed simply by replacing the **-er** ending of the infinitive with **é**:

voyager → **voyagé**; **réserver** → **reservé**; **organiser** → **organisé**

Despite the change, the participle usually sounds the same as the infinitive.

As an adjective, the participle agrees with its noun:

Suzie est très fatiguée, *Suzy is very tired* (see Module 9).

Ces réseaux sont compliqués, *These networks are complicated.*

COMPARATIVE ADJECTIVES

Comparative adjectives (*more, less,* etc.) are easier to form in French than in English because they do not depend on the number of syllables in the word. Use **plus** for *more* (comparative of superiority) and **moins** for *less* (inferiority).

Cette ville est plus/moins grande, *This city is bigger/smaller.*

Use **que** to introduce the thing you are making the comparison with:

Le livre est plus intéressant que le film, *The book is more interesting than the movie.*

For a comparison of equality, use **aussi** before the adjective and **que** after it:

Cette ville est aussi grande que Paris, *This city is as big as Paris.*

The negative forms are regular (**n'est pas plus intéressant, n'est pas moins grand, ne sont pas aussi chers**).

RE-: THE "REPEAT" PREFIX

As in English, the prefix **re-** can be added to a verb in order to convey the idea of repeating an action or returning to a prior location or situation. It can also replace the adverb *again*: **prendre**, *to take* → **reprendre**, *to retake, to start again*; **venir**, *to come*

→ **revenir**, *to return, to come back*. If the verb begins with a vowel or a silent **h**, an acute accent is usually added to the **e**: **écrire**, *to write* → **réécrire**, *to rewrite*. (But be careful to look at the context: **réserver** simply means *to reserve* and **réduire**, *to reduce*.) There are a couple of other slight variations, but you get the idea.

▲ CONJUGATIONS

TALKING ABOUT THE PAST: *LE PASSÉ COMPOSÉ*

The **passé composé**, or "compound past", is the perfect form of a verb, used to talk about actions that took place in the past and are now complete ("perfected"). It is formed with either **avoir** or **être** and the past participle.

In this module, we look at regular, non-reflexive verbs in the first group (**-er**).

j'ai voyagé	I travelled	nous avons voyagé	we travelled
tu as voyagé	you travelled	vous avez voyagé	you travelled
il/elle a voyagé	he/she/it travelled	ils/elles ont voyagé	they travelled

j'ai n'ai pas voyagé	I did not travel	nous n'avons pas voyagé	we did not travel
tu n'as pas voyagé	you did not travel	vous n'avez pas voyagé	you did not travel
il/elle n'a pas voyagé	he/she/it did not travel	ils/elles n'ont pas voyagé	they did not travel

est-ce que j'ai voyagé… ?	did I travel…?	est-ce que nous avons voyagé… ?	did we travel…?
est-ce que tu as voyagé… ?	did you travel…?	est-ce que vous avez voyagé… ?	did you travel…?
est-ce qu'il / elle a voyagé… ?	did he/she/it travel…?	est-ce qu'ils / elles ont voyagé… ?	did they travel…?

In everyday French, we use the first and second forms of the interrogative most of the time. With the third form, the inversion, we need to pay attention to the liaisons in the third person singular and plural. For the plural, the final **t** of **ont** is pronounced: **ont-elles** [ohntel]. The singular is a little more complicated because we have to avoid the hiatus **a il / a elle**. To do so, we place a hyphenated **-t-** between the two

aller loin *to go far*
apprécier *to enjoy, to appreciate*
nager *to swim*
organiser *to organise*
reprendre *to restart, to resume*
réserver *to reserve*
retrouver *to get back to, to find (again)*
terminer *to end* ("terminate")

à l'avance *in advance, ahead of time* (Don't confuse with **en avance**, *early*; Module 7)
agréable *pleasant, nice* ("agreeable")
au calme *resting, quiet*
au milieu (de) *in the middle (of)*
aussi... que *as...as*
chouette *nice, great*
de loin *by far*

dur *hard, tough*
fascinant *fascinating*
finalement *finally, in the end*
malheureusement *unfortunately*
si *so*

un appartement *a flat, apartment* (note the double /p/)
la foule *the crowd*
une île *an island, an isle*
un jardin *a garden*
une moto *a motorbike*
un palais *a palace*
le vélo *cycling* (also: *the bike*)
la voile *sailing* (also: *the sail*)

Ça y est ! *That's it! Done it!*
C'est / C'était comment ? *How is/ was it?*

vowels: **a-t-il... ? / a-t-elle... ? A-t-il téléphoné hier ?**, *Did he phone yesterday?* **Combien de fois a-t-elle appelé ?**, *How many times did she call?* For simplicity, therefore, the first two interrogative forms are standard in conversations and informal writing.

Although **le passé composé** is not the equivalent of the present perfect tense in English (*I have visited*), which has no equivalent in French, it can sometimes be used with the same meaning. So, for example, **Je l'ai appelé** can be translated as *I called him* or *I have called him*. It all depends on the context.

Some of the most common verbs take **être** rather than **avoir** as the past auxiliary. We will see these in the next module.

▲ EXERCISES

1. PUT THESE VERBS INTO THE PAST TENSE

a. Nous (*réserver*: …………………..) un appartement en Corse pour les vacances.

b. Je (*nager*, negative: …………………..) la semaine dernière mais je (*faire*: …………………..) du vélo.

c. Où vous (*passer*: …………………..) vos vacances cette année ?*

d. J'espère que vous (*aimer*: …………………..) le Vieux-Port. C'est magnifique.

e. Nous (*trouver*, negative: …………………..) les jardins du palais.

* 2nd and 3rd interrogatives

2. FORM A PAST PARTICIPLE ADJECTIVE FROM THESE VERBS (AND MAKE IT AGREE!)

a. Après les vacances, nous sommes tous (*fatiguer*: …………………..).

b. Elles sont extrêmement (*compliquer*: …………………..), les questions qu'il me pose.

c. Ça y'est, le film est (*terminer*: …………………..).

d. Ces femmes sont (*aimer*: …………………..) dans le monde entier.

e. Le palais de Versailles est un endroit très (*visiter*: …………………..).

3. PUT THESE ADJECTIVES INTO THE APPROPRIATE COMPARATIVE FORM

a. Le livre est beaucoup (*intéressant*) le film. (superiority) →

b. Je pense que Paris est (*grand*) Londres. (inferiority). →

c. Le ski est (*cher*) que la voile. (negative, superiority) →

d. Le chinois est (*difficile*) l'arabe. (equality) →

4. TRANSLATE INTO FRENCH

15

a. How was Bastia? – It's a beautiful city but less beautiful than Calvi.

b. We go skiing every year in January. It's really great.

c. There are a lot of people on the beach this morning. – Yes, everyone loves swimming.

d. Did the travel agent phone yesterday? (*inversion*) – No, unfortunately.

e. Do you know Corsica well? (*2 forms*) – No, I never travel. It's too tiring.

14.
FINDING A FLAT

TROUVER UN APPARTEMENT

AIMS	NOTIONS

- TALK ABOUT THE PAST
- MAKE COMPARISONS
- DESCRIBE A CITY

- PERFECT TENSE OF *-IR* VERBS
- INTERROGATIVE PRONOUNS
- SUPERLATIVE ADJECTIVES
- IRREGULAR COMPARATIVES AND SUPERLATIVES

WHEN CAN YOU MOVE?

(Élodie is talking to her father)

— I have finished my studies and I now have to move [house]. I have already chosen the suburb where I want to live.

— Which [one]? It's not too far from the town centre, I hope!

— No, dad, it is *(at)* less than 5 kilometres from *(home)* you and mum. It's the quietest *(most calm)* and greenest *(the most green)* place in the entire *(all the)* region.

— That's all very well, but have you found a place to live *(lodging)*?

— Not quite *(all at done)*. But there is one thing that interests me. Actually, it's an enormous garage converted into [a] block of flats. There's a furnished studio [flat] on the ground floor and a two roomed flat *(two rooms)* on the third floor.

— Which is the nicest *(most agreeable)*?

— The flat on the third [floor]: it's the brightest *(most clear)* and the least noisy of the two.

— Are there [any] shops or a shopping *(commercial)* centre nearby *(in the surroundings)*?

— Yes, there's a small grocery at the bottom of the building and a supermarket not too far [away], and above all, a bakery that makes the best bread, the best baguette and the best pastries in *(the)* town.

— Indeed, it's not the worst spot! When can you move?

— In fact, I haven't managed *(succeeded)* to contact *(to join)* the estate agent by email or phone. But I filled in his form online and I supplied all the required *(obligatory)* information.

— One important question: have you thought about the question of the rent? It's the most expensive part *(the corner the most expensive)* of *(the)* town, and the flats cost an arm and a leg *(the eyes of the head)*.

— That's too bad! It's you who is paying!

(Élodie parle avec son père)

— J'ai fini mes études et je dois maintenant déménager. J'ai déjà choisi la banlieue où je veux habiter.

— Laquelle ? Elle n'est pas trop loin du centre-ville, j'espère !

— Non, papa, c'est à moins de cinq kilomètres de chez toi et maman. C'est l'endroit le plus calme et le plus vert de toute la région.

— Tout cela est très bien, mais as-tu trouvé un logement ?

— Pas tout à fait. Mais il y a un truc qui m'intéresse. En fait, c'est un énorme garage converti en immeuble. Il y a un studio meublé au rez-de-chaussée et un deux pièces au troisième étage.

— Lequel est le plus agréable ?

— L'appartement au troisième : c'est le plus clair et le moins bruyant des deux.

— Est-ce qu'il y a des magasins ou un centre commercial dans les environs ?

— Oui, il y a une petite épicerie en bas de l'immeuble, un supermarché pas trop loin, et surtout, une boulangerie qui fait le meilleur pain, la meilleure baguette et les meilleures viennoiseries de la ville.

— En effet, ce ne n'est pas le pire endroit ! Tu peux déménager quand ?

— En fait, je n'ai pas réussi à joindre l'agent immobilier par mail ou par téléphone. Mais j'ai rempli son formulaire en ligne et j'ai fourni tous les renseignements obligatoires.

— Une question importante : as-tu réfléchi à la question du loyer ? C'est le coin le plus cher de la ville, et les appartements coûtent les yeux de la tête.

— Tant pis. C'est toi qui paies !

■ UNDERSTANDING THE DIALOGUE

WORDS AND PHRASES

→ **une banlieue** is usually translated as *a suburb*: **la proche / la grande banlieue** = *inner / outer suburbs*. A *suburban resident* is **un(e) banlieusard(e)**. In recent times, however, **les banlieues** of France's big cities have become synonymous with urban unrest and problems similar to those found in British and American inner cities.

→ **un truc** is a useful placeholder word, equivalent to *a thing, a whatname*, etc. Although the register is familiar, **un truc** is widely used in spoken French: **C'est quoi, ce truc ?**, *What's this thingammy?* It can also replace **quelque chose**: **J'ai un truc à faire demain** → **J'ai quelque chose à faire demain**, *I've got something to do tomorrow*.

→ **tout à fait** means *absolutely, entirely* (note the liaison: [tootafay]): **Cet homme est tout à fait charmant**, *That man is absolutely charming*. **Je ne suis pas tout à fait prêt**, *I'm not entirely ready*. Both forms can be used alone in response to a question: **Es-tu d'accord ? – Tout à fait. / Pas tout à fait**, – *Do you agree? – Absolutely. / Not completely*.

→ **la viennoiserie** is a collective noun for breakfast pastries such as **un croissant** and **un pain au chocolat** (a sweet roll with chocolate sticks) sold in **une boulangerie**, *a bakery*. It can also be used in the definite singular form: **Tu veux une viennoiserie ?** (The word comes from **Vienne**, *Vienna*, the Austrian city and reputed birthplace of the croissant.) **Une baguette** is a French stick loaf; **le pain** means *bread* in general, and **un pain** is *a loaf of bread*.

→ **le mail** is the most widely used word for *e-mail*. It can also be a definite singular noun: **Je vous envoie un mail tout à l'heure**, *I'll send you an email later*. The "official" term is **un courriel** but most French speakers (except in Canada) use the English-derived term.

→ **Tant pis**, an idiomatic expression meaning *That's too bad* or *Never mind*, contains a variant of the comparative adjective **pire** (see Grammar).

→ **coûter les yeux de la tête**, "to cost the eyes of the head", is the equivalent of our familiar expression *to cost an arm and a leg*. That same idiom is echoed in a recent variant, **coûter un bras** "to cost an arm", which presumably arrived in French via Canada.

CULTURE NOTES

The property market, **le marché immobilier**, is always an important topic of conversation. Most city-dwellers in France live in a *flat* (**un appartement**) located in **un immeuble**, *a building* or *block of flats*. The size of the property is usually defined by the number of rooms, for example, **un appartement de trois pièces**, *a three roomed flat*. In everyday conversation, however, the main noun is generally dropped: **J'ai trouvé un petit trois pièces**, *I've found a small three rooms*. A rented property containing *furniture*, **les meubles**, is advertised as **meublé**, *furnished*. The easiest way *to rent* (**louer**) or buy a property is through **une agence immobilière**, *estate agency* (**un agent immobiler**, *an estate agent*). *A rental* is advertised as **une location** and *the rent* is **le loyer** (usually quoted on a monthly rather than an annual basis). Properties *for sale* are advertised as **à vendre**. Note how knowing a single word can help you understand its derivatives. For example, the adjective **mobilier**, *movable*, gives us **le mobilier** (*furniture* in general) and **un meuble** (*an item of furniture*); the opposite of **mobilier** is **immobilier** (*real property*, i.e. which cannot be moved). Likewise, the verb **louer** is the root of **le loyer** but also **un locataire**, *a tenant*, **la location**, *rental*, and **une location**, *a rental property* (no relation to the English property mantra "*Location, location, location*"!) and the adjective **locatif / -ve**, *rental*.

 ## GRAMMAR

INTERROGATIVE PRONOUNS: *LEQUEL*

Used as both an interrogative pronoun and a relative pronoun to mean *which / who*, **lequel** combines the definite article **le** and the interrogative adjective **quel**. It agrees in number and gender with the noun it refers to or replaces, hence **laquelle** (feminine singular), **lesquels** (masculine plural) and **lesquelles** (feminine plural).

This module looks at the interrogative form, in which the pronoun is used to ask a question without repeating a noun. This is often done with a single word:

Je vais lire un livre → Lequel ? (= **Quel livre ?**)
Je veux habiter dans une banlieue → Laquelle ? (= **Quelle banlieue ?**)
Les cousins arrivent ce soir → Lesquels ? (= **Quels cousins ?**)
Elle a de bonnes raisons → Lesquelles ? (= **Quelles raisons ?**)

These interrogative pronouns can be used to form longer questions. In this case, the inverted verb form is generally used with them:

Lequel des deux appartements t'intéresse ? *Which of the two flats interests you?*
Il y a plein de viennoiseries : lesquelles voulez-vous ? *There are loads of pastries: which ones do you want?* We will see later how **quel/quelle** is used in the combined form with the partitive article.

SUPERLATIVE ADJECTIVES

The superlative form of the adjective uses **plus** for superiority and **moins** for inferiority (Module 11), together with the definitive article **le / la / les**:

C'est cher → C'est plus cher → C'est le plus cher
It's expensive → It's more expensive → It's the most expensive
Il est dangereux → Il est moins dangereux → Il est le moins dangereux
He's/It's dangerous → He's/It's less dangerous → He's/It's the least dangerous
If a noun is used, it comes before the superlative word:
C'est l'appartement le plus grand de l'immeuble, *It's the largest flat in the building.*
Je veux la tablette la moins chère, *I want the cheapest tablet.*

IRREGULAR COMPARATIVES / SUPERLATIVES

As in English (*good → better*), some comparative and superlative adjectives are irregular in French. The two most common ones are **bon**, *good*, and **mauvais**, *bad*. The masculine singular and plural forms are:

bon	*good*	**meilleur**	*better*	**le(s) meilleurs**	*the best*
mauvais	*bad*	**pire**	*worse*	**le(s) pire(s)**	*the worst*

Ce sont les meilleurs croissants de la ville, *They are the best croissants in town.*
Le temps est pire aujourd'hui, *The weather is worse today.*
The feminine singular and plural forms are:

bonne	**meilleure**	**les meilleures**
mauvaise	**pire**	**les pires**

La faim est la pire chose au monde, *Hunger is the worst thing in the world.*
The relative **que** is used when comparing two things or groups of things:
La bande-dessinée de *Napoléon* est meilleure que le film, *The comic book of Napoleon is better than the movie.*
Les résultats de notre équipe sont pires que l'année dernière, *Our team's results are worse than last year.*
A word with a similar meaning to **mauvais** is the adverb **mal**. It is used only with verbs expressing existence (**être**, *to be*; **devenir**, *to become*, for example) or sensation (**entendre**, *to hear*; **sentir**, *feel* or *smell*; **sembler**, *seem*). **J'ai très mal aux pieds**, *My feet hurt.* In addition to a regular comparative and superlative (**plus mal**, **le plus mal**), **mal** has an irregular form (**pis / le pis**) that is rarely used in conversation, except in the expression **Tant pis**, *Too bad, Never mind.*

▲ CONJUGATIONS

LE PASSÉ COMPOSÉ FOR *-IR* VERBS

To form the perfect tense of regular verbs ending in **-ir**, drop the final **r**:
finir, *to finish*

j'ai fini	*I finished*	nous avons fini	*we finished*
tu as fini	*you finished*	vous avez fini	*you finished*
il/elle a fini	*he/she/it finished*	ils/elles ont fini	*they finished*

je n'ai pas fini	*I have not finished*	nous n'avons pas fini	*we have not finished*
tu n'as pas fini	*you have not finished*	vous n'avez pas fini	*you have not finished*
il/elle n'a pas fini	*he/she/it has not finished*	ils/elles n'ont pas fini	*they have not finished*

est-ce que j'ai fini... ?	*have I finished...?*	est-ce que nous avons fini... ?	*have we finished...?*
est-ce que tu as fini... ?	*have you finished...?*	est-ce que vous avez fini... ?	*have you finished...?*
est-ce qu'il'/elle a fini... ?	*has he/she/it finished...?*	est-ce qu'ils'/elles ont fini... ?	*have they finished...?*

The rule for avoiding a hiatus in the third person singular and plural forms of the interrogative is the same as for **-er** verbs: **A-t-elle fini ?**, *Has she finished?* , **Ont-ils fini ?**, *Have they finished?* (Remember that the first two interrogative forms – raised intonation and **est-ce que** – are standard in conversation and informal writing.)

▲ EXERCISES

1. PUT THESE VERBS INTO THE PAST TENSE

a. Nous avons (*fournir*: ....) tous les renseignements nécessaires.

b. Je (*réussir*, negative: ....) à parler avec l'agent immobilier hier.

c. Vous (*remplir*, interrogative: ....) le formulaire de rendez-vous sur notre site ?*

d. Ils (*convertir*: ....) la boulangerie en appartements

* Use the 2nd and 3rd interrogatives.

2. PUT THESE VERBS INTO THE THIRD INTERROGATIVE

a. Tu as fini de manger. →

b. Ils ont réussi à vendre leur studio →

c. Nous avons réfléchi à votre question. →

d. Elles ont fourni les bonnes réponses à nos questions. →

3. PUT THESE ADJECTIVES INTO THE COMPARATIVE OR SUPERLATIVE FORM

a. Le pain que tu fais est (*bon*, comparative: ....) que la baguette de la boulangerie en bas.

b. C'est l'appartement (*cher*, superlative superiority: ....) de l'immeuble.

c. Pourquoi est-ce que ses résultats sont (*mauvais*, comparative: ....) que ceux des autres ?

d. Je préfère les tablettes qui sont (*grand*, comparative inferiority: ....) et (*rapide*, comparative superiority: ....).

e. C'est vraiment (*mauvais*, superlative: ....) film de tous les temps !

16

4. TRANSLATE INTO FRENCH

a. Their team's results are worse than last week. – Never mind.

b. You've got something to do next week, Madeleine?* – I'm not quite ready.

c. The studio on the ground floor is noisier and less bright than the flat on the second floor.

d. That's all very well, but have you finished** your studies?

e. There's a grocery and two supermarkets in the neighbourhood. – You're (*familiar form*) not far from the town centre, I hope?

* Use the **vous** and **tu** forms.

** Use the 2nd and 3rd interrogatives.

VOCABULARY

convertir *to convert*
déménager *to move* (house, office, etc.)
fournir *to supply, to provide*
réfléchir (à) *to think about, to reflect on*
remplir *to fill (in)*
réussir *to succeed*

un agent immobilier *an estate agent*
une baguette *a stick loaf*
une banlieue *a suburb*
une boulangerie *a bakery*
un deux pièces *a two-room flat*
un centre commercial *a shopping centre*
le centre-ville *the town/city centre*
le coin *the corner/area/spot*
un garage *a garage*
une épicerie *a grocery*
un étage *a floor* (in a building)
les études *studies, education*
un formulaire *a (printed) form*
un immeuble *a block of flats*
un logement *accommodation, a place to live*
un loyer *a rent*
le mail *email*
maman *mum*
le pain *bread*
papa *dad*
une pièce *a room*
renseignement(s) *information* (see **renseigner**, Module 9)

le rez-de-chaussée *the ground floor*
un supermarché *a supermarket*
un studio *a studio flat*
un truc *a thing, a whatname*
la viennoiserie *pastries*

bruyant *noisy*
calme *calme* (masc. + fem.)
clair *clear, bright*
dans les environs *in the neighbourhood*
meilleur / le meilleur *best / the best*
pire / le pire *worse / worst*
vert *green*

Ça coûte les yeux de la tête *It costs an arm and a leg*
Tant pis *Never mind, Hard luck*

III

TELLING

STORIES

15.
LISTENING TO MUSIC

ÉCOUTER DE LA MUSIQUE

AIMS	NOTIONS

- TALK ABOUT THE PAST (CONTINUED)

- INDICATE POSSESSION

- DESCRIBE OWNERSHIP

- PERFECT TENSE OF *-RE* VERBS

- POSSESSIVE PRONOUNS

- ORDINALS

- POSITION OF ADJECTIVES

A BIGHEAD!

(Agathe and Julien are talking about a "great" artist)

— You know Laurent Lacombe?

— And how! I have followed his career from *(since)* the beginning.

— He is really very good *(strong)*: author, musician, composer, actor : he knows how to do everything *(everything to do)*, this guy!

— His only weak point is *(it is)* his lack of modesty. He has written ten or so books, directed [put on stage] more than six movies and translated four or five of the greatest foreign authors.

— *(Me)* I know him through *(by)* my girlfriend, who is [a] bookseller.

— I love *(the)* detective *(police)* novels and *(the)* his are among the best.

— I read his last book: it's very powerful *(strong)* but I didn't really understand his message.

— But have you seen his play *(piece of theatre)*? It's not very funny. Actually, it's horribly sad.

— Yes I know. But that's a bit normal. Lacombe lost his mother and his father in a car accident *(there is)* 20 years ago. But he continued to write and produce records — he's *(it's)* an excellent musician too.

— Yes, I learned that he plays the piano, the guitar and some African instruments.

— I listened [to] the record he recorded with his new group. Damn, I've forgotten the title: where did I put my tablet? Ah, here it is.

— Wait a minute *(instant)*: is that *(the)* mine or *(the)* yours?

— Sorry, I took *(the)* yours. This old thing *(here)* is *(the)* mine.

— Let's see: I've opened his website. His first record is called *(calls itself)* Me and his second is *Me Myself*. But it's his third [one] that's really the best: its title is: *Modesty: the Greatest of All Time (the times)*.

(Agathe et Julien parlent d'un « grand » artiste)

– Tu connais Laurent Lacombe ?

– Et comment ! J'ai suivi sa carrière depuis le début.

– Il est vraiment très fort : auteur, musicien, compositeur, comédien : il sait tout faire, ce type !

– Son seul point faible, c'est son manque de modestie. Il a écrit une dizaine de bouquins, mis en scène plus de six films et traduit quatre ou cinq des plus grands auteurs étrangers.

– Moi, je l'ai connu par ma copine, qui est libraire.

– J'aime les romans policiers, et les siens sont parmi les meilleurs.

– J'ai lu son dernier livre : c'est très fort mais je n'ai pas vraiment compris son message.

– Mais as-tu vu sa pièce de théâtre ? Ce n'est pas très drôle. En fait, c'est horriblement triste.

– Oui je sais. Mais c'est un peu normal. Lacombe a perdu sa mère et son père dans un accident de voiture il y a vingt ans. Mais il a continué à écrire et à produire des disques – c'est un excellent musicien aussi.

– Oui, j'ai appris qu'il joue du piano, de la guitare et des instruments africains.

– J'ai écouté le disque qu'il a enregistré avec son nouveau groupe. Zut, j'ai oublié le titre : où est-ce que j'ai mis ma tablette ? Ah, la voilà.

– Attends un instant : c'est la mienne ou la tienne ?

– Pardon, j'ai pris la tienne. Ce vieux truc ici est le mien.

– Voyons voir : j'ai ouvert son site internet. Son premier disque s'appelle *Moi* et son deuxième est *Moi-même*. Mais c'est son troisième qui est vraiment le meilleur : son titre est : *Modestie : le plus grand artiste de tous les temps.*

UNDERSTANDING THE DIALOGUE

WORDS AND PHRASES

→ **premier, deuxième, troisième**, etc. are ordinal numbers. With a couple of exceptions, they are formed by adding **-ième** (like -th in English) to the cardinal number:

un	→	**premier / première**	*1st*	**six**	→	**sixième**	*6th*
deux	→	**deuxième**	*2nd*	**sept**	→	**septième**	*7th*
trois	→	**troisième**	*3rd*	**huit**	→	**huitième**	*8th*
quatre	→	**quatrième**	*4th*	**neuf**	→	**neuvième**	*9th*
cinq	→	**cinquième**	*5th*	**dix**	→	**dixième**	*10th*

– The main exception is **premier**, the only ordinal to agree in number and gender with its noun when used as an adjective: **mon premier disque, ma première guitare, mes premiers films, mes premières pièces de théâtre.** (There is also a difference between **deuxième** and **second**, the latter referring to one out of two, but in everyday French, **deuxième** can be used in both cases.)
– There are some minor spelling changes: the final **e** of **quatre** is dropped before adding the ending; the **f** of **neuf** changes to **v: quatrième, neuvième**; and a **u** is added to **cinq → cinquième**.
– For the ordinals from 11 upwards, the basic pattern is the same (**onzième, douzième**, etc.) with a couple of important exceptions, notably *21st* → **vingt et unième**, *31st* **trente et unième**, etc. (not **premier**).
– The abbreviation of **-ième** is a simple **e: 2ᵉ, 4ᵉ**, etc. (**1ᵉʳ / 1ʳᵉ** for *1st*). This ordinal letter is always written in superscript.
– Ordinal adjectives always come before the noun: **le premier jour**, *the first day*, **le troisième homme**, *the third man*, etc.

→ Don't confuse **écouter**, *to listen to*, and **entendre**, *to hear* (Module 9). Neither verb takes a preposition: **Écoutez cette chanson**, *Listen to this song*; **J'ai entendu beaucoup de choses sur ce chanteur**, *I've heard a lot about this singer*.

→ **une librairie**, *a bookshop*, and **un libraire**, *a bookseller*, are two very common – and deceptive – false cognates (see Module 5). They resemble, respectively, *a library* and *a librarian*, but the French words for these are **une bibliothèque** and **un(e) bibliothécaire** (the latter can be masculine or feminine). Another false cognate is **un comédien**, which means *an actor* (feminine: **une comédienne**). The English word *a comedian* translates as **un(e) comique**. A word of advice: **Faites très attention aux faux amis !**, *Be very careful of false friends!*

→ **fort** usually means *strong*: **Le vent est très fort aujourd'hui**, *The wind is very strong today.* That same notion of strength can be extended to mean *great, powerful, competent*, etc. **C'est un film très fort**, *It's a very powerful film.* The opposite is **faible**, *weak*, and, by extension, *small, low*, etc. **Mon salaire est beaucoup trop faible**, *My wages are much too low.* (The feminine of **fort** is **forte**, but **faible** is both masculine and feminine singular.)

→ **Voyons voir** (literally "Let's see to see") is almost identical to its English cognate *Let's see*, used to indicate that the speaker is thinking about or planning what to say next. **Passe-moi le bouquin. – Voyons voir, où est-ce que je l'ai mis ?**, *Pass me the book – Let's see, where did I put it?*

CULTURE NOTES

France is inordinately proud of its contribution to the field of la **culture** (*culture*). It has a special government department, **le Ministère de la culture**, set up in 1959 to oversee a very broad field of artistic, creative and heritage-related activities. These include **le cinéma** (*film*), **la musique** (*music*), **l'art** (*art*), **la danse** (*dance*) and **le théâtre** (*theatre*). France boasts a wealth of creative talent, including **les écrivains** (masc., *writers*), **les musiciens** (masc. *musicians*), **les metteurs en scène** (masc. *movie and theatre directors*), **les scénaristes** (masc. *scriptwriters*), **les chorégraphes** (masc. *choreographers*) and **les plasticiens** (masc. *visual artists*). But **la culture** is a very broad church that also encompasses rap, graffiti, comic books and many other disciplines. One of the emblematic cultural events is **la Fête de la musique** "the music party", a day-long celebration of music held on 21 June all over the country, from prestigious concert venues to impromptu street-corner bandstands. Launched by the ministry in 1983, it is now celebrated in more than a hundred countries worldwide. **Le Ministère de la culture** is also responsible for protecting and preserving the French language by limiting and regulating the use of other languages –notably English – in broadcasting, advertising and other sectors.

◆ GRAMMAR

POSSESSIVE PRONOUNS: *LE MIEN,* ETC.

Possessive pronouns can replace nouns, generally to avoid repetition (*my girlfriend* → *mine*). They look like this:

	masc. singular	fem. singular	masc. plural	fem. plural
mine	**le mien**	**la mienne**	**les miens**	**les miennes**
yours	**le tien**	**la tienne**	**les tiens**	**les tiennes**

his/hers	le sien	la sienne	les siens	les siennes
ours	le nôtre	la nôtre	les nôtres	les nôtres
yours	le vôtre	la vôtre	les vôtres	les vôtres
theirs	le leur	la leur	les leurs	les leurs

In contrast to English, they are always accompanied by the definite article. There are four forms for each of the singular pronouns but only three for the plural (and formal singular, **vous**). Note also that **nôtre** and **vôtre** are both written with a circumflex, to distinguish them from the possessive adjectives **notre** and **votre**. One very important point is that possessive pronouns agree in gender and number with the noun they are describing, not the person who "owns" it. So, if either a man or a woman is asking about the location of their tablet (**une tablette**), both would say: **Où est la mienne ?**, *Where's mine?*. Likewise, in the third person, **Ce livre est le sien** can be translated both by *This book is his* AND *hers*.

IL Y A MEANING "AGO"

We know that **il y a** means *there is / there are* (Module 5). However, if used with a verb in the past tense and an expression of time, it means *ago*. In this case it comes before, not after, the time period:
J'ai lu *Les Misérables* il y a vingt ans, *I read* Les Misérables *20 years ago*.
As in English, the expression can be used at the beginning of a clause:
Il y a dix ans, elle a perdu son mari, *Ten years ago she lost her husband*.

▲ CONJUGATIONS

LE PASSÉ COMPOSÉ FOR THE THIRD GROUP OF VERBS

The verbs in this group end in **-re**, **-ir** or **-oir** (plus **aller**). Most are irregular, but they can be subdivided into several groups that follow identical patterns, so you only have to learn a limited number of forms. In this module, we see different types of **-re** verbs in the perfect tense, formed with **avoir** and the past participle.
Regular verbs in this group that end in **-re** form the past participle by adding **-u** to the stem.

attendre	to wait	attendu
connaître	to know	connu
descendre	to come down	descendu

entendre	to hear	entendu
perdre	to lose	perdu
répondre	to answer	répondu

Nous avons attendu plus de trois heures, *We waited for more than three hours.*
Avez-vous répondu à la lettre de votre frère ?, *Have you answered your brother's letter?*
Il n'a pas entendu le téléphone, *He didn't hear the phone.*
Among the irregular verbs ending in **-re**, there is a group based on **prendre,** *to take,* which form their past participles by adding **-is** to the stem:

prendre	to take	pris
apprendre	to learn	appris
comprendre	to understand	compris

Other verbs that use **prendre** as a root, such as **surprendre,** *to surprise,* usually follow the same pattern – but always check!
Another group forms the past participle by replacing **-re** with a **t**

conduire	to drive	conduit
écrire	to write	écrit
traduire	to translate	traduit

The irregular verb **mettre** has **mis** as a past participle. It is also the root word for more than ten other verbs, which follow the same pattern. These include **admettre** → **admis** (*to admit*), **permettre** → **permis** (*to allow, permit*), and **transmettre** → **transmis** (*to transmit, to send*).
As in English, past participles can be used as adjectives and therefore agree with their noun. For example, **une chose permise,** *a permitted thing,* something that is allowed.
As we said before, the perfect can be translated in English by both the simple past or the present perfect (*have* + participle) because the latter tense does not exist in French.

● EXERCISES

1. PUT THESE VERBS INTO THE PERFECT TENSE

a. Il (*apprendre*: …………………..) le piano et la guitare avec un excellent professeur.

b. (*répondre* , interrogative*, toi: ………………..)* à sa lettre ? - Oui je (*répondre*: ………………..) hier.

c. Je (*lire*, negative: ……………………..) son dernier livre.

d. Comment (*connaître*, interrogative**, vous:………………………………..) ce musicien ? – Par mon copain, Gilles.

e. Je (*apprendre*: …………………………..) le texte mais je (*comprendre*, negative……………..) son message.

* 3rd interrogative
** 2nd interrogative

2. REPLACE THE UNDERLINED WORDS WITH A POSSESSIVE PRONOUN

a. Est-ce que je peux prendre cette tablette ? J'ai perdu ma tablette. →

b. Ceci est mon couteau n'est-ce pas ? – Non, c'est mon couteau.→

c. J'ai oublié mes cartes. Est-ce que tu as tes cartes ?→

d. Ce sont mes bouquins ? Non, ce sont nos bouquins.→

e. Je vais prendre ce gâteau. Je n'aime pas leurs gâteaux.→

3. MAKE THESE ADJECTIVES AGREE AND PUT THEM IN THE RIGHT PLACE, BEFORE OR AFTER THE NOUNS

a. **vieux(vieille) / bleu(e)** : Michel est un _ _ _ copain_ _ _ qui habite la _ _ _ maison _ _ _ là-bas.→

b. **intelligent(e) / sympathique** : C'est une _ _ _ _ femme _ _ _ _ et elle a un _ _ _ _ mari _ _ _ _ .→

c. **mauvais(e) / grand(e)** : J'ai une _ _ _ nouvelle _ _ _ : le _ _ _ _ musicien _ _ _ Hugo Prat est mort.→

d. **petit(e) / rouge** : Les _ _ _ verres _ _ _ sont dans le _ _ _ placard _ _ _ .→

e. **deuxième / meilleur** : *Modestie* est son _ _ _ _ disque _ _ _ _ . C'est aussi son _ _ _ _ disque _ _ _ _ .→

⬤ VOCABULARY

enregister *to record*
jouer *to play*
mettre en scène *to direct* (play, movie)
oublier *to forget*
perdre *to lose*
produire *to produce*
suivre *to follow*
traduire *to translate*

un(e) auteur(e) *a (male/female) author*
un bouquin *a book* (fam.)
un(e) comédien(nne) *a (male/female) actor*
un compositeur *a composer*
un copain/une copine *a mate/a boyfriend/girlfriend*
un disque *a record* (think: "a disc")
un(e) libraire *a bookseller (male/female)*
une librairie *a bookshop*
un manque *a lack*
la modestie *modesty*
un(e) musicien(nne) *a (male/female) musician*
une pièce de théâtre *a play*
un roman (policier) *a novel/a detective novel*
une tablette *a tablet* (computer)
un titre *a title*
un type *a guy, a bloke*

africain(e) *African*
étranger *foreign*
drôle *funny*

fort *strong, powerful*
horrible(ment) *horrible/-ly*
triste *sad*

Voyons voir *Let's see*
Zut ! *Damn!*

17

a. Where did he put his tablet? – Here it is. – But it's not his; it's mine.

b. What did he tell you?* – That he lost his mother 20 years ago.

c. Armand is a librarian during the week but he works in a bookshop on Saturday and Sunday.

d. And what does his wife do? – She's an excellent actress.

e. I saw his/her first play last week but I didn't really understand the message.

* familiar form only

Since the aim of this book is to teach you everyday French, we regularly include words and phrases which, while not actually slang, are nevertheless familiar in the grammatical sense of the term. In this module, for example, we learned:

- **un bouquin**, a synonym of **un livre**, *a book*
- **un copain / une copine**, *a male friend* or *boyfriend*, *a female friend* or *girl-friend*
- **un type**, *a guy*, *a bloke*
- **Zut !**, equivalent to *Damn!* or *Heck!*

The reason for including these turns of phrase is that you are bound to hear and read them when interacting regularly with native speakers, so it's important to know them. However, we do not recommend that you use them until you feel totally at home in the language!

16.
A LIFE STORY

L'HISTOIRE D'UNE VIE

AIMS	NOTIONS

- TALK ABOUT THE PAST (CONTINUED)
- DESCRIBE A SEQUENCE OF EVENTS
- DISCUSS YEARS

- PERFECT TENSES FORMED WITH *ÊTRE* INSTEAD OF *AVOIR*
- *TOUT/TOUTE/TOUS/TOUTES*

HE'S REALLY GIFTED!

— Have you heard the news? Paul Vandertramp died *(is dead)* yesterday at the age of 99 *(years)*.

— Vandertramp, the scientist? You're sure?

— Absolutely *(all to done)*. I read it a little while ago *(all to the hour)* on lesinfos.fr. Here [is] the article: "*(The)* Dr Paul Vandertramp was *(is)* born in Germany on 1st March 1925 of a German father and a French mother. All the family — three girls/daughters and one boy/son — and both parents *(is)* left in 1936. The passed through *(by)* South America and arrived eight months later in Canada."

— And after?

— "[A] brilliant student, Paul studied law initially *(in a first time)*. He *(is)* entered *(the)* university at the age of 17 *(years)*, and he *(is)* left two years later with a degree in [his] pocket. In less than five years, he *(has)* obtained his master's and his doctorate. He *(is)* became afterwards one of the youngest lawyers in the country, specialised in human rights *(the rights of Man)*."

— He's truly gifted!

— "He *(is)* fell in love with a French [woman], a young scientist met in 1956 in Paris, and they were *(are)* married at Christmas. The *(are)* came back to *(in)* France, and Paul *(has)* changed career[s] completely. He did *(is)* not go back to [the] university but *(is)* went to a grande école *(grand school)* in Lyon. *(The)* Dr and Mrs Vandertramp *(are)* went up together to Paris, where they *(are)* stayed for [some] 30 years. They worked ceaselessly, every day *(all days)* and every week *(all weeks)*, to invent medicines. Dr Vandertramp *(is)* fell ill suddenly and died *(is dead)* shortly *(little time)* after[wards]."

– As-tu entendu la nouvelle ? Paul Vandertramp est mort hier à l'âge de quatre-vingt-dix-neuf ans.

– Vandertramp, le scientifique ? Tu es sûre ?

– Tout à fait. Je l'ai lu tout à l'heure sur lesinfos.fr. Voici l'article : « Le docteur Paul Vandertramp est né en Allemagne le 1er mars mil neuf cent vingt-cinq d'un père allemand et une mère française. Toute la famille – trois filles et un garçon ainsi que les deux parents – est partie en mil neuf cent trente-six. Ils sont passés par l'Amérique du sud et sont arrivés huit mois plus tard au Canada ».

– Et ensuite ?

– « Brillant élève, Paul a étudié le droit dans un premier temps. Il est entré à l'université à l'âge de dix-sept ans, et il est sorti deux ans plus tard avec une licence en poche. En moins de cinq ans, il a obtenu sa maîtrise et son doctorat. Il est devenu ensuite un des plus jeunes avocats du pays, spécialisé dans les droits de l'Homme. »

– Il est vraiment doué !

– « Il est tombé amoureux d'une Française, une jeune scientifique rencontrée à Paris en mil neuf cent cinquante-six, et ils se sont mariés à Noël. Ils sont revenus en France, et Paul a changé complètement de carrière. Il n'est pas retourné à la fac mais est allé dans une grande école à Lyon. Le docteur et madame Vandertramp sont montés ensemble à Paris, où ils sont restés pendant une trentaine d'années. Ils ont travaillé sans cesse, tous les jours et toutes les semaines, à inventer des médicaments. Le docteur Vandertramp est tombé malade soudainement et il est mort peu de temps après. »

■ UNDERSTANDING THE DIALOGUE
WORDS AND PHRASES

→ **un point** (pronounced [pwa]) has several meanings, one of which is *a full stop*. In an email address, it means *a dot*. Domain names are pronounced more or less as in English: either as single letters (**.fr** → [pwa eff err]) or, where possible, as a syllable (**.com** → [pwa kom]). The @ symbol is often pronounced as the English word *at* but the French printing term **arobase** [arowbaz] (a feminine noun) is preferred, so an address ending **@dmail.com**, for example, would be pronounced [arowbaz dee-mayl pwa kom].

→ French uses cardinal numbers in dates, so, for instance, *the 25th of February* is **le vingt-cinq février**. Easy! The only exception is the first day of the month, for which the masculine ordinal **le premier** is used: **le premier mars**, *the 1st of March*, etc.

→ Years can be spoken about in two ways. The most common way is as a regular number, so 728 is **sept cent vingt-huit**, 1066 **mille soixante-six**, and 2019 **deux mille dix-neuf** (**mille** is sometimes written **mil** for years between 1001 and 1999; the pronunciation is identical). An alternative for the years from 1100 to 1999 is to break the four-digit number into pairs, separated by the word **cent**, *hundred*: 1536 **quinze cent trente-six**, 1756 **dix-sept cent cinquante-six**, etc. This method obviously does not work for the present century (2022, for instance, is **deux mille vingt-deux**). To specify the era – *BC* or *AD* – we write, respectively, **av. J-C** (**avant Jésus-Christ**, pronounced [zhayzoo kree]) and **ap. J-C** (**après Jésus-Christ**). The alternative, "neutral" forms *Before Common Era (BCE)* and *Common Era (CE)* also exist in French, **avant l'ère commune (ACE)** and **de l'ère commune (EC)**, but are less common than in English. Lastly, when referring to a specific year, for instance *the year 2026*, we use **l'année**: **l'année 2026**. But years ending in zero are designated by **l'an** (e.g. **l'an 2000**).

→ French has two words for *the law*: **la loi**, which refers to the rule of law (and also to a specific statute), and **le droit**, meaning the general concept or field of law. The latter word also means *a right*: **J'ai le droit de prendre des vacances**, *I have the right to take a holiday*. The common expression **les droits de l'Homme**, *human rights* (lit. "the rights of Man") is increasingly being replaced by a more modern (and accurate) term: **les droits humains**.

→ Many masculine nouns ending in **-e** have no feminine form as such and can be "feminised" simply by changing the article. This is especially the case for professions and jobs. So, for instance, **un détective**, *a (male) detective*, **un juge**, *a (male) judge* and **un scientifique**, *a (male) scientist*, become **une détective**, **une juge** and **une scientifique** if the person holding the position is female. French, like English, is constantly seeking single-form words to encompass both sexes, but the process is complicated by the fact that all French nouns are either masculine or feminine. For that reason, the topic can get highly political (should you say **une professeur, une professeure** or use another word altogether?). The jury is still out on many of these issues, so in this course we will stick to the time-honoured rules, pointing out any exceptions as they arise.

→ We learned in Module 12 that **tout à l'heure** means *later*, but, if used with a verb in the past tense, it means *earlier*. **Je te rappelle tout à l'heure**, *I'll call you back later*; **Elle m'a rappelé tout à l'heure**, *She called me earlier*. Obviously, the context will make the meaning clear.

CULTURE NOTES

Most of *the students*, **les étudiants**, entering *higher education*, **les études supérieures**, in France go to *a university*, **une université** (sometimes referred to as **une faculté**, *a faculty*, or, in everyday language, **une fac**). As in most European countries, the diploma system has three levels: **la licence** (equivalent to *a bachelor's degree*), **une maîtrise** (*a master's*) and **le doctorat** (*doctorate*). The general term for a higher-education qualification is **un diplôme**, *a diploma*, which can be used in expressions such as **Elle est diplômée de Sciences Po**, *She holds a qualification from* (or *is a graduate of*) *Sciences Po*.

In parallel to the universities, there are several elite higher-education institutions called **les grandes écoles** (literally "grand schools", although the term is hard to translate precisely) that offer degrees in subjects ranging from business to political science. One of the most prestigious **grandes écoles** is **l'École nationale d'administration**, or **l'ENA**, whose high-flier graduates, called **les énarques**, are to be found at the upper echelons of business and politics. France also has a state-regulated system of ongoing vocational training, **la formation professionnelle continue** (from the verb **former**, *to train*), funded by central government, regional authorities and firms. The importance of education in general is aptly summed up in the proverb **Sans éducation, l'enfant est orphelin**, *Without education, the child is an orphan*.

◆ GRAMMAR

ALL ABOUT *TOUT*

Tout and its derivatives are among the hardest-working words in French, acting as adjectives, adverbs, pronouns and, in some cases, nouns.

The basic meaning is *all*, *each*, *every*, and in some cases, *very*.

The adjectival form always agrees in gender and number with the qualified noun and always precedes it. The four forms are **tout** (masculine), **toute** (feminine singular), **tous** (masculine plural) and **toutes** (feminine plural). Memorise this sentence:

Les amis sont à la maison tous les jours (masc. plu.) **et toutes les semaines** (fem. plu.) : **ils mangent tout le pain** (masc. sing.) **et toute la confiture** (fem. sing.).

Tout qualifies not only nouns but also possessive and demonstrative adjectives:

Toute ma famille vit dans le Midi, *All my family lives in the south of France.*

Tous ces gens sont ici pour nous aider, *All these people are here to help us.*

As regards pronunciation, **tout** and **tous** are identical ([too]) as are **toute** and **toutes** ([toot]).

As an adverb, **tout** is nearly always invariable:

Allez tout droit et tourner à gauche, *Go straight on and turn left.*

If used with another adverb, it means *very*:

Le dimanche matin, elle se réveille tout doucement, *She wakes up gradually on Sunday morning.*

Three other very common expressions in which **tout** is an adverb are **tout droit**, *straight on* (Module 5), **tout à l'heure**, *later* (see above), and **tout à fait**, *absolutely* (Module 14).

As a pronoun, there are only three forms: **tout, tous** and **toutes**:

Tout est possible !, *Everything/Anything is possible!*

Où sont les enfants? – Ils sont tous dans la chambre, *Where are the children?, They're all in the bedroom.*

Elles sont toutes arrivées en retard, *They (i.e. females) all arrived late.*

In terms of pronunciation, **tout** and **toutes** are pronounced in the same way as the adjectival forms [too/toot] but the final **s** of **tous** is voiced: [tooss].

Remember also the expressions **pas du tout** (Module 1) and **rien du tout**, *nothing at all*.

We have also seen a number of useful expressions with **tout** so far in this course, notably **tout le monde**, *everybody*, and **en tout cas**, *in any case* (Module 5); **tout de suite**, *right away* (Module 6), **tout le temps**, *all the time* (Module 10); and **tout à l'heure**, meaning *earlier* (see Dialogue).

PEU

Don't confuse the adverbs **un peu** and **peu de** (see Module 5). The first can be used only with an uncountable noun and expresses a presence whereas **peu de** (no article) can be used with countables and uncountables but expresses an absence or limitation. Compare **J'ai un peu de temps**, *I've got a little time* and **J'ai peu de**

temps, *I have very little time.* **Peu** can be used on its own after a verb to convey the same meaning. **Il lit très peu,** *He reads very little.*

▲ CONJUGATIONS

LE PASSÉ COMPOSÉ USING *ÊTRE* INSTEAD OF *AVOIR* FOR AN AUXILIARY

We know that the majority of verbs use **avoir,** *to have,* as an auxiliary to form the perfect tense. But a group of common intransitive verbs use **être.** How to remember them? That's why we've introduced you to DR & MRS P. VANDERTRAMP:

Devenir *(to become);* **R**evenir *(to come back);* **M**ourir *(to die);* **R**etourner *(to return);* **S**ortir *(to go out);* **P**artir *(to leave);* **V**enir *(to come);* **A**rriver *(to arrive);* **N**aître *(to be born);* **D**escendre *(to come down, descend);* **E**ntrer *(to enter);* **R**entrer *(to come back);* **T**omber *(to fall);* **R**ester *(to rest);* **A**ller *(to go);* **M**onter *(to go up);* **P**asser *(to pass)*

These 17 verbs all express either movement or a change of place or condition (notably in the case of **naître** and **mourir**!). There are several more members of the group, but they are used less frequently.

In the perfect tense, they agree in number and gender with the subject(s):

Le docteur est allé à la conférence hier BUT **Le docteur et son collègue sont allés à la conférence hier** *(The doctor / doctor and his colleague went to the lecture yesterday)*

Paul est tombé amoureux de Marie, mais Marie n'est pas tombée amoureuse de Paul, *Paul fell in love with Marie, but Marie did not fall in love with Paul.*

Est-ce que les filles sont rentrées ? – Non, elles sont sorties il y a seulement deux heures, *Have the girls come back? – No they went out only two hours ago.*

Remember that **vous** can be both singular and plural: **À quelle heure êtes-vous arrivé ?** (masc. singular) BUT **À quelle heure êtes-vous arrivés ?** (masc. plural). Of course, the pronunciation is the same.

In a sentence with a plural masculine and feminine subject, the past participle takes the masculine gender: **Paul et sa femme sont rentrés hier soir,** *Paul and his wife got back last night.*

Five of the 17 have irregular past participles. They are: **venir (venu)** and its derivatives: **revenir (revenu)** and **devenir (devenu);** along with **naître (né)** and **mourir (mort).**

Lastly, half a dozen intransitive verbs also have a transitive form, meaning that they can take a direct object. For instance: **Nous avons passé trois jours à Nîmes à Noël,** *We spent three days in Nîmes at Christmas* (transitive) BUT **Trois bus sont**

passés sans s'arrêter, *Three buses passed without stopping.* Since this dual format is quite infrequent, you will be able to remember the verbs in question quite easily. And even if you make a mistake, your sentence will be clear enough to be understood!

● EXERCISES

1. PUT THESE VERBS INTO THE PERFECT TENSE

a. J'attends nos filles. Elles (*sortir*: …………………………..) tout à l'heure mais elles (*rentrer*, negative: …………………………..) encore.

b. Est-ce que le docteur Bellier (*partir*: …………....…………………………..) ? – Oui, il (*partir*: …………………………..) il y a une heure.

c. Les deux sœurs (*naître*: …………………………..) en 1901 et elle (*mourir*) en 1999.

d. Nous* (*sortir*: …………………………..) à pied ce matin mais nous (*aller*, negative: …………………………..) très loin.

e. Le directeur et sa femme (*arriver*: …………………………..) ce matin mais ils (*partir*: …………………………..) déjà.

* Masculine

2. USE THE CORRECT FORM OF *TOUT*

a. Madame Vandertramp est (*tout*) seule à la maison car son mari est parti (*tout*) à l'heure en voyage d'affaires. →

b. Comme (*tout*) le monde, il se réveille (*tout*) doucement le dimanche matin. →

c. (*tout*) mes cousins et (*tout*) mes cousines habitent au Canada. →

d. Est ce qu'ils viennent te voir (*tout*) les semaines ? – (*tout*) à fait ! →

e. (*tout*) ces gens sont venus pour t'aider. En (*tout*) cas, c'est ce qu'ils m'ont dit. →

3. READ THESE YEARS ALOUD

a.	1984*	f.	1999*
b.	827	g.	1555*
c.	1832*	h.	1066
d.	2019	i.	1600*
e.	1100*	j.	2000

* two possibilities

● VOCABULARY

changer *to change*
entrer *to enter*
étudier *to study*
inventer *to invent*
naître *to be born**
obtenir *to obtain, to get*
mourir *to die**
monter *to go up**
passer *(intransitive) to pass**
retourner *to return**
tomber *to fall**
tomber amoureux/-se *to fall in love*
* *conjugated with être as the auxiliary in the perfect tense*

l'Amérique du sud *South America*
une carrière *a career*
un doctorat *a doctorate, PhD*
le droit *law*
les droits *rights*
une faculté, une fac *a faculty, a university*
la loi *the law* (i.e. rule of law), *a statute*
une licence *a bachelor's degree*
une maîtrise *a master's degree*
un médicament *a drug, a medicine*
Noël *Christmas*
une nouvelle *a news item, a piece of news*
une poche *a pocket*
un professeur *a professor* (also a teacher, Module 2)
un(e) scientifique *a (male / female) scientist*

une université *a university*

brillant(e) *brilliant*
doué(e) *gifted, talented*
sans cesse *constantly* ("ceaselessly")
soudainement *suddenly*
tout à l'heure *earlier* (with a verb in the past tense)
dans un premier temps *initially, "in the first instance"*

Tout à fait *Absolutely*

18

a. I think that all students have the right to take holidays at Christmas. – Absolutely.

b. She studied law and she became one of the youngest lawyers* in France.

c. We fell in love, and we stayed together for about 20 years.

d. Have you** heard the news? The actress Jeanne Morteau has died at the age of 92.

e. She got her master's in less than three years. – She's really gifted!

* **un avocat** can be used for a male or a female lawyer, but the feminine form **une avocate** has now become the standard usage.

** Use the formal pronoun/verb form

Remember that learning numbers and dates is largely a question of reflexes. Years can be particularly awkward when you start learning French, so don't hesitate to read dates aloud whenever you come across them, or flip through a thick book – anything with more than 2,000 pages – to get into training. Start with today's date!

17.
LET'S GO TO THE MARKET!

ALLONS AU MARCHÉ !

AIMS	NOTIONS

- TALK ABOUT SHOPS AND SHOPKEEPERS
- DISCUSS FRIENDS AND PLANS
- LEARN ABOUT REGIONAL ACCENTS

- *Y* AND *EN*
- INDIRECT OBJECT PRONOUNS

FRIENDS IN TOULOUSE (PART 1)

(Bruno, the Parisian, is visiting (render visit to) his friends Émilie and Marc in Toulouse)

– Have you *(are you)* already been *(gone)* to the market this morning, Émilie?

– Not yet: I'm going there in an hour or two while *(that)* Marc [is] working.

– Can I go with *(I can accompany)* you "shopping" please? I don't know at all the Pink City.

– But the whole *(all the)* city knows the Saint Cyprien hall [covered market]! Everyone goes there at [the] end of the week. Outside *(at the exterior)*, you *(one)* find*(s)* fishmongers, butchers and fruit and vegetable sellers *(merchants)*. Inside *(at the interior of)* the building, there are regional products, pork butchers, florists, cheesemongers, and loads *(a pile)* of other things. This morning I have to *(must)* get *(take)* butter, milk and eggs. I really must think of it because we don't have any more *(of it/them)* at home. Lend me a pen please. I have to make a list.

– I don't have [one] on me. I am going to look [for] one in my bedroom.

– Forget it *(let drop)*, it's not important. Let's go *(go, we there go)*.

(On the way, the two friends are talking)

– By the way, have you had *(do you have)* [any] news from Raphaël and Claudie?

– Yes, they called me [on] Tuesday to tell me that they are in Toulouse this week.

– Me, I have been *(am)* waiting [for] them in Paris for months and months. I wrote [to] them a long time ago and I gave them my new address.

– Did you give your new contact details *(coordinates)*?

– To Raphaël, no, but to Claudie, yes. And I gave him my email and my mobile number. But she hasn't contacted me.

– What a pity *(damage)*! We visited them *(render visit)* three months ago. They lent us their spare room *(friends' room)* and we had a good time *(pass a good moment)* together. Raphaël is like Marc: he resembles him like two drops of water *(they're like peas in a pod)*.

– What do you mean *(that is to say)*?

– I talk to him, but he doesn't listen to me!

(Bruno, le Parisien, rend visite à ses amis Émilie et Marc à Toulouse.)

— Es-tu déjà allée au marché ce matin, Émilie ?

— Pas encore : j'y vais dans une heure ou deux pendant que Marc travaille.

— Je peux t'accompagner faire les courses ? Je ne connais pas du tout la Ville rose.

— Mais toute la ville connaît la halle Saint Cyprien ! Tout le monde y va en fin de semaine. À l'extérieur, on trouve des poissonniers, des bouchers et des marchands de fruits et légumes. À l'intérieur du bâtiment, il y a des produits régionaux, des charcutiers, des fleuristes, des fromagers, et un tas d'autres choses. Ce matin je dois prendre du beurre, du lait et des œufs. Il faut vraiment que j'y pense car on n'en a plus à la maison. Prête-moi un stylo s'il te plaît. Je dois faire une liste.

— Je n'en ai pas sur moi. Je vais en chercher un dans ma chambre.

— Laisse tomber, ce n'est pas important. Allez, on y va.

(En route, les deux amis discutent.)

— À propos, as-tu des nouvelles de Raphaël et Claudie ?

— Oui, ils m'ont appelée mardi pour me dire qu'ils sont à Toulouse cette semaine.

— Moi, je les attends à Paris depuis des mois et des mois. Je leur ai écrit il y a longtemps et je leur ai donné ma nouvelle adresse.

— As-tu donné tes nouvelles coordonnées ?

— A Raphaël, non, mais à Claudie, oui. Et je lui ai donné mon mail et mon numéro de portable. Mais elle ne m'a pas contacté.

— Quel dommage ! Nous leur avons rendu visite il y trois mois. Ils nous ont prêté leur chambre d'amis et on a passé un bon moment ensemble. Raphaël est comme Marc : il lui ressemble comme deux gouttes d'eau.

— C'est-à-dire ?

— Je lui parle, mais il ne m'écoute pas !

■ UNDERSTANDING THE DIALOGUE
WORDS AND PHRASES

→ In Module 16, we saw **une nouvelle** in the singular, meaning *an item of news*. In the plural, with the partitive article **des**, it has a more general sense: **As-tu des nouvelles de Sacha ?**, *Have you heard from* (i.e. *had any news from) Sacha?* A common (and easily recognisable) proverb goes **Pas de nouvelles, bonnes nouvelles**, *No news is good news.*

→ **pendant** is a preposition meaning *during* or *for a period of time* (Module 5). Followed by **que**, it forms a conjunctive phrase that means *while* (or *whilst*). **Pendant que** is used in phrases like **Pendant que j'y pense, peux-tu me donner tes coordonnées ?**, *While I think of it, can you give me your contact details?* (The feminine plural noun **les coordonnées** is a mathematical term for *coordinates*. But it is used in everyday French to mean *address and phone number* or, more broadly, *contact details*. **Je vous laisse mes coordonnées**, *I'm leaving you my name, address and phone number/my contact details.*)

→ The precise meaning of **la fin de semaine**, literally "the end of week", depends on the context but generally refers to Friday and/or either Thursday or Saturday. (It is a corruption of **à la fin de la semaine**, <u>at</u> *the end of <u>the</u> week.*) As we know, the French have adopted **le week-end** because the consecutive two-day break is purportedly an English invention – so much so that a five-day workweek used to be known as **la semaine anglaise** – but French-speaking Canadians tend to shun such loan words, using **la fin de semaine** for Saturday/Sunday. If in doubt, always ask!

→ **une course**, *an errand*, is generally used with the verb **faire**: *to get something from the shops* or *run an errand*. In the plural, **faire les courses** means *to go food shopping*. Don't confuse this expression with **faire du shopping**, seen in Module 11. (Note that **une course** also means *a race*, which might suggest a link between shopping, speed and competition…)

→ **laisser tomber** means *to drop* ("to let fall"): **Zut, j'ai laissé tomber mes clés**, *Damn, I've dropped my keys.* The idiomatic expression **Laisse tomber !** means *Forget it!* (a little like the English expression *Drop it.*)

→ The masculine noun **dommage**, the root of our word *damage*, means *harm* or *injury*. It is one of a group of nouns that can be either singular or plural, unlike their English equivalents. In everyday speech, however, it means *a shame*, *a pity*, and is used in expressions like **Quel dommage !**, *What a pity/shame!* or a phrase such as **C'est vraiment dommage de perdre le match**, *It's really a shame to lose the* *match*. In a subsequent module, we will see a group of collective nouns, including **dommage**, that are singular in English but can take a plural in French.

CULTURE NOTES

Toulouse is the capital of the **Occitanie** region of southwestern France. It is located between the Mediterranean and Atlantic coasts and traversed by the **Garonne** river and the 240-km **Canal du Midi**. The city is not only a historical and cultural landmark; it is also a hi-tech centre and the hub of the European aerospace industry. Toulouse is known as the **La Ville rose**, *the Pink City*, because of the reddish terracotta buildings dotted around the historic town centre. (Other French cities are often referred to by their sobriquets, notably **Paris** – **La Ville lumière**, *the City of Lights*; **Marseille** – **La Cité phocéenne**, *the Phoenician City*; and **Saint Malo** – **La Cité corsaire**, *the Pirate City*.)
Another distinctive characteristic of Toulouse, and southwestern France in general, is a distinctive local accent derived from the local Occitan language, which natives call **la langue d'oc** (see Module 8). The accent has several distinctive features: syllables carry a heavier stress than in standard French; vowels are more nasal; and the terminal "e" on words such as **femme** is pronounced ([fam-ë] instead of [fam]). The poet and singer **Claude Nougaro**, a Toulouse native, described the accent as **un torrent de cailloux [qui] roule** (literally "a rolling stream of pebbles", or gravelly). Try listening to Nougaro's love song to his native city: **Ô Toulouse**.

◆ GRAMMAR
Y AND *EN*

These two words can sometimes cause problems for beginners, but once you understand how they work, you will appreciate their elegance in avoiding repetition – one of the basic rules of good French.

• **y**
Often translated as *there*, **y** replaces prepositional phrases followed by **à** (**au, aux**, etc.) or **dans**. It is placed before a verb, replacing the final vowel in a pronoun or the negative adverb **ne** if necessary:
Tu vas au marché? – Oui, je vais au marché tout à l'heure → Oui, j'y vais tout à l'heure.
Est-ce qu'il habite dans la rue Balzac ? – Non, il n'habite pas dans la rue Balzac → Non, il n'y habite pas.

While **y** is not always translated – *Yes, I am going [there] later on / No, I've never been (there)* – it cannot be omitted.

Y can also be used as a pronoun in sentences like these:

Vous pensez à votre voyage ? – Oui, je pense à mon voyage. → **Oui, j'y pense.**
Est-ce que tes collègues sont dans le bureau – Non, ils ne sont pas dans le bureau → **Non, ils n'y sont pas.**

It also allows us to avoid repetition in sentences like the one seen in Module 5:
Le musée est près de la Seine. Vous pouvez y aller à pied.

• The pronoun **en** has a similar function to **y**. It replaces **du, de la, des**, and the singular or plural noun that follows, to avoid repetition. We came across it in Module 4:
Avez-vous des sœurs ? – Oui, j'ai deux sœurs → **Oui, j'en ai deux.**
Do you have any sisters? – Yes, I have two.

Like **y**, **en** is not always translated (*I have two* rather than *I have two of them*).
Je n'ai plus de cigarettes. Est-ce que tu as des cigarettes? → **Est-ce que tu en as?**
I don't have any more cigarettes. Do you have any?

Likewise, **en** is used as a pronoun with verbs followed by **de**. This mechanism may seem complicated at first, but it is actually quite intuitive.
Si tu as des idées, tu peux m'en parler (i.e. **parler des idées**),
If you have any ideas, you can talk to me about them.
Est-ce que vous pouvez me prêter votre stylo? J'en ai besoin (i.e. **besoin de votre stylo**). *Can you lend me your pen? I need it.*

It is important not to confuse the pronoun and the preposition (**Il habite en Bretagne**, **Je vais en car**, etc.).

Both **en** and **y** come usually come before the verb they modify. One very common exception to this rule, which we see in the next module, is the imperative form: **Allez-y**, *Go ahead*; **Prenez-en**, *Take some*.

INDIRECT OBJECT PRONOUNS

We are already familiar with direct object pronouns (Module 5).

Here are the pronouns used for indirect objects, which "receive" the action of a verb indirectly (like *whom* or *to/for what* in English).

me*	*(to/for) me*	**nous**	*(to/for) us*
te**	*(to/for) you*	**vous**	*(to/for) you*
lui	*(to/for) him/her/it*	**leur**	*(to/for) them*

* **m'** before a vowel or a mute **h**
** **t'** before a vowel or a mute **h**

Indirect object pronouns replace personal nouns that follow the preposition **à**. They are always used with a particular group of verbs, several of which appear in the second part of the dialogue in this module, especially **écrire à** (*to write to*), **dire à** (*to say to*) and **parler à** (*to talk to*). These pronouns always come before the verb.

Je parle à Marc → **Je lui parle.**

Émilie a écrit à Raphaël et Bruno → **Émilie leur a écrit.**

In a negative construction, **ne** comes before the pronoun and **pas** is placed after the verb or auxiliary:

Émilie n'a pas écrit à Raphaël et Bruno → **Émilie ne leur a pas écrit.**

Remember that **lui** is both masculine and feminine, so **Je lui ai dit** means *I told him* OR *I told her*. Likewise for **leur**. Always pay close attention to the context!

Also remember that **à** becomes **au** or **aux**, depending on the indirect object (**J'ai parlé au directeur / aux copains** → **Je lui / leur ai parlé**).

The slight complication is that some French verbs take direct objects whereas their English equivalents take indirect objects, and vice versa. This group includes **rendre visite à** (*to visit*), **ressembler à** (*to resemble*), **prêter à** (*to lend*) and **téléphoner à** (*to phone*).

Raphaël ressemble à son père, *Raphaël resembles his father* → **Raphaël lui ressemble**

Je n'ai pas prêté mon portable à Marc, *I didn't lend my mobile to Marc* → **Je ne lui ai pas prêté mon portable**

Conversely, common English verbs that take an indirect object require a direct object in French *to look at* (**regarder**), *to wait for* (**attendre**), *to look for* (**chercher**), *to listen to* (**écouter**)

Je cherche mes clés, *I'm looking for my keys* → **Je les cherche.**

Il a écouté le message, *He listened to the message* → **Il l'a écouté.**

Lastly, although indirect object pronouns usually come before a verb, they follow it if the sentence expresses an order: **Répondez-moi !**, *Answer me!*, **Téléphonez-lui !**, *Phone him/her.*

● EXERCISES

1. REPLACE THE UNDERLINED WORD(S) WITH Y. PAY ATTENTION TO THE WORD ORDER!

a. Vous allez au bureau cet après-midi ? – Oui, nous allons au bureau vers quatorze heures. →

b. L'année dernière il habitait à Lyon mais il n'habite plus à Lyon. →

c. Est-ce qu'ils pensent aux vacances ? – Oui, ils pensent aux vacances tout le temps. →

d. Marc and Élodie adorent le sud-ouest. Ils passent leurs vacances dans le sud-ouest chaque année. →

e. Le Louvre est près des Tuileries. – Est-ce que je peux aller au Louvre à pied ? →

2. REPLACE THE UNDERLINED WORDS WITH EN. PAY ATTENTION TO THE WORD ORDER!

a. Nous avons des croissants chauds. – Excellent. Je veux deux croissants s'il vous plaît. →

b. Est-ce que Paul et Marie ont des enfants ? – Oui, ils ont deux enfants. →

c. Si vous avez des problèmes, vous pouvez me parler des problèmes. →

d. Prête-moi de l'argent. – Pourquoi ? – J'ai besoin de l'argent. →

e. Vous avez entendu la nouvelle ? Tout le monde parle de la nouvelle. →

3. REPLACE THE UNDERLINED NOUNS WITH THEIR EQUIVALENT INDIRECT OBJECT PRONOUN

a. Raphaël a écrit à Bruno la semaine dernière. → Raphaël (.........) a écrit la semaine dernière.

b. Nous allons rendre visite à mes cousins. → Nous allons (...........) rendre visite.

c. Est-ce que tu as donné ton adresse à Anne ? → Est-ce que tu (..............) as donné ton adresse ?

d. L'agence a téléphoné à ma femme et à moi hier. → L'agence (.........) a téléphoné hier.

e. Ils ont vendu leur vieille voiture à moi. → Ils (...........) vendu leur vieille voiture.

● VOCABULARY

accompagner *to go with, to accompany*
contacter *to contact*
faire les courses *to go food shopping*
prêter *to lend*
rendre *to give back*
rendre visite *to (pay a) visit*
ressembler (à) *to look like, resemble*
se ressembler comme deux gouttes d'eau *to be alike as (two) peas in a pod*

un bâtiment *a building*
le beurre *butter*
un boucher *a butcher*
un charcutier *a pork butcher*
les coordonnées *contact details* (lit. "coordinates")
une course *an errand*
un fleuriste *a florist*
un fromager *a cheesemonger*
une goutte *a drop* (liquid)
le lait *milk*
un légume *a vegetable*
une liste *a list*
un marchand *a merchant, a seller*
un marché *a market*
un œuf *an egg**
un poissonnier *a fishmonger*
une pomme *an apple*
un produit *a product*
un stylo *a pen*
* Pronounced [euf] in the singular but [eu] in the plural

régional/-aux *regional*

à l'extérieur *(on the) outside ("exterior")*
longtemps *(for) a long time*
il y a longtemps *a long time ago*

Allez, on y va ! *Let's go!*
À propos *By the way*
C'est à dire ? *What are you saying?*
Laisse tomber *Forget it*
On y va *Let's go (there)*
Quel dommage ! *What a pity/shame!*

a. Can you give me your contact details please?

b. Has Bruno written to you? Answer me! If not, phone him quickly.

c. They lost the football match. – What a pity!

d. Can I go with you to the market? – Of course, everyone goes there at the weekend.

e. No news is good news.

You may have noticed that the grammar is getting a little trickier as we advance. That's why we're giving fewer items in the grammar section, so that you can spend more time learning them. Don't try to rush things. Take your time, and go back over the notes and the dialogue, and don't move on until you feel that everything is clear.

18.
DIETS

LES RÉGIMES

AIMS	NOTIONS

- TALK ABOUT FUTURE ACTIONS
- BUY FOOD IN A MARKET
- EXPLAIN AN INTENTION

- THE FUTURE TENSE
- VERBS CONJUGATED WITH BOTH *ÊTRE* AND *AVOIR*
- EMPHATIC PRONOUNS (CONTINUED)

FRIENDS IN TOULOUSE (PART 2)

(Bruno and Émilie are at Saint Cyprien market)

— Who's turn is it *(it is to whom, the turn)*? Madam, [what] do you want *(you desire)*?

— I'll take some potatoes, some onions, some carrots and [a] few leeks.

— How much do you want *(I you put of them how much)*? One pound? One kilo?

— A half-kilo please. And also some thyme and a little *(of)* parsley. How much is that *(I you owe how much)*? Now, we're going to buy some sausages, some cheese and a bottle of wine.

— Not for me: I must lose some weight — at least, a little weight, so I am going to *(make a)* diet.

— You'll *(make a)* diet, you? That will be difficult because you like your food *(you are "gourmand")*.

— Yes, yes: from now on, I will no longer eat charcuterie and I'll drink no more wine. I will no longer take sugar in my coffee and I won't snack *(nibble)* between meals. I'll go jogging every morning and I'll go to the gym twice a week, if not more [often]. Alice will help me: she'll stop preparing desserts and she'll learn to cook more lightly *(a lighter cooking)*. We'll buy an exercise bike *(bicycle of apartment)* and, together, will *(do)* exercise. That way *(like that)*, I'll be in better health, I'll lose *(some)* weight, and we will be able to save *(make some savings)*. It's tough, but it's necessary to have confidence in yourself.

— But you'll get bored, I'm sure of it. Me, I have already tried to do a little exercise every day. Yesterday morning, I brought up the shopping to the second floor, I took down the rubbish, and I brought in the bin, which was outside. Next, I vacuumed and ironed all Marc's shirts. But that made me hungry *(gave me hunger)* so I turned over the whole house to find a bit of chocolate and a biscuit.

— So that's *(It is that)* your balanced diet: something to eat in each hand?

(Bruno et Émilie sont au marché Saint Cyprien)

— C'est à qui, le tour ? Madame, vous désirez ?

— Je prendrai des pommes de terre, des oignons, des carottes et quelques poireaux.

— Je vous en mets combien ? Une livre ? Un kilo ?

— Un demi-kilo s'il vous plaît. Et aussi du thym et un peu de persil. Je vous dois combien ? Maintenant, on va acheter des saucisses, du fromage et une bouteille de vin.

— Pas pour moi : je dois perdre du poids — du moins, un peu de poids, donc je vais faire un régime.

— Tu feras un régime, toi ? Ça sera trop difficile car tu es gourmand.

— Si, si : à partir de maintenant, je ne mangerai plus de charcuterie et je ne boirai plus de vin. Je ne prendrai plus de sucre dans mon café et je ne grignoterai pas entre les repas. Je ferai un footing tous les matins et j'irai à la gym deux fois par semaine, sinon plus. Alice m'aidera : elle arrêtera de préparer des desserts et elle apprendra à faire une cuisine plus légère. Nous achèterons une bicyclette d'appartement et, ensemble, nous ferons de l'exercice. Comme ça, je serai en meilleure santé, je perdrai du poids, et on pourra faire des économies. C'est dur, mais il faut avoir confiance en soi.

— Mais tu t'ennuieras, j'en suis sûre. Moi, j'ai déjà essayé de faire un peu d'exercice tous les jours. Hier matin, j'ai monté les courses au deuxième étage, j'ai descendu les ordures, et j'ai rentré la poubelle qui était dehors. Ensuite, j'ai passé l'aspirateur et repassé toutes les chemises de Marc. Mais ça m'a donné faim, donc j'ai retourné toute la maison pour trouver un bout de chocolat et un biscuit.

— C'est ça, ton régime équilibré : quelque chose à manger dans chaque main ?!

■ UNDERSTANDING THE DIALOGUE

WORDS AND PHRASES

→ We know that some proper nouns for professional occupations can be either masculine or feminine (Module 16). A handful of other nouns also have two genders – and two different meanings. For example, **un tour** can mean *a tour* (of a city, for example) or, by extension, *a turn*. But **une tour** means *a tower*. Likewise, **un livre** is *a book* but **une livre** means *a pound* – either sterling or weight (500 grams). And **une voile**, *a sail* (Module 12) has a masculine equivalent, **le voile**, which means *a veil* or *headscarf*!

→ **désirer**, *to desire*, is commonly used in formal French instead of *to want*. You will often hear the verb used by sales assistants or restaurant waiting staff, either in the very formal phrase **Que désirez-vous ?**, or, more informally, **Vous désirez ?** In an upscale restaurant, the server might ask **Désirez-vous un café ?** but in a bistro he or she would say either **Vous voulez un café ?** or simply **Un café ?**

→ **la charcuterie** (derived from the somewhat less appetising term **la chair cuite** or *cooked flesh*) refers to pork delicatessen products such as **le pâté**, **le jambon**, *ham*, **le saucisson**, *sausage*, and **les rillettes** (fem. plu.), *potted pork*. The **-erie** ending can be added to a root noun to transform a profession into a shop: **un boulanger → une boulangerie**, *baker → bakery*; **un boucher → une boucherie**, *butcher – butcher's*; **un fromager → une fromagerie**, *cheesemonger → cheese shop*; and, of course, **un charcutier → une charcuterie**. (Don't confuse the **-ère** ending with **-erie**.)

→ We know **si** can mean both *if* and *so* (**Si tu viens, je serai si heureuse**, *If you come, I'll be so happy*) and can also use in apposition (Module 6). It is also commonly used when contradicting a statement in the negative form, a bit like saying "No you're wrong; yes I am/do/will, etc.". The nearest English equivalent is the repetition of the auxiliary. For example, **Tu n'es pas français. – Si, je suis de Rouen**, *You're not French. – Yes I am, I'm from Rouen*. To really insist on the contradiction, the word is often repeated: **Si si, je suis de Rouen**.

→ Another useful word derived from **si** is **sinon**, meaning *if not* (the literal translation) or *otherwise*. **Mets tes clés dans ta poche, sinon tu les perdras**, *Put your keys in your pocket, otherwise / if not you'll lose them.*

→ The feminine singular noun **l'économie** means both *the economy*: **L'économie française est en bonne santé**, *The French economy is healthy*; and *economics*: **Elle étudie l'économie à l'université de Toulouse**, *She's studying economics at Toulouse university*. In the plural, however, **les économies** (f.) means *savings* and is often used with the verb **faire** to mean *save up*: **Nous faisons des économies pour**

partir en vacances, *We're saving up to go on holiday.*

→ We learned **le bout** in Module 10. It can also be used idiomatically to mean *a bit of*: **Tu veux un bout de gâteau ?**, *Want a bit of cake?* An idiomatic expression combining this word with the ones above is **faire des économies de bout de chandelle**, meaning *to penny-pinch.*

CULTURE NOTES

Le jogging, and its close relative **un footing**, are prime examples of **le franglais**, where words and phrases that look and sound like English are used in ways that English speakers have never dreamt of! In some cases, the link between the original meaning and its **franglais** interpretation is tenuous: **les baskets** for *trainers* presumably comes from *basketball boots*; **un flipper** for *pinball machine* refers to the plastic bats used to propel the player's ball; not to mention **un smoking,** a *dress* or *dinner suit.* Other egregious examples include **un planning** (*a schedule*), **faire un brushing** (*to blow-dry one's hair*) and **un break** (*an estate car,* derived from the English term "a shooting brake").

Some of these borrowed words, like **le week-end**, are so deeply embedded in French that they will presumably never be eradicated. Others were originally imported as proper or product names (**le scotch**, for *adhesive tape,* and **un caddie**, *supermarket trolley*), and are therefore unlikely to change. But some **franglais** terms have entered the language by the back door. It is these intruders that academics, the authorities and many ordinary French-speakers are anxious to expel. **L'Académie française**, the three-century-old guardian of the French language, regularly publishes lists of 'official' translations (**les contre-vérités** rather than **les fake-news,** for example*), not all of which gain traction. French-speaking Canadians, with 325m Anglophones on their doorstep, understandably take a more proactive approach, giving us **le courriel** for *email* and **le clavardage** for *chat* (not to mention the slightly tongue-in-cheek **le chien chaud** for *hotdog*). Some of these neologisms will take root, just as **un ordinateur**, a *computer,* has done. Others will die a death, like **la vacancelle**, a mooted replacement for **le week-end**.

* www.academie-francaise.fr/la-langue-francaise/terminologie-et-neologie

◆ GRAMMAR

VERBS CONJUGATED WITH BOTH *ÊTRE* AND *AVOIR*

In Module 16, we learned the verbs that are conjugated with **être** instead of **avoir** in the past. As mentioned, some of them can take both auxiliaries, depending on whether they have a direct object. To help you remember these verbs, meet another physician:

DR PREMS: Descendre, Rentrer, Passer, Retourner, Entrer, Monter, Sortir

Here, in context, are the transitive and intransitive uses of each verb:

Intransitive (no direct object)*		Transitive (with direct object)*	
Je suis descendu du bus.	*I got off the bus.*	**J'ai descendu le sac.**	*I have taken down the bag.*
Il est rentré très tard.	*He got back very late.*	**Simon a rentré la poubelle.**	*Simon brought in the dustbin.*
Je suis passé plus tôt.	*I came past earlier.*	**J'ai passé un bon moment.**	*I had a great time.*
Il est retourné en France.	*He has returned to France.*	**Il a retourné le matelas.**	*He turned over the mattress.*
Je suis entré dans le magasin.	*I went into the shop.*	**Simon a entré les informations.**	*Simon entered the information.*
Il est monté dans la voiture.	*He got into the car.*	**Il a monté les courses.**	*He brought up the shopping.*
Je suis sorti à dix heures.	*I went out at 10am.*	**J'ai sorti mon téléphone.**	*I took out my phone.*

* Depending on the context, the verb can be translated in English by the present perfect or the past simple.

As you can see, the meanings are related but quite different. Remember: the intransitive form is followed immediately by a preposition or an adverb (e.g. **tôt**, **tard**) and the transitive form by a direct object.

MORE ON EMPHATIC PRONOUNS

We first came across emphatic pronouns (**moi**, **toi**, etc.) in Module 6.

We have seen them used in a "disjunctive" form:

Qui veut un café ? – Moi. *Who wants a coffee? – Me.*

These pronouns are used more widely in French than in English, which tends to prefer the auxiliary form for emphasis (*Who wants a coffee? I do.*). They are often placed at the beginning or end of a sentence expressing a contrast. In many cases, they do not need to be translated: **Moi, je suis gourmand ; lui, il mange trop**, *I am fond of food; he eats too much*; **Bruno m'aide, lui.**, *Bruno helps me* (i.e. you don't help me).

The trickiest pronoun of this type is the impersonal **soi**, which literally means *oneself* but is usually translated by a less formal pronoun such as *yourself* or *themselves*. You will find it in sentences like **Chacun pour soi !**, *Everyone for themselves!* or, as in our example, **Il faut avoir confiance en soi**, *You have to have confidence in yourself*. (English has adopted the expression **soi-disant** – literally: "saying of itself" – to mean *self-styled* or *so-called*.)

MORE ON THE POSSESSIVE (FORM, ADJECTIVES)

You will have realised by now that French has no equivalent to the so-called Saxon genitive (*Tom's job, Sally's flat*). This means that possession always has to be expressed using a direct object followed by the subject. So:

la femme de Bruno → *Bruno's wife*
le travail d' Émilie → *Emilie's job*

Simple. The only real difficulty comes when we replace the third person singular subject noun by a pronoun: **la femme de Bruno** → **sa femme; le travail d'Émilie** → **son travail**. Remember that the possessive adjective always agrees with the gender of the noun.

▲ CONJUGATIONS

THE FUTURE TENSE

The future tense is formed by adding the following endings to the infinitive of **-er** and **-ir** verbs:

manger, *to eat*

je mangerai	I will eat	nous mangerons	we will eat
tu mangeras	you I will eat	vous mangerez	you will eat
il/elle mangera	he/she/it I will eat	ils/elles mangeront	they will eat

Those that end in **-re** drop the final **e** before the endings are added:

perdre, *to lose*

je perdrai	I will lose	nous perdrons	we will lose
tu perdras	you will lose	vous perdrez	you will lose
il/elle perdra	he/she/it will lose	ils/elles perdront	they will lose

Apart from the **nous** and **vous** forms, the endings are those of the present tense of **avoir**. There are some slight spelling changes for certain verbs, which we will review in the next module.

• The negative and interrogative forms follow the same patterns as the present tense:

je ne perdrai pas, elle ne mangera pas, etc.
est-ce que je mangerai ?, perdront-ils ?, etc.

With the third, inverted form of the interrogative, we use the same hyphenated **-t-** as we used for the past tense (**a-t-elle appelé ?**, Module 13) to avoid a juxtaposition of final and initial vowels in the third person singular: ~~perdra il~~ → **perdra-t-il ?**, etc. However, as with the past tense, the first and second interrogative forms are more common than this inverted form in conversations and informal writing.

• The future is used in much the same way as in English, remembering that we can use the present tense of **aller** + infinitive for actions in the immediate future (**Je vais acheter des carottes; Il va arrêter de manger ce soir** – see module 4).

Il repassera ses chemises tout à l'heure, *He'll iron his shirts later on.*

À partir de demain, je ne prendrai pas de sucre dans mon café, *As from tomorrow, I won't take sugar in my coffee.*

Est-ce que tu boiras du thé ? *Will you have (drink) some tea?*

• Of course there are some irregular forms, especially with **être** and **avoir**, which should be learned right away:

être		avoir	
je serai	nous serons	j'aurai	nous aurons
tu seras	vous serez	tu auras	vous aurez
il/elle sera	ils/elles seront	il/elle aura	ils/elles auront

• Here are three other important irregular verbs in this module:

aller		faire		pouvoir	
j'irai	nous irons	je ferai	nous ferons	je pourrai	nous pourrons
tu iras	vous irez	tu feras	vous ferez	tu pourras	vous pourrez
il/elle ira	ils/elles iront	il/elle fera	ils/elles feront	il pourra	ils pourront

● EXERCISES

1. CONJUGATE THESE REGULAR VERBS IN THE FUTURE TENSE

a. Je (*prendre:* ....) deux kilos de poireaux, s'il vous plait.

b. Bruno n'a pas faim maintenant. Il (*manger:* ....) tout à l'heure.

c. Nous devons finir demain. Sinon, nous (*perdre:* ....) beaucoup d'argent.

d. Jacques et Christine (*passer:* ....) Noël avec nous cette année.

e. J'espère que vous m'(*aider:* ....) à terminer cet exercice. – Mais bien sûr !

● VOCABULARY

avoir confiance *to have confidence, to trust*
descendre* *to take/bring down*
désirer *to want, to desire*
devoir *to owe* (see Module 7)
faire un régime *to diet*
grignoter *to nibble, to snack*
monter* *to take/bring up*
passer* *to pass* (something)
rentrer* *to bring in*
repasser* *to iron*
retourner* *to turn over, to turn upside down*
* in the transitive form

une bicyclette *a bicycle*
une bicyclette d'appartement *an exercise bicycle*
un biscuit *a biscuit*
une bouteille *a bottle*
une carotte *a carrot*
la charcuterie *deli meats, charcutier's shop*
une / les course(s) *an errand, shopping*
le fromage *cheese*
un / le footing *a jog / jogging*
les économies *savings*

la gym *a gym / exercices*
un oignon* *an onion*
une livre *a pound*
les ordures *the rubbish, garbage*
le persil *parsley*
le poids *weight*
un poireau *a leek*

une pomme de terre *a potato ("apple of the earth")*
une poubelle *a rubbish bin*
un régime *a diet*
la santé *health*
une saucisse *a sausage*
le thym *thyme*
le vin *wine*
* Also spelled un **ognon** but pronounced the same way

léger/-ère *light*
gourmand *fond of food*
dehors *outside*
du moins *at least*
sinon *otherwise, if not*

C'est à qui le tour ? *Whose turn is it?*
Vous désirez ? *What do you want/would you like?*
Je vous dois combien ? *How much do I owe you?*

Not all the native speakers you meet will stick strictly to standard grammar rules. You will often come across familiar words, as well as idiomatic turns of phrase, such as those used by the market gardener in this module, who says **C'est à qui, le tour ?**, **Vous désirez ?** and **Je vous en mets combien ?** rather than, respectively, **À qui est-ce le tour ?**, **Que désirez-vous ?** and **Combien vous en mets-je ?** which, although perfectly correct, would sound much too formal in this setting. Our aim is not only to teach "correct" French but to get you acquainted with the language you will hear every day. However, don't use these familiar words and phrases until you feel totally at home in French. **C'est clair ?** (*Is that clear?*)

2. PUT THESE IRREGULAR VERBS INTO THE NEGATIVE OR SECOND INTERROGATIVE FUTURE FORMS

a. Tu <u>es</u> là demain. (inter.). →

b. Nous <u>avons</u> assez d'argent. (neg.) →

c. Émilie <u>peut</u> nous aider si on lui demande gentiment. (inter. with **est-ce que**) →

d. Je pense qu'ils <u>font</u> beaucoup de progrès (neg.) →

e. Vous <u>allez</u> directement au marché. (inter. with **est-ce que**) →

3. PUT THE VERBS IN BRACKETS INTO THE PERFECT TENSE

a. Je (*passer:* ....) trois semaines en Corse cette année.

b. Marine (*retourner*, negative: ....) en France à Noël.

c. Les enfants (*rentrer:* ....) tard hier.

d. Nous (*sortir:* ....) les couteaux et les fourchettes pour mettre la table.

e. Il (*entrer:* ....) dans le bureau et, ensemble, ils (*entrer:* ....) les informations dans l'ordinateur.

4. TRANSLATE INTO FRENCH

a. Fabien's wife turned over the whole house to find her mobile (phone).

b. In our new neighbourhood, we'll have two cheese shops, three bakeries and a butcher's.

c. I think that you're* not happy Marion. – Oh yes I am; everything is fine, thanks.

d. Put your keys in your** pocket, otherwise you'll lose them.

e. Benjamin says that he won't buy any more chocolate. – He's penny-pinching!

* Familiar
** Formal

19.
BOOKING

LA RÉSERVATION

AIMS	NOTIONS

- ENQUIRE ABOUT ROOMS AND PRICES
- ASK / SUGGEST
- BE NON-COMMITTAL

- PREPOSITIONS AT THE BEGINNING OF QUESTIONS
- *CHAQUE / CHACUN / CHACUNE*
- *FALLOIR*: A NEED OR REQUIREMENT

IT'S NO BARGAIN

– The Marais Hotel, Camille speaking *(at the apparatus)*. How may I help *(be useful to)* you?

– I would like to know your prices *(tariffs)* for a double room and a single *(simple)* room.

– For what date do you wish to book *(reserve)*, and for how many people?

– It will be the last weekend of the next month, for a couple and two children.

– That *(We)* will be the 26th and 27th *(it me seems)*.

– That's right *(it is well that)*, Easter Sunday and the Monday, which is a public holiday.

– We still have some space *(place)* for those dates but you must hurry *(need make quick)*. Each of the rooms has *(is equipped of)* a private bathroom, *(of)* a large bed, or twin beds, and *(of)* a wifi connection. The children will be in the room next to yours and each will have his [her] own bed. At what time do you think you [will] arrive, more or less? Where will you [be] coming from?

– We will not arrive before 6.30pm because we will be in Grenoble.

– What else *(of what of else)* do you need: a parking space *(place)*, maybe?

– No thanks. We will take the train and find a taxi at the station. But we will have to leave very early [on] the Tuesday morning. Will it be possible to have *(take)* breakfast?

– No worries. A buffet is served as from *(to leave from)* 6am for customers who get up early. You need *(it must)* to simply order it the day before.

– I forgot to ask you: *(at)* how much are the rooms?

– Each room is *(at)* 560 euros, breakfast not included.

– Ah, I see … I will call you tomorrow to confirm and I will pay at that time *(there)*.

– I'm going to take some details *(information)*, if you don't mind *(like it well)*. What are your surname, first name and date of birth?

– I will tell you all that tomorrow. Without fail *(mistake)*….

– Hôtel le Marais, Camille à l'appareil. Comment puis-je vous être utile ?

– Je voudrais connaître vos tarifs pour une chambre double et une chambre simple.

– Pour quelle date souhaitez-vous réserver, et pour combien de personnes ?

– Ça sera le dernier week-end du mois prochain, pour un couple et deux enfants.

– Nous serons le vingt-six et le vingt-sept, il me semble.

– C'est bien ça, le dimanche de Pâques et le lundi, qui est férié.

– Nous avons encore de la place pour ces dates mais il faut faire vite. Chacune des chambres est équipée d'une salle de bain privée, d'un grand lit ou de lits jumeaux, et d'une connexion wifi. Les enfants seront dans la chambre à côté de la vôtre et chacun aura son propre lit. À quelle heure pensez-vous arriver, à peu près ? D'où viendrez-vous ?

– Nous n'arriverons pas avant dix-huit heures trente car nous serons à Grenoble.

– De quoi d'autre avez-vous besoin : une place de parking, peut-être ?

– Non merci. Nous prendrons le train et trouverons un taxi à la gare. Mais nous devrons partir très tôt le mardi matin. Sera-t-il possible de prendre le petit déjeuner ?

– Pas de soucis. Un buffet est servi à partir de six heures pour les clients qui se lèvent tôt. Il faut simplement le commander la veille.

– J'ai oublié de vous demander : à combien sont les chambres ?

– Chaque chambre est à cinq cent soixante euros, petit déjeuner non compris.

– Ah, je vois… Je vous appellerai demain pour confirmer et je paierai à ce moment-là.

– Je vais prendre quelques informations, si vous le voulez bien. Quels sont vos nom, prénom et date de naissance ?

– Je vous dirai tout ça demain. Sans faute…

UNDERSTANDING THE DIALOGUE
WORDS AND PHRASES

→ **un appareil**, a *device* or a *piece of equipment*, is used in compound words such as **un appareil-photo**, a *camera* (false-cognate alert: **une caméra** is a *cine-camera*) or terms such as **un appareil électroménager**, a *home appliance*. It is also commonly used when using or answering the phone (which used to be called **un appareil téléphonique**): **Qui est à l'appareil ?** *Who's calling?* (lit. "Who is at the apparatus?"). Likewise, when receiving a call, you can give your name, like this: **Michel à l'appareil**, *Michel speaking*. But now that mobile telephony is the norm, most people answer simply **Allô ?**, except in more formal contexts.

→ The first person singular of **pouvoir**, *to be able to* (see Module 3) is **je peux** and the second − most common − interrogative is **est-ce que je peux ?**. In formal contexts, however, **je peux** cannot be inverted so you will hear or read an older, literary form, **puis** (pronounced [pwee]), in polite first-person phrases like **Puis-je vous aider ?**, *May I help you?* or **Comment puis-je vous être utile ?**, *How may I be of assistance ("useful to you")?*

→ In addition to **un prix** (pron. [pree]), *a price* (Module 5), another commonly used word is **un tarif** (one "f" only), *a rate* or *a fare*. In a hotel, you can ask **Quel est votre meilleur tarif ?**, *What is your best rate?* The word is also used in contexts such as transport or entertainment: **un billet à plein tarif / à tarif réduit**, a *full-fare / reduced-fare ticket*; **tarif étudiant**, *student rate*. There is some overlap between **un prix** and **un tarif** so, if in doubt, use the former.

→ **souhaiter** (pron: [soo-è-tay]: remember that the **h** is not aspirated) means *to wish (for)*. The verb is used in formal contexts when expressing a desire, **Je souhaite avoir des informations**, *I would like some information*, or asking a question: **À quelle heure souhaitez-vous venir ?**, *What time would you like to come?* (The usual response when someone sneezes is **À vos souhaits !** − "To your wishes" − or, familiarly, **À tes souhaits !**, the likely origin of the English exclamation: *Atishoo!*)

→ The adjective **propre** has two meanings: *clean*, usually placed after the noun: **Les chambres de cet hôtel ne sont pas très propres**, *The rooms in this hotel aren't very clean*; and *own*, which generally precedes it: **Ce sont mes propres photos**, *They're my own photos*. Remember this distinction because **propre** is one of several adjectives than change meaning depending on where they are placed in a sentence.

→ **près**, *near*, is used in the adverbial phrase **à peu près**, "to little near", meaning *about* or *almost*. The phrase generally comes before an adjective or a noun: **Le sens de cette phrase est à peu près clair**, *The meaning of the sentence this almost* *clear*, but it can also be used after a statement or question: **Le petit déjeuner coûte combien, à peu près ?** *How much does breakfast cost, more or less?*. Whatever the context, the phrase expresses an approximation.

→ Yet more **franglais**! **Un parking** is *a carpark* so, by extension, **une place de parking** means *a parking space*. However, the verb *to park* is translated by **(se) garer**: **Nous avons garé la voiture derrière l'hôtel**, *We've parked the car behind the hotel.* Hence the word **un garage**, *a garage.*

→ **un souci**, *a worry, a concern*, is widely used in the phrase **Pas de soucis** (or **souci**), more or less equivalent to the Anglo-Australian *No worries*. It is a more colloquial substitute for **Pas de problème**.

CULTURE NOTES

When looking for a hotel in France, make sure that the one you find does actually offer accommodation. That's because the masculine noun **un hôtel** also means a large, usually stately building. **Un hôtel particulier** (lit. "a private hotel") is a mansion, often of historical importance. These sumptuous dwellings began to appear in the 14th century, notably in the **Le Marais** district of Paris, where some of the more "recent" ones, such as **l'Hôtel de Carnavalet**, which dates from the 1600s, still stand. **Le Marais**, "the marsh", is one of the capital's oldest districts, housing not only mediaeval buildings but also prestigious museums, cutting-edge galleries, and a diversity of communities.

Many other buildings bearing the name **hôtel** have an official function, such as **l'Hôtel de la Monnaie**, *the national mint*, or **un hôtel de police**, *a police HQ*. In big cities, **l'hôtel de ville** is equivalent to *a town hall* or *guildhall* in the UK. (In smaller towns and villages, the centre of local government is **la mairie**, the office of **le** or **la maire**, *the mayor*.)

The university city of **Grenoble**, in southeastern France, is a major centre for scientific research and hi-tech industry. It is also the gateway to the mountainous Alpine region, hence its nickname, **la Capitale des Alpes** (*the capital of the Alps*).

◆ GRAMMAR

QUESTIONS WITH INITIAL PREPOSITIONS

By now you should be thoroughly familiar with the three forms of the interrogative. Let's now look at how to ask questions using interrogative pronouns combined with the prepositions **à** and **de**. With the second and third forms, we start the question with a preposition rather than dropping it or placing it at the end, as in English:

J'arrive à dix heures.	I arrive at 10.00	→	À quelle heure arrives-tu / est-ce que tu arrives ?	What time do you arrive (at)?
Ils arrivent de Grenoble.	They're arriving from Grenoble.	→	D'où arrivent-ils / est-qu'ils arrivent ?	Where are they arriving from?

As in English, though, many French speakers prefer the first, rising-intonation interrogative because it is simpler to construct and less formal: **Tu arrives à quelle heure ? / Ils arrivent d'où ?** All three forms are grammatically correct, of course.

It is very important to pay attention to the preposition because it will be placed before the question word (**... à dix heures → À quelle heure ?**; **... de Grenoble → D'où ?**). Take **combien** (*how much/many*): **À combien sont les chambres ? – Les chambres sont à deux cents euros; De combien avez-vous besoin ? – Nous avons besoin de deux chambres.**

The same rule applies to **qui** (*who*) and **quoi** (*what*):
De qui vient cette lettre ? – Cette lettre vient de Camille; À qui voulez-vous parler ? – Je veux parler à Camille.

Remember that **à** may be "disguised" as **au: Je veux parler au directeur → À qui voulez-vous parler ?**

De quoi ont-ils besoin ? – Ils ont besoin de mon aide. Likewise, **de** may be disguised as **du / des: Ils ont besoin des clés → De quoi ont-ils besoin ?**

À quoi penses-tu ? – Je pense à mes vacances.

Here, too, we can rephrase the questions and make them less formal by putting the interrogative pronoun at the end:
Cette lettre vient de qui ? Ils ont besoin de quoi ?
Vous voulez parler à qui ? Tu penses à quoi ?
Nonetheless, the preposition remains the same.

CHAQUE / CHACUN / CHACUNE

We've already come across **chaque**, *each*, *every*, an indefinite adjective that refers to people or things in general and is always paired with a singular noun: **chaque chambre**, *each room*, **chaque pays**, *every country*.

The adjective blends with **un** or **une** to form the indefinite pronouns **chacun** (masculine) and **chacune** (feminine), meaning *each / every one*. Both are used to "singularise" a statement and must agree with the noun they qualify: **Chacune des chambres a une salle de bain**, *Each of the rooms has a bathroom*. **Chacun des enfants aura un grand lit**, *Each of the children will have a big bed*.

The pronoun can also be used on its own, after a noun: **Nous avons dix chambres, chacune avec une salle de bain**, *We have ten rooms, each [one] with a bathroom*. In this form, it can also be translated as *everyone*, **J'ai donné une pomme à chacun**, *I gave each one / everyone an apple*. (If the group of people receiving the object comprises men only or men and women, use **chacun**; if it is composed only of women, use **chacune**).

Lastly, **chacun(e)** can be used in indefinite expressions such as **Chacun pour soi !**, *Everyone for themselves*, or **Chacun sait que Grenoble est une belle ville**, *Everyone knows that Grenoble is a beautiful city*. In this context, it is synonymous with **tout le monde: Tout le monde sait que...**, etc. There are a couple of other uses, which we shall see later on. Remember that there is no plural form because **chacun(e)** means *each one*.

▲ CONJUGATIONS
FALLOIR

Falloir is an impersonal verb used only in the infinitive or with **il** (meaning *it*). The good news is that there are only half a dozen forms, notably **il faut**, compared with as many as 20 for an ordinary verb. **Falloir** expresses a necessity or requirement and is usually translated by *to need*, in the case of a person, or, in a general sense, *to take*. **Il faut une connexion wifi pour accéder à Internet**, *A wifi connection is needed to get onto the internet*.

Pour aller de Grenoble à Forcalquier, il faut deux heures, *It takes two hours to go from Grenoble to Forcalquier*.

Although impersonal, the verb is often translated "personally". The pronoun used will depend on the context, for example **Il faut téléphoner au bureau**, *We / you need to phone the office*. In the text for this module, Camille tells the customer **Il faut simplement nous demander la veille**, which means *All you need to do is ask us the evening before*.

Any verb immediately following **falloir** is in the infinitive: **Il faut partir tout de suite**, *You / We have to leave immediately*. We'll see some other constructions in a later module.

FUTURE TENSE: SPELLING CHANGES

We know that the future is formed by adding **-ai, -as, -a, -ons, -erez**, and **-ont** to the infinitive of **-er** and **-ir** verbs and to the root of **-re** verbs. There are a couple of exceptions which affect certain groups of verbs. Here are two of the most important:

1) Almost all verbs ending in **-eler**, such as **appeler**, double the "l": **j'appellerai, tu**

appelleras, il/elle appellera, nous appellerons, vous appellerez, ils/elles appelleront.

Similarly, most of those ending in **-eter**, like **jeter**, *to throw*, take a double "t": **je jetterai, tu jetteras**, etc.

In both cases, the pronunciation changes very slightly. For example, the "e" in **nous appelons**, which sounds the same as the final "e" of *father*, becomes the "e" of *bell* in **appellerai**. Listen carefully to the fourth exercise in this module but for the time being, it's important simply to recognise the spelling changes.

2) Verbs like **lever**, *to lift*, take a grave accent over the first "e", as does **acheter**, *to buy*: **je lèverai, tu lèveras**, etc.

Here, too, the pronunciation of the "e" changes, from *father* (**lever**) to *b<u>e</u>ll* (**lèverai**).

Lastly, the future tense of verbs ending in **-yer**, like **payer**, *to pay*, can be written in two ways: **je payerai** or **je paierai**. Both are correct, and the pronunciation is the same.

These details are important because the same types of changes occur in other tenses. But remember that, for the time being, it's more important to speak and understand than to write.

● EXERCISES

1. TURN THESE SENTENCES INTO QUESTIONS STARTING WITH A PREPOSITION

a. Les oignons sont à 2 euros le kilo. →

b. Marion arrive à 22 heures. →

c. Elles veulent parler à Jean-Philippe. →

d. J'ai besoin de deux places. →

e. Nous pensons à nos vacances d'été. →

2. MAKE THESE QUESTIONS LESS FORMAL

a. De qui vient ce mail ? → …………………………………… ?

b. À qui veut-il parler. → …………………………………… ?

c. De quoi ont-ils besoin ? → ……………………………… ?

d. À quoi pensez-vous ? → …………………………………… ?

e. D'où arrivent-ils ? → …………………………………… ?

VOCABULARY

commander *to order*
confirmer *to confirm*
falloir (il faut) *to have to, to need*
sembler *to seem*
souhaiter *to wish*

une bonne affaire *a bargain, a good deal*
une connexion *a connection*
un nom *a (sur)name*
un couple *a couple* (spouses, etc.)
un jumeau/-elle *a male/female twin*
des lits jumeaux *twin beds*
la naissance *birth*
Pâques *Easter* (think "pascal")
un prénom *a first name*
un taxi *a taxi*
la veille *the day before*

double *double*
privé(e) *private*
propre *clean, own*
simple *single (room)*
chacun(e) *each one* (individually)
chaque *each, every*
prochain(e) *next*
à ce moment-là *at that time, moment*

C'est bien ça *That's absolutely right*
Comment puis-je vous être utile ? *How may I help you?*
Il me semble *I think ("it appears to me")*
Pas de souci(s) *No worries*
Sans faute *Without fail / Definitely*
Si vous voulez bien *If you don't mind*

3. USE *CHAQUE, CHACUN* OR *CHACUNE*

a. Je l'appelle (......................) jeudi pour avoir de ses nouvelles.

b. (..................) des enfants fait de l'exercice tous les matins.

c. J'ai trois boîtes de chocolat, mes filles. Vous aurez une boîte (.......................)

d. (..................) sait que cet hôtel est beaucoup trop cher.

e. Nous avons deux marchés dans notre ville, (..................) avec un boucher et un poissonnier.

4. TRANSLATE INTO FRENCH

a. This cine-camera costs only 200 * euros. − It's a bargain!

b. Sophie asked me to call her at 10.00. − Call her, you're late.

c. It takes two hours to go from Paris to Bordeaux by train. − That's all?

d. Who's speaking? − It's me, Arnaud. − I'll call you** back in half an hour.

e. I still have rooms, but you need to be quick. − No worries.

* Write out in full - and don't forget the plural "s"!

** Familiar

In this module, you have learned the kind of formal language you might read on a website or hear on the phone when contacting a service provider. Contrast the first couple of lines with the way that the market vendor speaks to a customer in Module 18. We don't expect you to talk like Camille just yet, but it is useful to be able to recognise different registers, even when you are a beginner.

20.
SPORT

LE SPORT

AIMS	NOTIONS

- **MAKE A POLITE INVITATION**
- **ACCEPT POLITELY**
- **REFUSE AN OFFER**

- **VERBS + PREPOSITION**
- **IRREGULAR NOUN PLURALS**
- **VERBS THAT CHANGE MEANING**

A HANDFUL OF PLAYERS, LOADS OF REFEREES

— I follow the French soccer championship every year. I read the sports newspaper every week. I watch *(the)* most of the matches on *(the)* TV or, at worst, I listen to them on the radio. But this time, my favourite *(preferred)* team is in [the] final and I'm going to see them tomorrow evening. Do you fancy coming with me? I've managed *(succeeded)* to get two tickets for *(to attend)* the match.

— You know, I don't know [anything] about *(the)* soccer. I'm from the southwest and I prefer *(the)* rugby. Where is the match being played *(it happens where, this match)*?

— It's taking place at the Stadium of France. It's really worth it, I assure you. The players had a huge success two weeks ago when they played against Nice. They won four *(to)* two, whereas the time before, they drew *(made a null match)*.

— And André? It seems [to] me that he loves soccer. Doesn't he want to come with you?

— I suggested *(proposed to him)* that he *(to)* comes with me, but he refuses to out in [the] week. He says that he has umpteen *(36,000)* things to do and that he can't spend the evening *(to)* enjoying himself. In general, we get on well but he's starting to annoy me *(break the feet)*.

— You have *(it's necessary)* to learn to be patient.

— You're right. I'll make an effort. So, are you coming, yes or no?

— If it makes you happy *(pleasure)*. But I'm going to pay [for] my seat, I insist.

— Out of *(it's of it no)* the question I'm inviting you — even if you don't like *(the)* games with round balls!

— Where do we meet *(find each other)*?

— I'll wait [for] you in front of the stadium at 6.30 pm. Be careful: there is work *(are works)* on the RER line.

— That works [for me]. So see you tomorrow evening. [Do] you think that there will be a lot of people?

— And how! There will be 22 players and 50,000 referees.

— Je suis le championnat de France de football chaque année. Je lis les journaux sportifs toutes les semaines. Je regarde la plupart des matchs à la télé ou, au pire, je les écoute à la radio. Mais cette fois-ci, mon équipe préférée est en finale et je vais les voir demain soir. Ça te dit de venir avec moi ? J'ai réussi à avoir deux billets pour assister au match.

— Tu sais, je ne m'y connais pas en foot. Je suis du sud-ouest et je préfère le rugby. Ça se passe où, ce match ?

— Il a lieu au Stade de France. Ça vaut vraiment la peine, je t'assure. Les joueurs ont fait un tabac il y a deux semaines quand ils ont joué contre Nice. Ils ont gagné quatre à deux, alors que la fois d'avant, ils avaient fait match nul.

— Et André ? Il me semble qu'il adore le foot. Il ne veut pas venir avec toi ?

— Je lui ai proposé de m'accompagner mais il refuse de sortir en semaine. Il dit qu'il a trente-six mille choses à faire et qu'il ne peut pas passer la soirée à s'amuser. En général, on s'entend très bien mais il commence à me casser les pieds.

— Il faut apprendre à être patient.

— Tu as raison. Je ferai un effort. Alors, tu viens, oui ou non ?

— Si ça te fait plaisir. Mais je vais payer ma place, j'insiste.

— Il n'en est pas question. Je t'invite — même si tu n'aimes pas les jeux de ballon rond !

— Où est-ce qu'on se retrouve ?

— Je t'attendrai devant le stade à dix-huit heures trente. Attention : il y a des travaux sur la ligne du RER.

— Ça marche. À demain soir, alors. Tu penses qu'il y aura beaucoup de monde ?

— Et comment ! Il y aura vingt-deux joueurs et cinquante mille arbitres.

■ UNDERSTANDING THE DIALOGUE
WORDS AND PHRASES

→ As you know, **je suis** is the first person singular of **être**. But it is also the singular present tense of **suivre**, *to follow*, which we saw in Module 15 (**je suis, tu suis, il/elle suit, nous suivons, vous suivez, ils suivent**). It's important to note down words with the same spelling but different meanings to make sure that you use them correctly. Another tricky word is **inviter**, *to invite*. **Il m'a invité à la fête**, *He invited me to the party*. But it can also mean *to treat*. So if someone says **Je t'invite** or **C'est moi qui invite**, they are offering to pay for you!

→ **dire**, *to say*, can be used idiomatically as a synonym for *to like, to please*, etc. It is often found in the impersonal form with **ça: Ça vous dit de voir le match?** *Do you fancy watching the match?* **Ça ne me dit rien**, *I really don't feel like it*. Remember that the subject of **dire** in this case is **ça**, so the verb is conjugated in the third person singular.

→ **assister à** is a false cognate: it means *to attend, to witness*. **Le premier ministre a assisté au débat au Sénat hier**, *The prime minister attended the debate in the Senate yesterday*. It can often be translated by *to be at*, **Combien de spectateurs ont assisté au match ?**, *How many spectators were at the match?* In this context, the verb is always followed by **à** (or **au /aux**). Without the preposition, **assister** can mean *to assist* or *give aid to*. (See Grammar below)

→ **s'y connaître en** (literally "to know oneself in") is used idiomatically to mean *to know about (something)*. Note how the expression is used: **Je m'y connais en sport automobile**, *I know about motorsport*. **Est-ce qu'il s'y connait en rugby?**, *Does he know about rugby?* **Elle ne s'y connaît pas en peinture**, *She doesn't know anything about painting*.

→ **la peine** (the origin of our word *pain*) literally means *sorrow, sadness*. **Cet homme me fait de la peine**, *That man makes me sad / I feel sorry for that man*. But the word is commonly used with the verb **valoir** in the sense of *to be worth (doing something)*, with the indefinite article **de. Ça vaut la peine d'arriver de bonne heure au stade**, *It's worth arriving early at the stadium*. The negative form, **ça ne vaut pas la peine**, is often shortened to **ce n'est pas la peine: Ça ne vaut pas la peine / Ce n'est pas la peine d'arriver avant deux heures**, *It's not worth arriving before 2 o'clock*.

→ **faire un tabac** (literally "make a tobacco") is an idiom meaning *to be a big hit, a great success*. It comes from an old naval expression meaning a clap of thunder. **La chanteuse a fait un tabac avec son nouvel album**, *The (female) singer had a big hit with her new album*. (See also Module 24, Culture Notes). Another common idiom is **casser les pieds** (literally "to break the feet"), which basically means *to annoy* or *get on someone's nerves*. **Elle me casse les pieds avec ses problèmes**, *She bores*

/ *annoys me with her problems*. We'll learn some more common idioms in the upcoming modules.

→ **trente-six**, *thirty-six*, is used as an indeterminate number in several idiomatic expressions. It can mean a large and indefinite number, as we saw in the dialogue: **Je ne peux pas faire trente-six** (or **trente-six mille**) **choses à la fois**, *I can't do umpteen things at the same time*. Or a very long period of time, **Je la vois tous les trente-six du mois parce qu'elle habite très loin**, *I see her once in a blue moon because she lives very far away*. The origin of these and other 36-related idioms is disputed. Suffice it to say that whenever you hear **trente-six**, it might not mean three times twelve!

→ **Il n'en est pas question** means *It is out of the question*. Listen carefully to the recording and be careful not to put a second negative adverb before **est** (**il n'en n'est pas**).

→ **Ça marche !** (literally "That walks") is a very common expression, similar to *That works (for me)*. It basically indicates agreement or affirmation: **Tu peux venir dîner mardi ? – Ça marche !** *Can you come to dinner on Tuesday? – Sure.* You will often hear it when placing an order in a café or restaurant: **Deux cafés et un thé, s'il vous plaît. – Ça marche !** *Two coffees and one tea, please. – Coming up.* (One alternative is the ubiquitous **OK!**)

CULTURE NOTES

Le sport, *sport*, plays an important part in French life. The most popular sport is **le football** (often abbreviated to **le foot**), although the southwestern part of the country is the spiritual home of **le rugby**. Other sports that enjoy a wide following are **le tennis, le cyclisme**, *cycling*, **la natation**, *swimming*, **l'escrime** (fem.), *fencing* and, of course, **le ski** (France has the world's largest skiable area). And, with some 3,400 km of coastline, it's hardly surprising that **la voile**, *sailing*, is both a sport and a pastime. One typically French game that does not require Olympic-level skills is **la pétanque**, a game that is related to bowls (and is also known as **le jeu de boules**). A high-profile international event that attracts worldwide interest is the annual three-week-long cycle race, **Le Tour de France** (literally "tour of France" – be careful: **la tour** means *the tower*), in which teams of riders travel the length and breadth of the country, with incursions into neighboring Italy, Spain, Belgium and the UK.

In addition to the noun **le foot**, much of the sports-related vocabulary in French comes directly from English: **la boxe, le hockey, le golf, le steeple** (*steeplechase*), **le squash, le tennis, le volley** (*volleyball*) and **le water-polo** (not to mention **le match, le penalty**, and **tacler**, *to tackle*). Nonetheless, French is one of the official languages of **les Jeux olympiques**, *the Olympic Games* and France was a precursor in certain sports, including tennis (the English word comes from **tenez**, the imperative of **tenir**, and the game was originally called **le jeu de paume**, or "palm game") and, possibly, even the typically English game of cricket (from **un criquet**, a *stick*, which gave us a *wicket*). **Allez les Bleus !** (Go, France! – the name **les Bleus** comes from the colour of the national team's official jersey).

Le Réseau express régional, abbreviated to **le RER** [er-eu-er], is the rapid transit system (*regional express network*) serving the Paris suburbs.

◆ GRAMMAR

In this grammar section we give some rules covering issues that you have already assimilated naturally from previous modules by reading the dialogues and grammar rules and by doing the associated exercises.

VERB-PREPOSITION COMBINATIONS

When learning a new verb, it is just as important to learn the preposition, if any, that usually accompanies it. One of the reasons is to avoid interference with English. Unfortunately, there is no single rule governing such combinations, but here are a few guidelines:

Verbs with a direct object plus a preposition in English but not in French:

approuver	*to approve of*	**Elle approuve mon choix.**	*She approves of my choice*
attendre	*to wait for*	**Nous attendons le bus.**	*We're waiting for the bus.*
chercher	*to look for*	**Vous cherchez le métro ?**	*Are you looking for the metro?*
demander	*to ask for*	**Demandez le programme.**	*Ask for the programme.*
écouter	*to listen to*	**J'écoute la radio**	*I'm listening to the radio*
regarder	*to look at, watch*	**Elle regarde ses mains**	*She's looking at her hands.*
payer	*to pay for*	**Il a payé mon billet**	*He paid for my ticket*

Verbs followed by a preposition in French but not in English:

appuyer sur	*to press*	**Appuyez sur ce bouton.**	*Press this button.*
assister à	*to attend*	**Il assiste à tous les matchs.**	*He attends every match.*

changer de	to change	Je change de sujet.	I'm changing the subject.
commencer à	to start	Il commence à pleuvoir	It's starting to rain.
douter de	to doubt	Elle doute de moi.	She doubts me.
finir de	to finish	J'ai fini de manger.	I've finished eating.
manquer de	to lack	Nous manquons de personnel	We lack staff.
jouer à jouer de	to play a sport to play an instrument	Je joue au golf. Elle joue du piano.	I play golf. She plays the piano.

Verbs that can be followed by an infinitive with no preposition:

aimer	to like/love	Elle aime travailler seule.	She likes to work alone.
détester	to hate	Ils détestent attendre.	They hate waiting.
devoir	must/to have to	Tu dois arriver avant neuf heures.	You have to arrive before 9 am.
espérer	to hope	Nous espérons aller en vacances en mars.	We hope to go on holiday in March.
pouvoir	can/to be able to	Peux-tu répondre au téléphone ?	Can you answer the phone?
préférer	to prefer	Je préfère partir demain.	I prefer to leave tomorrow.
savoir	to know	Il sait faire la cuisine.	He knows how to cook.
vouloir	to want, wish	Nous voulons acheter cette maison.	We want to buy that house.

Because the rules governing the use or omission of prepositions are so complex, it is easier to learn verbs in groups (followed by **à**, by **de**, by an infinitive, etc.).

"DUAL" VERBS: REFLEXIVE AND TRANSITIVE

We know that a transitive verb is made into a pronominal (or reflexive) verb by adding **se** and a reflexive pronoun: **Je réveille ma femme, Je me réveille** → *I wake my wife/I wake up* (see Module 10). In some cases, however, the meaning changes. Look at these examples:

Je vais demander trois billets pour le match mais je me demande si André viendra.

I'll ask for three match tickets but I wonder whether André will come.

Le film se passe **à Nice, où nous** passons **nos vacances tous les ans.**
The movie takes place in Nice, where we spend our holidays every year.
Je vous entends **très mal. – J'ai dit : "Nous** nous entendons **bien avec tout le monde".** *I can't hear you very well. – I said "We get on well with everybody".*
J'ai trouvé **sa maison sur la carte : elle** se trouve **près de la banque.**
I've found his house on the map. It's near the bank.
Here are some other common "dual" verbs:

amuser	to amuse	s'amuser	to enjoy
battre	to beat	se battre	to fight
tromper	to trick, deceive	se tromper	to make a mistake
servir	to serve	se servir	to help oneself

PLURAL NOUNS (CONT.)

We know that most nouns form their plural by adding a final **s** (unless they already end in **s**, or in **x** or **z**, see Module 2). There are some, exceptions, however.
Nouns ending in **-al** usually form their plural by replacing the **l** with **-ux**:
un animal, *an animal* → **des animaux**
un journal, *a newspaper* → **des journaux**
The same rule applies to words ending in **-eau, -au,** and **-eu**:
un bateau, *a boat* → **des bateaux**
un tuyau, *a pipe* → **des tuyaux** (plumbing, hose, etc.)
un jeu, *a game* → **des jeux**
A handful of nouns ending in **-ail** follow a similar rule. The most common one is **le travail,** *work, job* → **les travaux,** *works* (eg *roadworks*).
Finally, there are seven nouns ending in **-ou** that form their plural with an **x** (all the others take a final **s**). The most useful of these are probably **un chou,** *a cabbage* → **des choux**; and **un genou,** *a knee* → **des genoux**.
In every case, the final **x** is silent.

⬢ EXERCISES

1. PUT THE CORRECT PREPOSITION, IF ANY, AFTER THE VERB

a. Le chanteur joue aussi _ _ _ _ piano. J'espère _ _ le voir en concert à Nantes.

b. Est-ce que vous voulez assister _ _ _ la réunion demain ?

c. J'ai appuyé _ _ le bouton mais la machine ne marche pas.

d. Nous espérons _ _ _ te voir _ _ match ce soir.

VOCABULARY

avoir lieu *to take place*
assister *to attend*
casser les pieds *to annoy*
connaître *to know*
s'y connaître *to know about, to be well up on*
entendre *to hear*
s'entendre *to get on with*
faire plaisir *to please*
faire un tabac *to have a hit, to be very successful*
gagner *to win*
inviter *to invite, to treat*
passer *to pass, to spend* (time)
se passer *to happen*
préférer *to prefer*
proposer *to offer, to propose*
refuser *to refuse*
retrouver *to find again*
se retrouver *to meet up*
réussir *to manage* (see also Module 6)
sortir *to go out, to leave*

un arbitre *a referee*
un championnat *a championship*
un ballon *a ball* (soccer, rugby, etc.)
une équipe *a team*
une finale *a final* (sport, etc.)
le football / le foot *soccer, "footy"*
un joueur/une joueuse *a player*
un match / des matchs *a match/ matches*
un match nul *a draw*
une place *a seat, a place* (theatre, etc.)
un stade *a stadium*

la télé *the TV, the "telly"*
des travaux *work* (construction, repair, etc.)

au pire *at worst*
contre *against* (think "counter")
en général *in general*
la plupart (de) *most (of)*

Attention ! *Be careful! Watch out!*
Ça marche ! *OK!, That works for me!*
Ça vous/te dit de...? *Do you fancy...?*
Et comment ! *And how! I should say so!*
Il n'est pas question *Out of the question*

e. Ils préfèrent _ _ aller en vacances en octobre parce qu'il y a moins _ _ monde.

f. Je joue _ _ _ golf et _ _ _ la guitare.

g. Vous avez fini _ _ faire cet exercice ?

2. TRANSLATE THESE NOUNS THEN PUT THEM INTO THE PLURAL

a. an animal → ....

b. a boat → ....

c. a newspaper → ....

d. a pipe → ....

e. a knee → ....

3. FORM SENTENCES WITH THESE PAIRS OF VERBS

a. Nous (se demander) si ce projet vous intéresse.
Nous vous (demander) de ne pas être en retard.

b. Avez-vous (trouver) votre journal ?
Où (se trouver) votre bureau ?

c. La ligne est mauvaise : je te (entendre) mal
Je (s'entendre) avec ta famille.

d. (Passer) nous voir si vous venez à Paris.
Le film (se passer) en mil neuf cent quarante-trois à Paris.

4. TRANSLATE INTO FRENCH

22

a. I don't know anything about rugby, but I'll make an effort if it makes you* happy.

b. You have to/It's necessary to learn to be patient. – That's out of the question.

c. Do you* feel like seeing a film tonight? It's worth arriving early at the cinema.

d. Can you* help me to finish this job? – I can't do umpteen** things at the same time.

e. Are you looking for the metro? – No, we're waiting for the bus. – Come with me. – Sure thing!

* Use the **tu** and **vous** forms
** Use both forms of the idiomatic expression

21.
SICKNESS

LA MALADIE

AIMS	NOTIONS

- TALK ABOUT HEALTH
- EXPLAIN SYMPTOMS
- EXPLAIN AN INTERACTION

- PRONOUN ORDER
- *MEILLEUR / MIEUX*
- FUTURE TENSE AFTER TIME CONJUNCTIONS

I'M NOT FEELING VERY WELL...

– Apparently *(it appears)* that you're not feeling *(yourself)* very well. Is it true *(that)*?

– Absolutely. I *(me)* feel very ill *(bad)*: I have a temperature *(fever)*– nearly 38°– and a cough. I think I have the *(a)* 'flu or something like that. I contacted my primary care *(treating)* doctor and he told me to stay in bed. I explained the symptoms to him and asked [for] some advice and he gave me some, with clear explanations about my illness.

– You talked to him about it? What do you mean *(How that)*?

– He asked me [for] my mobile number and I gave it to him.

– What? You gave him your personal number? That's not the done thing!

– I know but I was feeling under the weather *(not in my plate)*. I didn't ask him [for] *(a)* sick leave but he gave me one all the same *(even)* . He answered: "Believe me, it's better for you. You will return to work when you are *(will be)* in better health. Then he sent me a prescription and the medical certificate.

– Did you send this certificate to your employer?

– Yes, I sent it to him straight away.

– But what's wrong with you *(do you have)* exactly? You don't look unwell to me. You seem on form.

– But I am unwell, I'm telling you. I'm not well at all. I may not look like it, but, according to the doctor I have *(suffer) (an)* angina, *(an)* otitis, *(a)* cephalalgia and abdominal pains. You see? It's rather serious, isn't it?

– Rubbish *(not matter what)*! You have a sore throat, an earache, a headache and a stomach ache.

– Phew! Now I feel much better. Thanks doctor!

— Il parait que tu ne te sens pas très bien. C'est vrai, ça ?

— Absolument. Je me sens très mal : j'ai de la fièvre – près de trente-huit degrés – et de la toux. Je crois que j'ai une grippe ou quelque chose comme ça. J'ai contacté mon médecin traitant et il m'a dit de rester au lit. Je lui ai expliqué les symptômes et demandé des conseils et il me les a donnés, avec des explications claires sur ma maladie.

— Tu lui en as parlé ? Comment ça ?

— Il m'a demandé mon numéro de portable et je le lui ai donné.

— Quoi ? Tu lui as donné ton numéro personnel ? Ça ne se fait pas !

— Je sais, mais je n'étais pas dans mon assiette. Je ne lui ai pas demandé un arrêt de travail mais il m'en a donné un quand même. Il m'a répondu : « Croyez-moi, c'est mieux pour vous. Vous retournerez au travail quand vous serez en meilleure santé ». Puis il m'a envoyé une ordonnance et le certificat médical.

— Est-ce que tu as envoyé ce certificat à ton employeur ?

— Oui, je le lui ai envoyé sans attendre.

— Mais, qu'est ce tu as précisément ? Tu ne m'as pas l'air souffrant. Tu as l'air en forme.

— Mais je suis souffrant, je te dis. Je ne vais pas bien du tout. Je n'en ai peut-être pas l'air, mais, d'après le médecin je souffre d'une angine, une otite, une céphalée et des douleurs abdominales. Tu vois ? C'est plutôt grave, non ?

— N'importe quoi ! Tu as mal à la gorge, mal aux oreilles, mal à la tête et mal au ventre.

— Ouf ! Maintenant je me sens beaucoup mieux. Merci docteur !

■ UNDERSTANDING THE DIALOGUE
WORDS AND PHRASES

→ **une fièvre**, *a fever*, is used in everyday French to mean simply *a temperature*: **Ma fille a beaucoup de fièvre**, *My daughter has a high temperature*. In a technical context, however, we translate it by the cognate: **la fièvre jaune**, *yellow fever*. The noun **la température** refers to the measured temperature of the body but also the atmosphere. (Remember that the Fahrenheit scale is unknown in France: all temperatures are in Celsius.)

→ To talk about illnesses, we can use the verb **souffrir (de)**, which literally means "to suffer (from)" but is often less dramatic than it may sound: **Je souffre d'un mal de tête**, *I have a headache*. **Ma sœur souffre de l'estomac**, *My sister has stomach pains*. As always, context is key. The adjective **souffrant** means *unwell, poorly*. Another, more common way of describing illness or discomfort is **avoir mal**, (literally "to have bad") followed by **à** (in the correct form) and the ailing part body part(s). **J'ai mal à la tête**, *I have a headache*; **Elle a mal au ventre**, *She has a tummy ache*; **Ils ont mal aux oreilles**, *They have earache*. (Remember, however that doctors tend to use technical expressions, such as **une otite**). Lastly, a common idiomatic way of saying that one feels unwell is **ne pas être dans son assiette**, literally "not to be in one's plate", which is as idiomatic as the equivalent expression *to feel under the weather*.

→ **Comment ça ?** expresses puzzlement and demands an explanation, like *How so? Comment ça : tu as oublié d'acheter le pain ?* What do you mean, you forgot to buy bread? Not to be confused with **Comment ça va ?**, *How are you doing?*

→ The reflexive form **se faire**, which we saw in Module 10 with the literal meaning of *to make oneself*, is used in a number of idiomatic expressions. One of the most common ones is **Ça ne se fait pas**, meaning *It / That is not the done thing*. It can be used with a complement: **Ça ne se fait pas de refuser une invitation**, *It's not right to refuse an invitation*.

→ **avoir** can be used in the same way as *to matter* in English: **Qu'est-que vous avez? Vous vous sentez mal ?**, *What is the matter? Don't you feel well?* A standard answer would be **Je n'ai rien**, *Nothing's the matter*, or, for example, **J'ai mal à la tête**, *I have a headache*.

→ **avoir l'air** refers to what a person perceives about someone or something. It can be translated as *to look like* or, more broadly, *to seem*. **Il a l'air fatigué**, *He looks tired*; **Les hommes ont l'air très contents de leur travail**, *The men seem very pleased with their work*.

CULTURE NOTES

The French health system, **le système de santé français**, is considered one of the best in the world. Primary care (**les soins de ville**, literally "city care") is provided by a comprehensive system of public hospitals (**des hôpitaux publics**), state-approved private hospitals (**des cliniques**), emergency care (**la médecine d'urgence**) and out-patient care (**soins ambulatoires**). The bulk of treatment costs is funded by the social security system (**la Sécurité sociale**, often referred to familiarly as **la Sécu**), with the rest covered by independent health insurers (**des mutuelles**). The first line of healthcare is provided by a general practitioner (**un médecin généraliste**). Everyone is required to register with a GP of their choice, who becomes their **médecin traitant** ("treating" or primary care doctor). Note that **un médecin** means a *doctor* (male or female), and the word **docteur** is used only as a title (**le Docteur Bellier**, for example) or when addressing the practitioner directly: **Bonjour docteur**. Most doctors work independently or in small practices (**un cabinet**) and, where necessary, will refer a patient (**un patient**) to a specialist (**un/une spécialiste**). If a doctor prescribes drugs (**les médicaments**, not to be confused with **la médecine**, the science of medicine), he or she will write a prescription (**une ordonnance** or **une prescription**), which the patient takes to a pharmacy (**une pharmacie**) to be filled. Everyone over 16 carries a health insurance smartcard, **une carte Vitale**, which is presented to the healthcare professional or pharmacist when making a payment. Lastly, the expression used when raising a toast to someone is **À votre / ta santé** (or simply **Santé !**), *Your very good health!*

GRAMMAR
PRONOUN ORDER

When a sentence contains both a direct object pronoun and an indirect object pronoun, there is a strict order to be followed. A good way to remember this sequence is to visualise it as a football team playing in a 5-3-2-1-1 formation (the last "1" being the ball):

me				
te	le			
se	la	lui	y	en
nous	les	leur		
vous				

All these pronouns have to precede the verb. Let's see what happens in practice (or "in play") when we use them to replace a noun:

Je te laisserai le numéro de téléphone. *I will leave you the phone number.*	→ **Je te le laisserai.** *I will leave it for to you.*
Il donnera l'ordonnance à Louise. *He will give the prescription to Louise.*	→ **Il la lui donnera.** *He'll give it to her.*
Nous envoyons les invitations à vous. *We're sending the invitations to you.*	→ **Nous vous les envoyons.** *We're sending them to you.*
Elles me parlent souvent de leur travail. *They often talk to me about their work.*	→ **Elles m'en parlent souvent.** *They often talk to me about it.*
Je vais aller à Rennes demain. *I'm going to go to Rennes tomorrow.*	→ **Je vais y aller demain.** *I'm going to go there tomorrow.*

The indirect pronouns in the first and third columns of the team table can never go together.

This may all seem quite complex, but in practice there are never more than two pronouns together. Just remember the 5-3-2-1-1 formation.

In the negative, the pronouns come immediately after the first negative particle, **ne**, while **pas**, as usual, comes after the verb: **Je ne te le donnerai pas, Il ne la lui donnera pas,** etc.

In a subsequent module, we'll see how the word order changes when we use the imperative form.

MEILLEUR / MIEUX

It is easy to confuse these words, both of which mean *better*. The problem is that *better* can be both an adjective and an adverb in English, whereas in French the distinction is much clearer: **meilleur** is an adjective, the comparative of **bon**, *good*; and **mieux** is an adverb, the comparative of **bien**, *good*, *well*. The superlative forms are **le meilleur** and **le mieux**, respectively.

In a comparison, the comparative adjective **meilleur** is usually followed by **que** and a noun, with which it agrees: **Ce magasin de vêtements est meilleur que celui d'en face**, *This clothes shop is better than the one opposite*; **Les femmes sont meilleures que les hommes dans ce domaine**, *Women are better than men in this field*. The same rule applies to the superlative: **Ma copine fait les meilleurs gâteaux au monde**, *My girlfriend makes the best cakes in the world*. In a superlative sentence or a question, **le/la/les meilleur(e)(s)**, can appear at the end of sentence: **Il y a trois films au cinéma ce soir. Lequel est le meilleur ?** *There are three films at the cinema this evening. Which is the best?*

The comparative adverb **mieux** is used with a verb (or an adjective): **Je parle bien le français mais tu l'écris mieux**, *I speak French well but you write it better*. The answer to the question **Comment vas-tu ?** is usually **Je vais bien** (or, colloquially, **Bien !**). But if you've been ill and are now feeling better, you say **Je vais mieux**.

And, since adverbs are invariable, **mieux** never changes: **Les femmes conduisent mieux que les hommes**, *Women drive better than men.*

Here's a simple phrase to help you remember the difference: **André est un bon cuisinier mais Gérard est meilleur. Ensemble, ils cuisinent mieux que moi**, *André is a good cook but Gérard is better. Together they cook better than me.*

▲ CONJUGATIONS

FUTURE TENSE AFTER *QUAND*

In a French sentence containing **quand** that describes two actions taking place in the future, both verbs are in the future tense. This contrasts with English, which uses a present tense after the conjunction *when*:

Je vous donnerai des nouvelles quand je vous verrai, *I will give you some news when I see you.*

This is an important rule to remember, especially where the sentence starts with **quand**:

Quand nous viendrons à Paris, nous irons au Louvre, *When we <u>come</u> to Paris, we will go to the Louvre.*

If you use a present tense for the **quand** clause, it would imply a regular action (**quand nous venons à Paris** = *each time we come to Paris*, etc.). This rule applies to several other time-related expressions, including **lorsque**, a formal synonym of **quand**, but for the time being, just memorise the examples above.

EXERCISES

1. USE AN OBJECT PRONOUN TO REPLACE THE WORDS IN BRACKETS

a. Je le donnerai (à *Jean*) → Je le .... donnerai demain.

b. Elle a dit (à *ses patients*) qu'elle serait absente vendredi. → Elle .... a dit qu'elle serait absente vendredi.

c. Le médecin a téléphoné (à *moi et ma femme*) → Le médecin .... a téléphoné.

d. Est-ce qu'il vous a parlé (*de son problème*) ? → Est-ce qu'il vous .... a parlé ?

e. Je ne dirai pas (*aux deux frères*) que leur père est malade. → Je ne .... dirai pas que leur père est malade.

2. ANSWER THESE QUESTIONS, REPLACING THE UNDERLINED NOUNS WITH A DIRECT OR INDIRECT PRONOUN

a. Est-ce que tu as donné l'ordonnance au patient ? → Oui, je .... ai donnée.

b. Est-ce que Simon va à Rennes demain ? → Non, il ....va pas.

c. Est-ce qu'elles te parlent de leur appartement ? → Oui, elles .... parlent.

d. Est-ce qu'elle donnera l'adresse à Marion ? → Non, elle ne ....donnera pas.

e. Est-ce que vous vendez les billets à Michel et Catherine. → Oui, nous .... vendons.

3. USE *MEILLEUR* (IN THE CORRECT FORM) OR *MIEUX* WHERE APPROPRIATE

a. Je parle très bien l'allemand, mais tu le parles beaucoup .... que moi.

b. Les hommes sont .... que les femmes en football.

c. Est-ce qu'André est toujours malade ? – Non, il va ....

d. J'ai deux disques de ce nouveau chanteur français. – Lequel est le .... ?

e. Ce sont les .... tartes aux fraises de toute la ville.

4. TRANSLATE INTO FRENCH

a. I don't have Marie's address with me. – I'll give it to you* tomorrow when I see you.

b. What do you mean, they refused my invitation? That's not the done thing.

c. What's the matter with her? Is she feeling ill? – Apparently, she has a temperature.

d. Did you send the report to your doctor? – Yes I sent it to him straight away.

e. You look on form. – Rubbish! I'm very ill.

* Use **vous** and **tu**

● VOCABULARY

avoir l'air *to look like*
croire *to believe*
expliquer *to explain*
paraitre *to seem*
retourner *to return*
(se) sentir *to feel*

une angine / un mal de gorge *a sore throat*
un arrêt de travail *sick leave*
une céphalée / un mal de tête *a headache*
un certificat médical *a medical certificate*
un degré *a degree* (temperature)
une douleur *a pain*
une explication *an explanation*
une fièvre *a fever*
avoir de la fièvre *to have a (high) temperature*
un hôpital/-aux *a hospital / hospitals*
une ordonnance* *a prescription*
une otite / un mal aux oreilles *an earache*
une maladie *an illness* (from **mal**, *bad*)
un symptôme *a symptom*
une toux *a cough*
* une prescription is also used

souffrant *unwell* ("suffering")
d'après *according to*
en forme *on (good) form*
personnel(le) *personal*
précis *precise*

précisément *precisely*
quand même *all the same / even so*
sans attendre *right away ("without waiting")*

Il parait que... *It seems that...*
À votre / ta santé ! *Your good health! Cheers!*
Ça ne se fait pas *It's not done*
Comment ça ? *What do you mean?*
Ouf ! *Phew!*

IV

ENJOYING

FREE

TIME

22.
WORKING LIFE
LA VIE PROFESSIONNELLE

AIMS	NOTIONS

- **TALK ABOUT A SEQUENCE OF EVENTS IN THE PAST**
- **TALK ABOUT CITIES AND COUNTRIES**
- **EXPRESS HESITATION**

- **THE IMPERFECT TENSE**
- **"MOBILE" ADJECTIVES**
- **AGREEMENT OF PAST PARTICIPLES**
- **PREPOSITIONS OF PLACE**

I KNEW NOTHING ABOUT IT.

– Good evening and welcome to your weekly programme *The Company on the Small Screen*, presented by Amélie Broutard. *(The)* Last week, we were talking to you about the building world. This week, I have the pleasure of introducing *(receive)* Baptiste Legrand, a former director of marketing and now one of the best known businessmen of the moment. Well, Baptiste, explain to our viewers your exceptional career.

– Thank you and good evening to you all. I've long *(since long time)* wanted to appear on *(pass at)* this show. I [used to] watch it all the time when I was young and I found it great.

– That's great! Tell *(talk)* me about Xavier Perrier, the man to whom you owe your success.

– I met him when he was running a very modern factory in Le Mans. Next, he left for Canada and, with his wife Élise, set up *(created)* a company specialized in *(the)* e-commerce. The outfit *(box)* very quickly became the number one in the sector, and the two partners became very rich.

At the time *(epoch)*, I was living in Le Havre, where I was working in a recruitment firm just next to the building where they had one of their offices. I had been *(was)* wanting to change jobs for months and months. They hired me as head of *(responsible for)* communication. I knew nothing about it but they took me [on] because we were childhood friends and they thought that I could manage on my own *(alone)*. It's still *(even same)* because of me that they became millionaires.

– Really? So what were they before?

– Er, they were billionaires!

– Thank you and good bye. That was the last show of this season. We'll see one another in January.

– Bonsoir et bienvenue à votre émission hebdomadaire *L'Entreprise au petit écran*, présentée par Amélie Broutard. La semaine dernière, nous vous parlions du monde du bâtiment. Cette semaine, j'ai le plaisir de recevoir Baptiste Legrand, un ancien directeur de marketing et maintenant un des hommes d'affaires les plus connus du moment. Alors, Baptiste, expliquez à nos téléspectateurs votre carrière exceptionnelle.

– Merci et bonsoir à tous. Je voulais depuis longtemps passer à cette émission. Je la regardais tout le temps quand j'étais jeune et je la trouvais formidable.

– Tant mieux ! Parlez-moi de Xavier Perrier, l'homme à qui vous devez votre succès.

– Je l'ai rencontré quand il dirigeait une usine très moderne au Mans. Ensuite, il est parti au Canada et, avec sa femme Élise, a créé une entreprise spécialisée dans le commerce numérique. La boîte est devenue très vite le numéro un du secteur, et les deux associés sont devenus très riches.

À l'époque, je vivais au Havre, où je travaillais dans un cabinet de recrutement juste à côté du bâtiment où ils avaient un de leurs bureaux. Je voulais changer de métier depuis des mois et des mois. Ils m'ont embauché comme responsable de communication. Je n'y connaissais rien mais ils m'ont pris parce que nous étions des amis d'enfance et ils pensaient que je pouvais me débrouiller seul. C'est quand même à cause de moi qu'ils sont devenus millionnaires.

– Ah bon ? Alors, qu'est-ce qu'ils étaient avant ?

– Ben, ils étaient milliardaires !

– Merci et au revoir. C'était la dernière émission de cette saison. Nous nous verrons en janvier.

UNDERSTANDING THE DIALOGUE
WORDS AND PHRASES

→ **bienvenue** is the literal translation of *welcome*. It is used as an invariable interjection, followed, where necessary by **à** for a place and **en** for a region, country, etc.: **Bienvenue à Paris / en France**, *Welcome to Paris / France*. In this role, it is invariable. Used as an adjective, **bienvenu** agrees with its noun: **un accord bienvenu**, *a welcome agreement*, **une offre bienvenue**, *a welcome offer*, etc. (French speakers in Canada use **Bienvenue** as back-translation meaning *You're welcome*, in response to a thank you.)

→ **une boîte**, literally "a box", is another very common slang term (see Module 15). In work-related language, it means *a company* or *business*: **Xavier travaille pour une grosse boîte au Mans**, *Xavier works for a big outfit in Le Mans*. But **une boîte** also means *a nightclub*: **Xavier sort en boîte tous les soirs**, *Xavier goes clubbing every evening*. Pay close attention to the context!

→ **hebdomadaire** is another example of the close links between French and English. Derived from the Greek for "seven", the word means a *seven-day period* or... "a hebdomad" (now used only by crossword fans!). In French, it can be an adjective: **une émission hebdomadaire**, *a weekly TV programme*, or a noun, **un hebdomadaire**, *a weekly publication*. This type of linguistic detective work is a good way of remembering new words.

→ **un cabinet**, mentioned in the Culture Notes of the previous module, is the noun used for a firm of independent professionals such as architects and lawyers (**un cabinet d'architectes, d'avocats**). **Ma femme travaille dans un cabinet dentaire**, *My wife works in a dental surgery*. In many instances, a French word will have several different translations, depending on the specific circumstances. Which makes it much easier when translating from English!

→ **tant** is an adverb meaning *so much*. **Je les aime tant**, *I love them so much*. Coupled with **mieux**, *better*, the comparative of **bien**, *well*, it forms the expression **Tant mieux**, literally "so much the better", which expresses approval. **J'ai gagné ! – Tant mieux !**, – *I won – Good for you!* Like so many idiomatic expressions, the translation will depend on the context.

→ **brouiller** means *to mix* or *muddle*: **les œufs brouillés**, *scrambled eggs*. Logically, **débrouiller** means *to untangle*. However, the most common usage is the reflexive verb **se débrouiller**, which means *to cope*, *to manage* or *to sort out* (i.e. to "untangle" problems). The actual translation will depend on the context, but remember expressions such as: **Je me débrouille en français**, *I can get by in French*; **Elle se débrouille toute seule**, *She can manage on her own*. A useful derivative is the adjective and noun **débrouillard(e)**, meaning *smart* or *resourceful*. **Tu penses qu'elle va réussir ? – Bien sûr, elle est débrouillarde**, *You think she'll succeed? – Of course, she's resourceful.*

CULTURE NOTES

France was one of the first countries in the world to introduce **la télévision**, or **la télé** in familiar French, often called **le petit écran**, *the small screen* (as opposed to **le grand écran**, *the big screen*, i.e. *the cinema*). The broadcast media – basically TV and radio, referred to collectively as **l'audiovisuel** (masc.) – have changed drastically over the past few decades with the advent of *cable* (**le câble**), *digital* (**le numérique**) and *satellite* (**le satellite**) broadcasting. Many media companies now offer a bundle, or **un bouquet**, of *channels* (**des chaînes**) accessible through **un décodeur**, *set-top box*. Despite these technological advances, though, many *viewers* – **les téléspectateurs** – still tune in to terrestrial television to catch *a news bulletin* or *weather report*, respectively **un journal télévisé** (masc. "televised newspaper") or **les informations** (fem. plu., *news*), and **un bulletin météorologique**. As befits such a fast-moving medium, these terms are generally shortened in everyday language to, respectively, **un JT** (pronounced [zheetay]), **les infos** and **la météo**. Likewise, **la publicité**, *advertising*, gets contracted to **la pub**.
In terms of content, the types of shows are easily recognisable, whether **un jeu télévisé** (*a game show*), **un dessin animé** (*a cartoon*), **un documentaire** (*a documentary*), or **une émission de sports** (*a sports programme*). Note that **un programme** means *a programme listing* or *schedule*, as opposed to **une émission**, *a programme* or *show*. But TV-related vocabulary is arguably becoming more anglicised: the term **un feuilleton** is making way for **une série** (plural: **des séries**) and **les heures de grande écoute** for **le prime time**, while **un sitcom** and **un talk-show** are often preferred to their equivalents **une comédie de situation** and **un débat-spectacle**. Fortunately, linguistic creativity is not dead: we have the wonderfully onomatopoeic verb **zapper**, *to channel-surf*, which is done using **une zappette**, *a remote control* (the "proper" word being **une télécommande**). The world of **la téloche** (*the telly*) still has much to offer the language student!

◆ GRAMMAR

THE IMPERFECT TENSE

The imperfect tense is used to talk about an action performed regularly or during an extended period of time in the past. (It is so named because the actions it describes are not "perfected", or completed.)

The nearest English equivalents, depending on the context, are the past continuous (*I was talking*, for example) or the past habitual (*he used to work, she would visit*).

To form the imperfect, we take the root of the verb and add the endings shown in colour. Here is the structure for **-er** group verbs:

je pensais	I was thinking	nous pensions	we were thinking
tu pensais	you were thinking	vous pensiez	you were thinking
il/elle pensait	he/she/it was thinking	ils/elles pensaient	they were thinking

See the appendix for the other two groups.

The negative and interrogative forms follow the usual pattern:

Il ne pensait pas à son travail, *He wasn't thinking about his work/job.*

Est-ce que vous pensiez que l'émission aurait du succès ?, *Did you think the programme would be successful?*

The only verb with an exceptional imperfect form is **être**, *to be*:

j'étais	I was + ing	nous étions	we were + ing
tu étais	you were + ing	vous étiez	you were + ing
il/elle était	he/she/it was + ing	ils/elles étaient	they were + ing

This is important to remember because, when translating an English sentence such as *She was happy in her job*, the French verb must be in the imperfect: **Elle était heureuse dans son travail.**

The imperfect tense is also used when describing an action that continued when another action took place. That second action is usually in the **passé composé**:

J'ai rencontré Serge quand je vivais à Paris.

I met Serge when I was living in Paris.

Elle ne travaillait pas dans son bureau quand le mail est arrivé.

She wasn't working in her office when the email arrived.

Another common use of the imperfect is in a narrative, in which case it is translated by *would* or *used to*:

Quand j'étudiais à Nantes, j'allais chaque semaine à l'Île de Versailles. Je me promenais dans le Jardin japonais, je mangeais des glaces et je regardais la vue pendant des heures. Parfois, je louais un bateau pour naviguer sur la rivière.

When I was studying in Nantes, I used to go every week to Versailles Island. I would walk through the Japanese garden, I would eat ice cream and look at the view for hours. Sometimes, I would rent a boat and sail on the river.

Some adverbs and adverbial phrases usually require the imperfect, particularly those describing repeated or regular actions: **toujours**, *always*; **d'habitude**, *usually*; **chaque jour**, *every day*; **en général**, *in general*, etc.

"MOBILE" ADJECTIVES

In Module 19 we saw that the meaning of the adjective **propre** depends on whether it comes before (*own*) or after (*clean*) the noun. Here are some more adjectives whose meanings shift or change according to their position.

un ancien employé	a former employee	un bâtiment ancien	an old building
un cher ami	a dear friend	un hôtel cher	an expensive hotel
le dernier train	the last (i.e. final) train	la semaine dernière	last week
un grand homme	a great man	un homme très grand	a very big/tall man
une jeune femme	a young woman	un visage jeune	a youthful face
la même ville	the same city	la ville même	the very city
un pauvre type	an unfortunate guy	un pays pauvre	a poor country
un seul homme	only one man	un homme seul	a man on his own

As a rule, when the adjective comes after the noun, it is attributive and has a literal meaning (**un bâtiment ancien**, *an old building*). But if placed before the noun, its meaning is either figurative (**un pauvre type**, *an unfortunate guy*) or slightly different from the attributive one (**un seul homme**, *only one man, i.e. not several*). There are about 40 adjectives like this, but the ones above are the most commonly used.

AGREEMENT OF THE PAST PARTICIPLE

In some cases, the past participle of a verb conjugated in the perfect tense will agree with either the subject or the direct object in which it is used. In spoken French, this poses very few problems because the plural **s** is never pronounced and the feminine ending **e** rarely changes the pronunciation. Since we are not focusing on the written language in this course, we have kept the discussion to a minimum, but here are some basic rules to remember:

– if the verb is conjugated with **avoir**, the participle generally does not agree with anything

– if the verb is conjugated with **être**, the participle agrees with the subject.

Thus, for a feminine subject, we write **Elle est allée au Canada, où elle a vu le Lac Champlain**, *She went to Canada, where she saw Lake Champlain*. If the subject is masculine, the sentence reads **Il est allé au Canada, où il a vu...**, etc. There is no difference in pronunciation between **allée** and **allé**.

Of course, reflexive verbs are conjugated with **être**, so the participle has to agree: **Michel s'est levé à dix heures et sa femme s'est levée à midi,** *Michel got up at 10am and his wife got up at noon.* The rules on agreement get more complex when the direct object of a reflexive verb is different from the subject but, for the purposes of this course, the above information is sufficient.

USE OF ARTICLES AND PREPOSITIONS WITH PLACE NAMES

Choosing the preposition to use before a toponym, or place name, can be a little complicated. With verbs describing position rather than movement (**vivre, travailler,** etc.), use **à**: **Je travaille à Paris,** *I work in Paris.* Before a toponym, containing the masculine definite article, the rule that **à** + **le** or **les** becomes **au** or **aux** applies. For instance: **Les bureaux de ma société sont aux Ulis mais je travaille au Mans,** *My firm's offices are at Les Ulis but I work in Le Mans.* (Note how the initial capital L becomes a small letter.)

As for country names, the prepositions vary depending on gender. For instance, **La France** is feminine so the proposition **en** is used: **Ma tante habite en France,** *My aunt lives in France.* But if she lives in Canada, **Le Canada,** we say: **Ma tante habite au Canada.** Some countries, like **les États-Unis,** *the United States,* are plural, so **Mon oncle habite aux États-Unis.**

The basic rule for identifying the gender of a country name is that the vast majority of those ending in **-e** are feminine and take the preposition **en**: **Notre cousine est née en Pologne,** *Our cousin was born in Poland.* All the remaining nouns are masculine and take **à** (+ definite article = **au/aux**): **... mais son père est né au Japon,** *...but her father was born in Japan.* However, if the name – whether masculine of feminine – begins with a vowel, then the article is dropped and the preposition **en** is used: **Il travaille en Équateur** (**L'Équateur,** *Ecuador*). As always, there are a few exceptions to the rule, and some countries, such as **Cuba** (*Cuba*), do not have a definite article. But as long as you get the country name right, you will be understood (note that **Mexico** is the capital city of **le Mexique** – one of the exceptions to the feminine "e" rule!)

You may feel that the devil is literally in the detail (**au Mans, en France** but **au Canada,** etc., not to mention the agreement of the past participle). And it's true that there is a lot to learn. But remember that the main aim of this course is to get you talking and reading (and to a lesser extent writing). What you are learning are the building blocks that will help you construct sentences that get more and more complex as you move forward. Don't forget that learning a language should be fun, which is why some of our dialogues have a slight twist in the tail. **Tant mieux !**

VOCABULARY

créer *to create, to establish*
(se) débrouiller *to manage, to get by, to sort out*
diriger *to direct, to run*
embaucher *to hire, to employ*
passer *to pass, to appear on* (TV)
présenter *to present*
recevoir *to receive, to play host to*
se voir *to see one another*

un(e) associé(e) *a (business) partner*
le bâtiment *the building trade*
un bâtiment *a building*
une boîte *a box,* (fam.) *a firm, an outfit*
une carrière *a career*
le commerce *commerce, trade, business*
le commerce numérique *e-commerce*
un métier *a profession, a trade*
une émission *a programme* (TV, radio)
l'enfance *childhood*
un homme / une femme d'affaires *a businessman/woman*
un milliard *a billion*
un(e) milliardaire *a billionaire*
un(e) millionnaire *a millionaire* (note the double "n")
un programme *a programme schedule or grid*
un(e) responsable *a person in charge*

une saison *a season*
le (un) succès *(a) success*
un(e) téléspectateur(-trice) *a (TV) viewer* (male/female)
une usine *a factory*

à cause de *because of*
ancien(ne) *former*
exceptionnel(le) *exceptional*
hebdomadaire *weekly*
formidable *great, super*

Ah bon ? *Really?, Is that right?*
À l'époque *At that / the time*
Ben… *Er…*
Bonsoir et bienvenue *Good evening and welcome*
Tant mieux *Great, Good for you, "So much the better"*

● EXERCISES

1. PUT THESE VERBS INTO THE IMPERFECT TENSE

a. À l'époque, nous (*vivre*) au Mans et je (*travailler*) dans une usine.

b. Tu (*vouloir*) me parler, peut-être ?

c. Le journaliste (*penser*) que je (*être*) un homme d'affaires.

d. Est-ce qu'ils (*être*) riches à l'époque ? – Oui, ils (*être*) milliardaires.

e. Nous avons rencontré Serge et Nathalie quand ils (*habiter*) à Paris.

2. PUT THE VERBS IN THIS PARAGRAPH INTO THE IMPERFECT

Quand nous sommes (**a.**) _ _ _ _ _ _ à Nantes, nous allons (**b.**) _ _ _ _ _ chaque semaine à l'Île de Versailles. Nous nous promenons (**c.**) _ _ _ _ _ _ dans le Jardin japonais, nous mangeons (**d.**) _ _ _ _ _ des glaces et nous regardons (**e.**) _ _ _ _ _ _ _ la vue pendant des heures. Parfois, Serge loue (**f.**) _ _ _ _ _ un bateau pour naviguer sur la rivière.

3. USE THE APPROPRIATE ARTICLE AND/OR PREPOSITION IF APPROPRIATE

a. J'habite _ _ Paris mais je travaille _ _ _ Le Havre.

b. Ma sœur est née _ _ _ l'Argentine et moi _ _ _ les États-Unis.

c. Est-ce que tu as étudié _ _ _ l'Angleterre ? Non, _ _ _ la France

d. Je vais _ _ _ Cuba en janvier. Je préfère _ _ _ le Canada.

e. Quelle est la capitale _ _ _ _ Mexique ? – _ _ _ Mexico, bien sûr.

4. TRANSLATE INTO FRENCH

a. Emmanuelle and her friends are working for a big outfit in Les Ulis. – They're managing well.

b. Michelle got up at ten o'clock and her husband got up at noon. – Really?

c. She became rich very quickly, and she bought a house in Le Mans.

d. They left for Canada when they were very young. – Good for them!

e. Did you* think those programmes would be successful? – Not really.

* Use the **tu** form

23.
PARTYING

FAIRE LA FÊTE

AIMS	NOTIONS

- TALK ABOUT BIRTHDAYS
- EXPRESS A CONDITION
- DISCUSS ALTERNATIVES

- FIRST CONDITIONAL
- *CE QUI / CE QUE*
- *ON* OR *NOUS*? (CONT.)

HAPPY BIRTHDAY!

– What's wrong *(What is it that doesn't go?)* Feeling down *(You have the cockroach)*?

– If I'm in [a] bad mood, it's because it's my birthday next month. I'm blowing out my 25 candles. [Can] you imagine? Already a quarter of [a] century! I'm going to organise a huge party *(feast)*, not the actual day but the next day or [the] day after.

– What [an] excellent idea. You have loads *(full)* of friends in Paris. If they're there, they will all come, that's [for] sure *(certain)*.

– What worries me is *(it's)* the weather. You know what they say: "In April, don't remove *(uncover yourself)* a thread". If it's fine, we will be able to picnic in Boulogne Wood. By contrast *(in revenge)*, if it rains, we will be obliged to stay at home and that will be less fun *(amusing)*. If there are many of us *(numerous)*, what's [for] sure *(and certain)* is that the neighbours are going to moan. They complain as a *(general)* rule, so, if we make some noise, they'll hit the roof *(jump to the ceiling)*. I don't know what is more *(most)* important: a successful party or peaceful neighbours.

– I see what you mean *(want to say)*. And if you invite them, you think they'll come?

– It would surprise me, but we can always try. There's no harm in it *(doesn't eat bread)*.

– You know what I think? They'll be delighted if you ask them nicely. If they say yes, we'll be cool *(tranquil)*. If not, it doesn't matter. We'll have fun anyway.

– By the way, I'm thinking about inviting Jacques, my ex. If he comes, I'll be very happy. I haven't seen him for a long time.

– You knew that he was going out with Christine? Ah, you weren't aware. That means that if he comes, I'm almost certain that Christine will come too.

– To be honest, it doesn't bother me too much. I don't love Jacques any more. And anyway, he always forgot my birthday, which really irritated me.

– But if he forgets it, it means he doesn't see you age!

— Qu'est-ce qui ne va pas ? Tu as le cafard ?

— Si je suis de mauvaise humeur, c'est parce que c'est mon anniversaire le mois prochain. Je souffle mes vingt-cinq bougies. Tu imagines ? Un quart de siècle déjà ! Je vais organiser une grosse fête ; pas le jour même mais le lendemain ou le surlendemain.

— Quelle excellente idée. Tu as plein d'amis à Paris. S'ils sont là, ils viendront tous, c'est certain.

— Ce qui m'inquiète, c'est le temps. Tu sais ce qu'on dit : « En avril ne te découvre pas d'un fil ». S'il fait beau, on pourra pique-niquer au Bois de Boulogne. En revanche, s'il pleut, on sera obligés de rester à la maison et ça sera moins amusant. Si on est nombreux, ce qui est sûr et certain c'est que les voisins vont râler. Ils se plaignent en règle générale, alors, si on fait du bruit, ils vont sauter au plafond. Je ne sais pas ce qui est le plus important : une fête réussie ou des voisins paisibles.

— Je vois ce que tu veux dire. Et si tu les invites, tu penses qu'ils viendront ?

— Ça m'étonnerait, mais on peut toujours essayer. Ça ne mange pas de pain.

— Tu sais ce que je pense ? Ils seront ravis si tu leur demandes gentiment. S'ils disent oui, on sera tranquilles. Sinon, ça ne fait rien : on s'amusera quand même.

— À propos, je pense inviter Jacques, mon ex. S'il vient, je serai très contente. Je ne l'ai pas vu depuis longtemps.

— Tu savais qu'il sortait avec Christine ? Ah, tu n'étais pas au courant. Ça veut dire que s'il vient, je suis presque sûr que Christine viendra aussi.

— Pour être honnête, ça ne me gêne pas trop. Je ne l'aime plus, Jacques. Et de toute façon, il oubliait toujours mon anniversaire, ce qui m'énervait beaucoup.

— Mais s'il l'oublie, ça veut dire qu'il ne te voit pas vieillir !

■ UNDERSTANDING THE DIALOGUE

WORDS AND PHRASES

→ **Qu'est-ce qu'il y a ?**, literally "what is it there?", is a useful phrase for enquiring about a problem or a situation. **Qu'est-ce qu'il y a ? – Je ne me sens pas très bien**, *What's the matter? – I'm not feeling very well.* If something is visibly amiss, the question is **Qu'est-ce qui ne va pas ?**, *What's wrong?*

→ **un cafard** means *a cockroach*, an insect that's bound to cause depression if found in a bathroom or mattress! Thus the idiomatic expression **avoir le cafard** means *to be feeling down in the dumps*. The best way to remember idiomatic expressions is to create one's own mnemonics – like feeling blue if you come across a nasty insect.

→ The feminine noun **l'humeur** is a false cognate. Despite sharing the same root as **l'humour**, *humour*, the word has the broader meaning of *mood* or *temper*. Two common expressions are **Tu es de bonne / mauvaise humeur**, *You're in a good/bad mood* and **Il / Elle est d'humeur changeante**, *He / She is moody.* The word for *humour*, **l'humour** (masc.), actually comes from English and was originally used in contrast to **l'esprit**, *wit*, considered a specifically French form of jocularity. **Ils ont un excellent sens de l'humour**, *They have an excellent sense of humour.*

→ **une revanche** is the origin of the English word *revenge*. The expression **en revanche**, generally used at the beginning of a clause, means *on the other hand*. **Je n'aime pas les films d'horreur. En revanche, j'adore les comédies romantiques**, *I don't like horror films. On the other hand, I love romcoms.* A synonymous expression is **par contre** (literally "by against"): There is much debate among learned grammarians about the difference between the two. The first is considered more elegant than the second but you can use either.

→ **le plafond**, *the ceiling.* If you are furious in French, you "jump to the ceiling": **Quand je lui ai donné la mauvaise nouvelle, il a sauté au plafond**, *When I gave him the bad news, he hit the roof.* (In some cases, the same expression can also mean *to jump for joy*, so pay close attention to the context!)

→ **Ça ne fait rien** (literally "It does nothing") is such a useful expression that it was once adopted in English as *San fairy ann!* It basically means *It doesn't matter* or *No problem* (although the latter is also used in French!). Another **ça** idiom is **Ça ne mange pas de pain**, "That doesn't eat bread", means *It can't do any harm* or *It won't hurt.* The expression dates from the time when bread was a staple foodstuff and had to be conserved. Anything that didn't consume bread was innocuous. As in English, there are many expressions that use **le pain**, including **On a du pain sur la planche**, "We have bread on the board", equivalent to *We have our work cut out.*

→ The adjective **courant(e)** is the root of our word *current*, in the sense of *standard*, *everyday*, etc. The expression **être au courant** indicates that one is aware of what is going on or is up to speed on a subject. **Ils viennent demain ? Je n'étais pas au courant**, *They're coming tomorrow? I wasn't aware.* Placed at the beginning of a clause, it is followed by **que**: **Il est au courant que le magasin a fermé**, *He is aware that the store has closed.* Used with the verb **tenir** instead of **être**, the expression means *to keep someone informed.* **Je te tiendrai au courant**, *I'll keep you posted.*

CULTURE NOTES

The close links between English and French are so evident that they can lull us into a sense of false linguistic security. In addition to the **faux amis** we have already learned, there are many sayings and proverbs in both languages that express the same sentiment but with slightly different wording. For example, **En avril ne te découvre pas d'un fil** (*In April, don't remove a thread*) anticipates by one month its English equivalent *Cast ne'er a clout 'till May is out.* Another "time-shifting" proverb is **Une hirondelle ne fait pas le printemps**, the English equivalent of which is *One swallow doesn't make a summer* (instead of the spring). By and large, the differences are confined to set phrases, and the changes follow certain patterns. This is particularly true of sayings involving animals. The French advise against waking a cat rather than dogs – **Ne réveillez pas le chat qui dort**/*Let sleeping dogs lie* – and believe that church rats, not mice, are destitute: **pauvre comme un rat d'église**/*poor as a church mouse.* Another trick is to change the verb or noun: what sells "like hot cakes" in English are "bread rolls" in French: **se vendre comme des petits pains**. And whereas we "rob Peter to pay Paul", the French will undress one to dress the other: **déshabiller Pierre pour habiller Paul**. Alternatively, phrases like "double or quits" and "safe and sound" are inverted: **quitte ou double, sain et sauf**.

Such differences are not simply anecdotal. They are important to identify and remember in order to appreciate the similarities and subtle differences between French and English.

One such difference lies in the significance of **la fête**, which, in everyday usage, means *a party.* However, it also means *a name day*, the day in the year that is associated with a particular saint of the Catholic church (put back the "s" represented by the circumflex to obtain *feast*). A person given the first name **Jean** will celebrate his own birthday as well as the Feast of Saint John on 21 June. This tradition has fallen by the wayside somewhat as French society becomes more secular and children are given forenames from other cultures or religions. Nonetheless, the name of each day's patron saint is still inscribed on calendars, displayed in the entertainment section of certain newspapers and even announced on the TV evening weather forecast. It was customary to wish one's friends or relatives **Bonne fête** (*Happy name day*) on their name day, although that tradition, too, is disappearing (in Canada, the phrase is used instead of **Joyeux anniversaire**, for *Happy birthday*). A word of warning, though: the interjection **Ça va être ta fête !** is not an invitation to party but a cautionary message: *You're in for it!*

◆ GRAMMAR

THE FIRST CONDITIONAL, WITH *SI*

We have already seen the first – or real – conditional (*if → then*), but it warrants another look because it is widely used. This type of construction comprises two parts: the **si** clause and the main clause.

• To talk about a habit or usual state of being, we use the present tense in both clauses:

Je suis de mauvaise humeur si on me pose trop de questions, *I get in a bad mood if people ask me too many questions.*

In this case, **si** has the same function as **quand**, *when*, which can be used instead (**quand on me pose...**). The two clauses can be inverted with no difference in meaning, but in this case a comma is needed after the first clause: **Si on me pose trop de questions, je suis de mauvaise humeur.**

• To talk about something that will definitely happen if a condition is satisfied, use the future tense in the main clause:

Si mes amies sont à Paris, elles viendront à ta fête, *If my girlfriends are in Paris, they'll come to your party.*

• With the real conditional, we can also use the perfect tense instead of the present in the **si** clause:

Si vous avez oublié votre mot de passe, vous pourrez le retrouver par mail, *If you have forgotten your password, you can recover it by email.*

The same type of construction is used with an imperative sentence:

Si tu vas à la boulangerie, achète-moi deux croissants et une baguette, *If you go to the bakery, get [buy] me two croissants and a bread stick.*

Remember: in a **si** clause, we can use only the present, the perfect, the imperfect and the pluperfect (which we will not see in this course). In the next module, we'll look at the second conditional.

CE QUI / CE QUE

These two indefinite relative pronouns, meaning *which* or *what*, can be problematic at first because they look very similar. They both introduce a subordinate clause, just like **qui** and **que**. But they are used in sentences where the antecedent – the noun or phrase referred to by a pronoun – is not expressed.

• **Ce qui** refers to the phrase – not the single noun – that is the subject of the verb.

Mes voisins font beaucoup de bruit, ce qui m'énerve, *My neighbours make a lot of noise, which annoys me.*

Je n'ai pas de ses nouvelles, et c'est ce qui m'inquiète le plus, *I've haven't heard from him, and that's what worries me most.*

• **Ce que** refers to the object of the verb:

Ce qu'elles font m'intéresse énormément, *What they do interests me hugely.*

Nous ne comprenons pas ce que vous voulez, *We don't understand what you want.*

Both pronouns can be used for emphasis. For this, we start the sentence with the **ce qui/ce que** clause, then introduce the second clause with **c'est**:

Ce qui nous intéresse, c'est que nos clients gagnent de l'argent, *What interests us is that our customers make money.*

Ce que je veux dire, c'est que j'ai vraiment besoin de vacances, *What I mean is that I really need a holiday.*

This is similar to the English construction *What* + verb + object pronoun, although the second part of the sentence begins with *that*.

ON VS. NOUS

We learned about the pronoun **on** in Module 6. As you will have noticed by now, it is very commonly used both in the impersonal form (*one*) and as an alternative to **nous**. One possible reason for the latter is that the first person plural form of a verb can be quite long: the three syllables of **nous préférons,** for instance, can be reduced to two: **on préfère.** Consequently, as the dialogue in this module shows, **on** is the spoken pronoun of choice, and the switch between the personal and impersonal is seamless: **On sera obligés,** *We'll be obliged* (personal); **Tu sais ce qu'on dit,** *You know what they say* (impersonal). **On** can also be used as the first person plural when writing informally, for example in a personal email. In this case, you can choose whether or not to make any adjectives agree with the subject (**on sera obligé / obligés**) because the rule is quite ambiguous. In formal French, however always use **nous** for the first person plural, keeping **on** for an indefinite pronoun.

INVARIABLE ADJECTIVES

Many singular adjectives have the same form in the masculine and the feminine. In this module, for example, we learned **tranquille**, *peaceful, calm, tranquil*. Other common adjectives that do not change include **large**, *broad*; **libre**, *free*; **magnifique**, *superb*; **malade**, *sick*; **mince**, *slim*; **moderne**, *modern*; **necessaire**, *necessary*, **pauvre**, *poor*; **riche**, *rich* and **rapide**, *fast, rapid*. Here's a quick way to remember them:

Si vous êtes riche ou pauvre, mince ou malade, vous pouvez admirer ce magnifique bâtiment moderne avec sa large porte d'entrée. L'accès est libre, mais il est nécessaire d'être rapide : il y a beaucoup de visiteurs. *If you're rich or poor, slim or sick, you can admire this magnificent building with its wide entrance door. Entry is free, but it's necessary to be quick: there are many visitors.*

Another category of invariable adjectives consists of colours. For example, **orange**, *orange*; **rose**, *pink*; and **marron**, *brown* are invariable. Adjectives derived from nouns relating to animals, flowers, fruit or gemstones do not generally vary. The most common of these are **argent**, *silver*; **émeraude**, *emerald green*; **marine**, *navy blue*; and **turquoise**. Compound colours follow the same rule: des **yeux gris clair**, *light grey eyes*; **une jupe vert pomme**, *an apple-green skirt*. However, since these idiosyncrasies have little effect on pronunciation, they do not need to be explained in detail at this stage.

⬢ EXERCISES

1. PUT THE VERBS IN THESE CONDITIONAL SENTENCES INTO THE CORRECT FORM

a. Si mes amis (*être*) à Paris le mois prochain, ils (*venir*) dîner à la maison.

b. Tu (*pouvoir*) retrouver ton mot de passe par mail si tu le (*perdre*).

c. Si vous (*aller*) au marché, (*prendre*)-moi un kilo de pommes, s'il vous plait.

d. Nous (*aller*) au Bois de Boulogne demain s'il (*faire*) beau.

e. Si tu (*inviter*) ton ex à la fête, tu penses qu'elle (*venir*) ?

2. USE *CE QUI* OR *CE QUE* TO COMPLETE THESE SENTENCES

a. (.......) est certain, c'est que les voisins vont se plaindre du bruit.

b. Dis-moi (......) tu comprends dans cette lettre : elle est écrite en arabe.

c. Son mari oublie toujours son anniversaire, (.......) l'énerve.

d. (.......) font Marie et Nicolas m'aide beaucoup dans mon travail.

e. Avoir un bon travail, c'est (.......) est le plus important.

● VOCABULARY

avoir le cafard *to be down in the dumps*
(s')énerver *to (get) annoy(ed)*
(s')étonner *to surprise/be surprised*
gêner *to bother*
(s')inquiéter *to worry* (see **inquiet**, Module 12)
inviter *to invite*
piqueniquer *to picnic*
se plaindre (de) *to complain (about)*
râler *to moan, to complain*
sauter *to jump*
~au plafond *to hit the roof*
souffler *to blow (out)*
vieillir *to age, to get old*
vouloir dire *to mean*

un anniversaire *a birthday*
un bois *a wood* (small forest)
le bois *wood* (material)
une bougie *a candle*
un cafard *a cockroach*
une fête *a party, a saint's day, a public holiday*
une humeur *a mood*
mauvaise humeur *a bad mood*
le lendemain *tomorrow*
le plafond *the ceiling*
le surlendemain *the day after tomorrow*
un(e) voisin(e) *a neighbour*

longtemps *a long time*
quand même *all the same, nonetheless*
amusant(e) *amusing, funny*

gentiment* *nicely, politely*
honnête *honest*
nombreux(-euses) *numerous*
paisible *peaceful, calm*
ravi(e) *delighted*
tranquille *peaceful, calm*

Ça ne mange pas de pain *It can't do any harm*
En revanche *On the other hand*
Joyeux anniversaire. *Happy birthday*
Qu'est ce qui ne vas pas ? *What's wrong?*
* Note the irregular spelling (**gentillement → gentiment**)

3. CHANGE THE SENTENCES FROM *NOUS* TO *ON* AND VICE VERSA

a. Nous sommes très contents de vous avoir ici avec nous*. →

b. Ce n'est pas grave : nous nous amuserons quand même. →

c. Nous ne l'avons pas vu vendredi dernier mais nous lui avons parlé le surlendemain. →

d. On préfère ne pas bouger d'ici car on attend nos amis à seize heures. →

e. Ce que nous pensons, c'est que nous devons vraiment aller à la fête de Jacques demain. →

* The second **nous** in this sentence does not change because it is an emphatic pronoun (see Module 6).

4. TRANSLATE INTO FRENCH

a. They hit the roof when we gave them the bad news. That's the reason that they are in a bad mood.

b. Are you aware that the stores will be closed tomorrow and Monday?

c. We've got our work cut out: we have to organise Nelly's party.*

d. What's wrong, Monique? – I'm down in the dumps because my ex is going out with my best friend.

e. Perhaps I'll invite them. – You can always try. It won't do any harm.

* Use both forms (**on**, **nous**)

24.
THE LOTTERY

LA LOTERIE

AIMS	NOTIONS

- DESCRIBE A CONDITION
- TALK ABOUT POSSIBILITIES
- USE COMMON IDIOMS

- THE SECOND CONDITIONAL
- POSITION OF ADVERBS
- IDIOMATIC PRONOMINAL VERBS

"ALL OUR WINNERS HAVE TRIED THEIR LUCK"

(A journalist is asking a guest some questions)

— Do you feel like playing a little game, just to take your mind off things? Yes? Then answer this question frankly: what would you do if you won the jackpot *(big lot)* at the lottery?

— If I won the jackpot? Honestly, I've never thought about it. And you?

— Me, I often think about it. But it's *(to)* you that I'm asking *(the question)*.

— I've never bought a lottery ticket, because I have realised that I've had little luck in my life. But if I won, what is certain is that I wouldn't continue working.

— Pardon, I misheard: you would continue working?

— No, on the contrary, I would resign and I would never return to the office. I would give *(offer)* presents to my whole family and my relatives and I would find a pretty country house for my girlfriend. I'm convinced that she would do the same if she was in my position. I would buy *(offer)* myself the very latest luxury hybrid car, the one that film stars drive. I saw one yesterday or the day before yesterday on the motorway and I fell in love with it. Normally I couldn't afford it because it costs an arm and a leg. But because I would be rolling in money, I would even-numbered buy two of them, one for even days and the other for odd days. I would live in a detached house in an upscale and trendy neighbourhood. I would have a chef who would cook delicious dishes, and someone who would do the housework.

— So you would spend everything, all at once? You should pay attention not to throw your money out the window.

— Rest assured: I would put part of it aside in a bank. And you, what would you do if you were in my position?

— Above all, if I wanted to win, I would buy a ticket!

* In these last few modules, the translation of the French text is much less literal than in the first part of the book. It's time to wean yourself off word-for-word equivalents as far as possible.

(Une journaliste pose des questions à un invité)

— Ça vous dirait de faire un petit jeu, juste pour vous changer les idées ? Oui ? Alors répondez franchement à cette question : qu'est-ce que vous feriez si vous gagniez le gros lot à la loterie ?

— Si je gagnais le jackpot ? À vrai dire, je n'y ai jamais pensé. Et vous ?

— Moi, j'y pense souvent. Mais c'est à vous que j'ai posé la question.

— Je n'ai jamais acheté un billet de loterie, parce que je me suis rendu compte que j'ai eu peu de chance dans ma vie. Mais si je gagnais, ce qui est sûr est que je ne continuerais pas à travailler.

— Pardon, j'ai mal entendu : vous continueriez à bosser ?

— Non, au contraire, je démissionnerais et je n'irais plus jamais au bureau. J'offrirais des cadeaux à toute ma famille et mes proches et je trouverais une jolie maison de campagne pour ma petite amie. Je suis convaincu qu'elle ferait pareil si elle était à ma place. Je m'offrirais la toute dernière voiture hybride de luxe, celle que conduisent les vedettes de cinéma. J'en ai vu une hier ou avant-hier sur l'autoroute et j'ai eu le coup de foudre. Normalement, je ne pourrais pas me la payer parce que ça coûte les yeux de la tête. Mais parce que je roulerais sur l'or, j'en achèterais même deux, une pour les jours pairs et l'autre pour les jours impairs. J'habiterais une villa dans un quartier chic et branché de la capitale. J'aurais un chef qui me cuisinerait des plats délicieux, et quelqu'un qui ferait le ménage.

— Donc vous dépenseriez tout, tout d'un coup ? Il faudrait faire attention à ne pas jeter votre argent par les fenêtres.

— Rassurez-vous : j'en mettrais une partie de côté, dans une banque. Et vous, que feriez-vous si vous étiez à ma place ?

— Avant tout, si je voulais gagner, j'achèterais un billet !

UNDERSTANDING THE DIALOGUE

WORDS AND PHRASES

→ The regular verb **dire**, *to say*, can be used to ask someone politely if they would like to do something: **Ça te dit de venir passer la soirée avec nous ?** *Do you feel like spending the evening with us?* In a more formal context, the verb is put into the conditional of politeness: **Ça vous dirait de visiter nos bureaux ?** *Would you like to visit our offices?* Another expression with **dire** is **à vrai dire**, *to tell the truth* (literally "to true to tell"). The phrase can be inverted, with no difference in meaning (**à dire vrai**).

→ **bosser**, *to work*, is another of those familiar words (see Module 15) that are widely used in everyday French but that have no precise equivalent in English. **Une bosse** is *a lump* or *a bump*, and the original meaning of **bosser** was that the person's back was bowed under the weight of their labour (**un bossu**, *a hunchback*). It is important to remember that some words do not have a direct translation.

→ The adjective **proche** means *close, nearby* (see Module 12, **la proche banlieue**, *the inner suburbs*). As a noun, usually a masculine plural, **les proches** means *close relatives* or, more formally, *next of kin*. A common end-of-year greeting is **Bonne année à vous et à vos proches**, equivalent to our *Happy new year to you and yours*.

→ **pareil** is an adjective with a comparable meaning to **même**, *same*, but it also means *similar* or *alike*. **J'ai une nouvelle écharpe. – J'en ai une pareille**, *I have a new scarf. – I've got one like it*. It can also be used as an adverb: **Elles s'habillent pareil**, *They dress alike*. (Remember the English adjective *nonpareil*, "having no equivalent".)

→ The noun **une vedette** (literally "someone who watches") means *a star* (stage, screen, etc.). In this meaning, it is often eclipsed by the "French" word **une star** (always feminine). But the word is also used as an adjective: **Giniaux est le joueur vedette de l'équipe**, *Giniaux is the team's star player*. (The word for *a star* as a celestial body is **une étoile**).

→ **branché** is an adjective meaning *plugged in*: **Est-ce que l'imprimante est branchée ?**, *Is the printer plugged in?* In a familiar register, the word means *trendy*: **Il y a plein de boutiques branchées dans le quartier du Marais**, *There are loads of trendy boutiques in Le Marais district*. (See Module 22 for the rule on definite articles in proper names.)

CULTURE NOTES

Games of chance, **les jeux du hasard**, are state-controlled in France. Probably the most popular is the *national lottery*, **loterie** (note the single "t") **nationale**, established in the 1930s to raise money for soldiers wounded or mutilated in the first world war. The weekly draw was later renamed **Le Loto**, under which name it operates today. *Scratch-card games*, **les jeux de grattage**, are also very popular. Cards can be bought in **un bureau de tabac**, a specially licensed café that also sells tobacco, (hence the name) or in a *newsagent*, **un marchand de journaux**. In recent years, much of this activity has migrated online. Another popular game of chance (or skill) is betting on *horse races*, **les courses** (fem.) **de chevaux**. This activity is controlled through an organisation called **le Pari mutuel urbain**, or **PMU**, named for a mutual betting system (**un pari**, *a bet*) also used in North America. Punters originally bet on a combination of three horses, hence the name **tiercé**. Although the system has been expanded to four or five winners, **le tiercé** is widely used as a generic term for horse betting. Much of the vocabulary connected with this activity comes from English, including **un bookmaker**, **un betting book**, **un trotteur** and **un steeple-chase**. But **le Loto** has made its mark in France and is known for its clever slogans, arguably the most famous of which is **Cent pour cent des gagnants ont tenté leur chance**, *100% of winners have tried their luck!*. **Bonne chance !** *Good luck!*

GRAMMAR

POSITION OF ADVERBS

Now that we are familiar with the formation of adverbs, let's look more closely at where to position them in a sentence.

The first rule is that, unlike in English, adverbs are never placed next to the subject of a sentence: *They always say no*, **Ils disent toujours non**.

Secondly, adverbs are placed immediately after a verb that consists of a single word, whatever the tense: **Je pense souvent à mon premier travail**, *I often think of my first job*. If the verb is negative, the adverb comes after the negative particle: **Sa voiture ne roule pas vite**, *His car doesn't drive fast*. Remember, however, that if the adverb contains the idea of negation, **pas** is unnecessary: **Il ne pensait jamais à moi**, *He never used to think of me*.

If the sentence contains a direct object noun, the adverb will come before it: **J'aime beaucoup ses romans**, *I like his novels very much*. It is important to remember this rule because in many cases, the word order differs from English.

For verbs conjugated with **avoir** or **être**, the adverb usually comes between that auxiliary and the participle: **Je n'ai jamais pensé qu'il était intelligent**, *I've never thought he was intelligent*. Most of these adverbs relate to quantity or frequency; they include **beaucoup**, *a lot*; **bien**, *well*, **mal**, *badly*; **vraiment**, *really*; **rarement**, *rarely*; **souvent**, *often*, and **toujours**, *always*.

Likewise, in the future immediate tense with **aller**, the adverb comes between this auxiliary and the infinitive: **Elle va certainement venir demain**, *She'll certainly come tomorrow.*

Some adverbs come after a compound verb, especially those relating to time and position: **Ils sont arrivés tôt ce matin**, *They arrived early this morning.* Other adverbs in this category include **tard**, *late*; **quelquefois**, *sometimes*; **longtemps**, *a long time*; as well as **aujourd'hui**, *today*; **hier**, *yesterday*; and **demain**, *tomorrow.*

Adverbs modifying an adjective or another adverb generally come before the word in question: **Le livre est très bien écrit**, *The book is very well written.* **Désolé, vous êtes trop en retard**, *Sorry, you're too late.*

IDIOMATIC PRONOMINAL VERBS

As mentioned in Module 10, some pronominal verbs are idiomatic and have to be learned. The mechanism is very simple and consists in putting a reflexive pronoun before an ordinary verb: **J'offre un cadeau à ma petite amie**, *I'm giving my girlfriend a present* → **Je m'offre un cadeau**, *I'm buying myself a present.*

Likewise, **payer quelque chose**, *to pay for something*; **se payer quelque chose**, *to buy something for oneself.*

For example, **rendre compte** means *to recount* or *account for*, *report* (literally "to render account"), whereas **se rendre compte** means *to realise**: **Il s'est rendu compte que le quartier était très branché**, *He realised that the district was very trendy* (remember that all pronominal verbs use **être** instead of **avoir** as an auxiliary).

Likewise, **se changer les idées**, "to change ideas", means *to think about something else* or *take one's mind off something*: **Viens boire un café avec moi: ça te changera les idées**, *Come and have a coffee with me: it will take your mind off things.*

It is important to learn these idiomatic forms because, in most cases, they cannot be understood via a literal translation.

* The French verb **réaliser** is a false cognate, meaning *to achieve*, *carry out.*

▲ CONJUGATIONS

THE SECOND CONDITIONAL

The second conditional corresponds to the English verb form with *would.* It is used to describe a hypothetical situation or as a form of polite address when asking for something. It can also be employed when giving advice or making a suggestion.

To form the conditional, add the endings of the imperfect tense (see Module 22) to the infinitive (deleting the final **e** for the **-re** group).

gagner, *to win, to earn*

je gagnerais	I would win	nous gagnerions	we would win
tu gagnerais	you would win	vous gagneriez	you would win
il/elle/on gagnerait	he/she/it/we would win	ils/elles gagneraient	they would win

mettre, *to put*

je mettrais	I would put	nous mettrions	we would put
tu mettrais	you would put	vous mettriez	you would put
il/elle/on mettrait	he/she/it/we would put	ils/elles mettraient	they would put

If the future tense of a verb has any irregular forms (notably the auxiliaries **aller, avoir** and **être**), they will also occur in the conditional. For example: **j'irai** → **j'irais**; **j'aurai** → **j'aurais**; **je serai** → **je serais**. However, both forms are pronounced identically. So be especially careful when writing in the first person: **je gagnerai** = future; **je gagnerais** = conditional: even native French speakers sometimes confuse the two! We have added the impersonal **on** to the table because it is often used instead of **nous**, considered rather formal (and a bit harder to pronounce!).

Two other common verbs are regularly found in the conditional because they are used in polite conversation: **pouvoir**, *to be able to*, and **vouloir**, *to want to*.

je pourrais	nous pourrions	je voudrais	nous voudrions
tu pourrais	vous pourriez	tu voudrais	vous voudriez
il/elle pourrait	ils/elles pourraient	il/elle voudrait	Ils/elles voudraient

Pourriez-vous nous aider s'il vous plait ? Nous voudrions louer une voiture, *Could you help us, please? We would like to rent a car.*

In two-part sentences using **si** and a dependent clause, the verb that follows the conjunction is in the imperfect tense:

Si je gagnais le gros lot, j'achèterais une maison, *If I won the jackpot, I would buy a house.*

Elles partiraient demain si elles pouvaient, *They'd leave tomorrow if they could.*

Care should be taken when using the conditional of politeness. When offering or accepting something in English, we use the verb *to like* in both the question and the answer: *Would you like a coffee? – I would like* (or *love*) *one, please.* Using the same response in French would imply that you would like to accept the invitation but cannot for some reason. Instead we use **vouloir** in the conditional for the question: **Voulez-vous** (or, very politely, **Voudriez-vous**) **un café ?** and an affirmative in the answer **Je veux bien** or, quite simply, **Avec plaisir**, *With pleasure*.

One peculiarity is that the conditional is used to express a conjecture or an action that the speaker is unable to confirm. In this sense, it is regularly found in news reports and translated by adding a conditional word such as *apparently*, *reportedly*, or *allegedly*: **Dix personnes seraient blessées dans un accident de car en Bourgogne**, *Ten people are reportedly injured in a coach accident in Burgundy*.

● EXERCISES

1. PUT THESE SENTENCES INTO THE SECOND CONDITIONAL WHERE NECESSARY

a. Dis-moi, qu'est ce tu (*faire*:………………..) si tu (*gagner*:………………..) le gros lot à la loterie ?

b. Je (*acheter*, negative:……………………………..) une voiture car j'en ai déjà deux.

c. Qu'est-ce que tu (*vouloir*:………………….) si tu (*avoir*:………………..) de l'argent? – Quelqu'un qui (*faire*:………………..) le ménage.

d. Elle m'a dit que son mari (*démissionner*:……………..) et (*aller*, negative:……………..) au bureau.

e. Ce qui est sûr, c'est que je (*habiter*, negative:…………………………..) Le Marais, même si je (*pouvoir*:…………………..).

2. PUT THESE ADVERBS IN THE CORRECT PLACE TO MODIFY THE UNDERLINED VERB(S)

a. **beaucoup** → Elle n'aime pas ses films car ils sont trop tristes. (2 times in this sentence)

b. **jamais** → Tu es égoïste : tu ne penses pas à moi.

c. **certainement** → Il m'a dit qu'il va partir demain.

d. **toujours** → J'ai pensé qu'ils étaient nos amis mais j'avais tort.

e. **souvent** → Nous l'avons vu à la télévision : c'est une star !

●VOCABULARY

bosser (fam.) *to work*
conduire *to drive*
(se) changer *to change (get changed)*
~ les idées *to think about something else*
convaincre *to convince*
démissionner *to resign*
dépenser *to spend*
jeter *to throw*
offrir *to offer, to give* (a present)
(se) rendre compte *to report, to realise*
rassurer *to reassure, to put someone's mind at rest*
rouler *to roll, to drive*

une autoroute *a motorway*
une banque *a bank*
un cadeau *a gift*
une étoile *star* (celestial)
une fenêtre *a window*
la foudre *lightning*
un gros lot, un jackpot *a jackpot*
un jeu *a game*
une loterie *a lottery*
le luxe *luxury*
de luxe *luxurious, "de luxe"*
l'or (masc.) *gold*
le ménage *housework*
un proche *a (close) relative*
une star *a star* (celebrity)
un(e) petit(e) ami(e) *a boyfriend/ girlfriend*
une vedette *a star, a speedboat*
une villa *a detached house, a villa*

branché(e) *trendy*
chic *chic, fashionable*
à côte *aside*
franchement *frankly*
impair *odd* (number)
pair *even* (number)
pareil *the same, similar*

Ça te/vous dirait… ? *Do you feel like…?*
Rassurez-vous *Rest assured*

3. COMPLETE THESE IDIOMS

a. Est-ce que son cadeau était cher ? – Oui ! Ça m'a coûté . . . .

b. Ne jette pas tout ton argent . . . .

c. Sortons au restaurant. Tu pourras . . . . . . changer . . . .

d. Je ne peux pas acheter une voiture neuve. Je ne roule pas . . . .

e. Je pense que Michel est tombé amoureux. – Oui, il a eu . . . .

4. TRANSLATE INTO FRENCH

26

a. Do you feel like spending the evening with us?* – To tell the truth, I don't have much time. (two possibilities)

b. I'm convinced that you would do the same if you were in our position.*

c. I've realised that their new neighbourhood is very trendy. – Frankly, we've never thought about it.**

d. He would leave tomorrow if he could, just to take his mind off things.

e. The two stores are the same: quite upscale and very expensive.

* Use both forms (**vous**, **tu**)

** Use both forms (**nous**, **on**)

We have started to learn some common idioms, like **rouler sur l'or, avoir le coup de foudre** and **coûter les yeux de la tête** (and the alternative form **coûter un bras**). It is important to recognise this type of expressions because they are widely used in everyday speech. However, we recommend that you refrain from using them until you feel comfortable with "regular" French.

25.
POLITICS

LA POLITIQUE

AIMS

- EXPRESS A COMMAND
- COMPARE MANNER/METHOD
- OFFER ADVICE

NOTIONS

- COMPARISON OF ADVERBS
- IMPERSONAL FORMS
- THE SUBJUNCTIVE OF *ÊTRE* AND *AVOIR*

THEY'RE ALL THE SAME!

(Two deputies are discussing the next elections).

— The minister of health is going to take her retirement soon. How long has she been in parliament?

— She was elected when she was 21, the youngest deputy for half a century.

— Until when is she there?

— Until the next legislative elections.

— And how do you find Dubuffet, the senator [in] charge of unemployment issues?

— He shots louder than the other elected officials but he expresses himself much less well than they [do]. It's he who should be unemployed.

— I'd say you don't appreciate him! Since when have *(do)* you known him?

— We used to be friends when we were young deputies, but at present we see each other much less than before. He will stand *(present himself)* in the elections, I'm sure of it, and he will perhaps win once again. All that interests him is power.

— Oh come on, you have to be optimistic and enthusiastic, and, above all, you have to have a positive attitude!

— If you insist, but I mustn't be idiotic either. Politics is something much too serious to be entrusted to politicians. It does happen that some male and female politicians are better than others, but that's the exception rather than the rule.

— It seems to me that you've become a bit cynical. Am I right?

— It's important, no, essential that we be very attentive. For that, it's enough to vote for the one *(he or she)* who will do the least damage. In any case, you know as well as me that the parties are all the same: the right is *(it's)* the exploitation of man by man, whereas the left is *(it's)* exactly the opposite.

(Deux députés discutent des prochaines élections).

– La ministre de la santé va prendre sa retraite bientôt. Depuis combien de temps est-elle au parlement ?

– Elle a été élue quand elle avait vingt-et-un ans, la députée la plus jeune depuis un demi-siècle.

– Jusqu'à quand est-elle là ?

– Jusqu'aux prochaines élections législatives.

– Et comment trouvez-vous Dubuffet, le sénateur chargé des questions de chômage ?

– Il crie plus fort que les autres élus mais il s'exprime nettement moins bien qu'eux. C'est lui qui devrait être au chômage.

– On dirait que vous ne l'appréciez pas ! Depuis quand le connaissez-vous ?

– Nous étions amis quand nous étions jeunes députés, mais à présent nous nous voyons beaucoup moins qu'avant. Il se présentera aux élections, j'en suis sûr, et il gagnera peut-être à nouveau. Tout ce qui l'intéresse, c'est le pouvoir.

– Mais voyons, il faut que vous soyez optimiste et enthousiaste, et, surtout, il faut que vous ayez une attitude positive !

– Si vous insistez, mais il ne faut pas que je sois idiot non plus. La politique est une chose beaucoup trop sérieuse pour être confiée aux politiciens. Il arrive que certains hommes ou femmes politiques soient meilleurs que d'autres, mais c'est l'exception plutôt que la règle.

– Il me semble que vous êtes devenu un peu cynique. Ai-je raison ?

– Il est important, non, essentiel que nous soyons très attentifs. Pour cela, il suffit de voter pour celui ou celle qui fera le moins de dégâts. De toute façon, vous savez aussi bien que moi que les partis sont tous pareils : la droite, c'est l'exploitation de l'homme par l'homme, alors que la gauche, c'est exactement le contraire.

■ UNDERSTANDING THE DIALOGUE
WORDS AND PHRASES

→ We learned in Module 2 that some nouns have both a masculine and a feminine form and that the language is constantly evolving in this respect. The political arena is a case in point. The masculine **un député**, a member of the French parliament, is used to apply to women as well as men. In recent years, however, the feminine **une députée** has become increasingly common. Likewise, **un ministre** is used for a man and **une ministre** for a woman.

→ **dire**, *to say*, and **voir**, *to see*, are used in a number of common expressions and interjections. The conditional **on dirait que** (literally "one would say that") expresses a perception: **On dirait qu'il va neiger**, *It looks like / seems as if it's going to snow*. The first person plural **Voyons**, used at the beginning of a sentence is similar in tone to the English *Oh come on!*, used to express disagreement or annoyance: **Voyons, tu sais bien que c'est impossible**, *Oh come on, you know it's impossible*. Another common exclamatory phrase is **Voyons voir** "let's see to see", which means. . .*Let's see*. **Voyons voir, qui m'a envoyé ce message ?**, *Let's see, who sent me this message?*

→ **le chômage**, *unemployment*, is derived from **chômer**, *to lie idle*. The noun is used with the verb **être**: **Éric est au chômage depuis six mois**, *Éric has been out of work for six months*. By extension, it can also mean *unemployment benefit*, **Je suis étudiant: est-ce que j'ai droit au chômage ?**, *I'm a student. Can I get* (literally: "Have I right") *unemployment benefit?* Note also **un chômeur / une chômeuse**, *an unemployed person* (male, female). In the same vein, **la retraite** (the root of the English word *retreat*) is most commonly used in **prendre sa retraite** or **être à la retraite**, *to retire, to be retired*. The noun is **un(e) retraité(e)**, *a retiree*. Like **le chômage**, **la retraite** can also have an extended meaning: *a pension*: **Mon père reçoit une retraite confortable**, *My father gets a comfortable pension*.

→ **arriver**, *to arrive* (Module 7), can also mean *to happen*. **L'accident est arrivé hier**, *The accident happened yesterday*. (A useful expression is **Ce sont des choses qui arrivent**, *These things happen*.) The verb can be used impersonally, as in English: **Il arrive que nous soyons en retard, mais c'est rare**, *It can happen that we're late, but it's rare*. In this type of sentence, the outcome is uncertain, which is why we use the subjunctive.

→ **combien de temps**, *how long*, is used with several prepositions, notably **depuis** and **pour**. **Depuis combien de temps habitez-vous ici ?** *How long have you been living here?*; **Pour combien de temps sont-ils à Paris ?**, *How long are they in Paris for?* In the familiar interrogative form, the two parts of the sentence are inverted:

Vous habitez ici depuis combien de temps ?; Ils sont à Paris pour combien de temps ?

CULTURE NOTES

Politics, **la politique**, is a topic of passionate debate in France. The country is a constitutional republic, **la République française**, whose motto is **Liberté**, **Égalité**, **Fraternité** (*freedom, equality, brotherhood*). The political system is organised around *the parliament*, **le parlement**, with a lower and an upper house, **la Chambre des deputés** and **le Sénat**, whose members, **les députés** and **les sénateurs**, are elected for five and nine years, respectively. *A general election*, **les élections législatives** (always plural), is held every five years. *A parliamentarian* is known as **un élu** (from the past participle of the verb **élire**, *to elect*). Executive authority is exercised on behalf of the people by the president, **le président de la République**, who serves a five-year term, known as **un quinquennat**. The president appoints his *ministers*, **les ministres (un(e) ministre)**, each of whom heads a *ministry* (**un ministère**) – be careful not to confuse the two words.

As in most countries, *political parties*, **les partis politiques** (masc.) cover a broad spectrum of philosophies that are often identified as being on either *the right*, **la droite**, or *the left*, **la gauche**.

GRAMMAR

COMPARATIVE AND SUPERLATIVE FORMS OF ADVERBS

We know that adverbs are invariable. To make positive and negative comparisons, we use the same structures as for adjectives: **plus ... que** and **moins ... que**:

L'inflation monte plus rapidement que mon salaire !
Inflation is rising faster than my salary!

J'apprends moins rapidement que toi, *I learn less quickly than you.*

The comparison of equality is formed with **aussi ... que**:

Le projet avance aussi rapidement que possible.
The project is moving ahead as quickly as possible.

Many adverbs do not end in **-ment**, but the same rule applies:

Le vent est fort aujourd'hui → Le vent est moins fort qu'hier.
The wind is strong today → The wind is less strong than yesterday.

And, of course, there are a couple of irregular adverbs. We saw **mieux**, the comparative of **bien**, in Module 21. Another form often considered as irregular is **peu**:

Il lit très peu → Il lit moins que moi. *He reads very little → He reads less than me.*

In all cases, the superlative is formed simply by adding the definite article **le**:

Il avance le plus rapidement possible, *It's moving ahead as quickly as possible.*

Je bosserai le plus longtemps possible, *I'll work for as long as possible.*

Il lit le moins de nous tous, *He reads the least of all of us.*

IMPERSONAL FORMS

We know impersonal verb forms, such as **Il pleut**, *It's raining*, as well as constructions formed with **il y a**. There are number of other impersonal structures, formed from the third person singular of the verbs **arriver**, **suffire**, **sembler**, **être** and **falloir**, that are used idiomatically and have to be translated according to the context.

• **Il arrive que…**, "*It happens that…*":

Il arrive que j'oublie mon mot de passe, *I sometimes forget my password*

• **Il est important / essentiel que…**, *It's important / vital that…*:

Il est important d'arriver toujours à l'heure, *It's important always to arrive on time.*

• **Il suffit de….**, "*It's sufficient to…*":

Il suffit d'entrer votre nom, puis valider, *Simply enter your name, then confirm.*

• **Il semble que…**, "*It seems that…*":

Il semble que vous êtes satisfait, *You seem to be satisfied.*

Some of these expressions, for example **il faut que**, *it is necessary that*, involve a supposition or a requirement. In this case, we have to use the subjunctive (see below).

▲ CONJUGATIONS

THE SUBJUNCTIVE OF *ÊTRE* AND *AVOIR*

The subjunctive mood allows you to express a feeling, a command or a wish. For that reason, it has to be used with certain constructions, notably **il faut que**, *it is necessary that*. For the time being, we will concentrate on the two most common – and, of course, irregular – verbs used in this type of construction: **être** and **avoir**:

être		avoir	
je sois	nous soyons	j'aie	nous ayons
tu sois	vous soyez	tu aies	vous ayez
il/elle soit	ils/elles soient	il/elle ait	ils/elles aient

Il faut que tu sois à la gare à neuf heures, *You have to be at the station at 9 o'clock.*

Il faut que nous ayons une discussion, *We need to have a talk.*

We'll learn more about the subjunctive in Module 26.

VOCABULARY

confier *to entrust*
crier *to shout*
discuter *to discuss*
(s') exprimer *to express oneself*
insister *to insist*
(se) présenter *to introduce oneself,*
to stand (in an election)
sembler *to seem*
voter (pour) *to vote (for)*

une attitude *an attitude*
le chômage *unemployment*
le contraire *the opposite* (see **au**
contraire, Module 10)
les dégâts *damage*
un(e) député(e) *a deputy, member*
of parliament
idiot *stupid, idiotic*
optimiste *optimistic*
exactement *exactly*
nettement *clearly, markedly*
une élection *an election*
un(e) élu(e) *an elected official*
(male/female)
une exception *an exception*

l'exploitation *exploitation*
un(e) ministre *a minister*
un ministère *a ministry*
le parlement *the parliament*
un parti (politique) *a (political)*
party
la politique *politics* (always singular
in this context)
le pouvoir *power*
la retraite *retirement*
un sénateur *a senator*

sérieux(-euse) *serious*
chargé(e) de *in charge of*
cynique *cynical*
enthousiaste *enthusiastic*

Ce sont des choses qui arrivent,
These things happen.
Depuis combien de temps ? *How*
long…? (followed by present
perfect)
Pour combien de temps ? *For*
how long…? (followed by present
tense)
Voyons ! *Oh come on!*
Voyons voir *Let's see*

Whenever you come across a new word, for instance a noun, see if it is related
to a verb that you may know (or vice versa). This is one of the simplest ways to
build up a good vocabulary.

● EXERCISES

1. USE THE SUPERLATIVE (SL) OR THE COMPARISONS OF SUPERIORITY (S), INFERIORITY (I) OR EQUALITY (E), AS INDICATED

a. E: Je travaille (*vite*: ....) ta collègue.

b. S: Son projet avance (*rapidement*: ....) le tien.

c. I: Mes amis gagnent (*peu*: ....) moi.

d. SL: Prononcez la phrase (*fort*: ....) possible.

e. S/I: Je vois mes amis (*souvent*: ....) avant.*

* *Two forms – superiority and inferiority – are possible.*

2. COMPLETE THE SENTENCES WITH THE IMPERSONAL FORM

a. **sembler** → .... vous n'aimez pas le fromage bleu.

b. **suffire** → .... appuyer sur ce bouton si vous voulez un café.

c. **arriver** → .... j'oublie les clés à la maison.

d. **être** → .... important de répondre à ses questions.

e. **falloir** → .... je sois à Paris après-demain au plus tard.

3. PUT *ÊTRE* AND *AVOIR* INTO THE SUBJUNCTIVE

a. Il faut que vous (*être*: ....) à l'heure pour l'avion.

b. Il faut que je (*avoir*: ....) une réponse le plus rapidement possible.

c. Il faut que nous (*être*: ....) nombreux.

d. Il faut que tu (*avoir*: ....) confiance en moi.

e. Il faut que Jean-Michel et Sylvie (*être*: ....) là pour ma fête.

🔊 4. TRANSLATE INTO FRENCH

27

a. How long have you been waiting* for me? – I've been here for two hours.

b. You know** as well as I do that unemployment is rising faster than before.

c. How long are you in Paris for? – As long as possible.

d. We have to be*** enthusiastic and optimistic. – Until when?

e. "Politics is something much too serious a thing to be entrusted to politicians." Charles de Gaulle

* Use the 2nd and 3rd interrogative.

** Use both **vous** and **tu**

*** Use the subjunctive

26.
RENTING A CAR

LOUER UNE VOITURE

AIMS	NOTIONS

- **GIVE ROAD DIRECTIONS**
- **EXPLAIN PREFERENCES**
- **MAKE RECOMMENDATIONS**

- **SUBJUNCTIVE WITH IMPERSONAL FORMS**
- **MULTI-WORD PREPOSITIONS**
- *AUTANT DE / QUE*

BETTER TAKE THE MOTORWAY.

— What type of vehicle do you wish to rent, madame?

— I would like a fuel-efficient car *(economical in fuel)* with a diesel engine, but it has to be fast and the price [must] be below 600 euros if possible.

— I can offer you the all-new Y70. It is *(drives)* as a fast as a sports car and it is as big as a van but it consumes as much as a small city [car] and there is as much room as in a saloon. We have an attractive *(advantageous)* package for four days at 630 euros, everything included.

— That's a bit above my budget, but I'll take it. Here's my driving licence.

— And I'll also need a credit card. Enter *(type)* your PIN please. Thank you.

— Perhaps you can help me? I'm going to Beaune but I don't know *(know little)* the region [very well]. What is the fastest route *(way)*?

— Have you *(are you)* already been *(come)* to *(in)* Burgundy?

— I went once to Vézelay but it [was] a long time ago.

— You had better take the motorway as far as Dijon and then the departmental road. Is that clear?

So here are the rental contract and the keys. The vehicle is parked at the back of the car park, which is *(finds itself)* opposite the post [office]. You can't miss it. Leave here, go to the end of the street and turn left. You will need this token so that you can exit the garage without paying. You have to fill up *(make the full)* before leaving because the tank is almost empty and you [should] also think to check the pressure of the tyres because I haven't had time to do it. Oh, you may *(it is possible that)* find a few scratches on the bonnet and the boot. It's a shame that you didn't come last week: all our vehicles were in good condition *(state)* but we are short of *(lack)* staff at the moment.

— Quel type de véhicule souhaiteriez-vous louer, madame ?

— Je voudrais une voiture économe en carburant avec un moteur diesel, mais il faut qu'elle soit rapide et que le prix soit en-dessous de six cents euros si possible.

— Je peux vous proposer la toute nouvelle Y70. Elle roule aussi vite qu'une voiture de sport et elle est aussi grande qu'une camionnette mais elle consomme autant qu'une petite citadine et il y a autant de place que dans une berline. Nous avons un forfait avantageux pour quatre jours à six cent trente euros, tout compris.

— C'est un peu au-dessus de mon budget, mais je la prendrai. Voici mon permis de conduire.

— Et il me faut aussi une carte de crédit. Tapez votre code s'il vous plaît. Merci.

— Vous pourriez peut-être m'aider ? Je vais à Beaune mais je connais peu la région. Quel est le chemin le plus rapide ?

— Êtes-vous déjà venue en Bourgogne ?

— Je suis allée une fois à Vézelay mais il y a très longtemps.

— Il vaut mieux que vous preniez l'autoroute jusqu'à Dijon et ensuite la route départementale. C'est clair ? Voici donc le contrat de location et les clés. Le véhicule est stationné au fond du parking, qui se trouve en face de la poste. Vous ne pouvez pas le manquer. Sortez d'ici, allez au bout de la rue et tournez à gauche. Vous aurez besoin de ce jeton pour que vous puissiez sortir du garage sans payer. Il faut que vous fassiez le plein avant de partir car le réservoir est presque vide et il faut aussi penser à vérifier la pression des pneus car je n'ai pas eu le temps de le faire. Oh, il est possible que vous trouviez quelques rayures sur le capot et le coffre. C'est dommage que vous ne soyez pas venue la semaine dernière : tous nos véhicules étaient en bon état mais nous manquons de personnel en ce moment.

■ UNDERSTANDING THE DIALOGUE

WORDS AND PHRASES

→ The adjective **économe**, literally *thrifty*, can be translated in different ways: **Ma mère est très économe**, *My mother is very careful with money*. Similarly, **un couteau économe** is *a vegetable peeler* (it removes only the thinnest layer of peel). The adjective is frequently used when talking about energy efficiency and consumption: **L'immeuble est économe en énergie**, *The building is energy-efficient*; **Cette nouvelle voiture est économe en carburant**, *This new car is fuel-efficient*. By contrast, **économique** means both *economic* and *economical*.

→ **un forfait** basically means *a fixed* or *set price*. It is frequently used for the pre-arranged or all-inclusive package, or deal, comprising a bundle of services: **Nous avons un forfait avion-hôtel**, *We have a flight-hotel package*. In winter sports, **un forfait de ski** (or simply **forfait ski**) is equivalent to *a ski pass*, i.e. a fixed sum covering the use of equipment and lift facilities. Mobile phone operators offer **un forfait illimité**, or *unlimited call plan*. Not to be confused with the English word *a forfeit*.

→ **une cité** is a literary word for *a city* (see Culture Note, Module 17), the common word being **une ville** (which covers both *a town* and *a city*). But **un(e) citadin(e)** means *a city dweller* or *urbanite*. **Une voiture citadine**, usually abbreviated to **une citadine**, means *a city car* or *a mini*. In contemporary French, however, **une cité** is also used to refer to a housing estate, often in a deprived peri-urban area: **Le problème des cités est très complexe**, *The problem of deprived housing estates is very complex*.

→ **une voiture**, *a car*, is often used interchangeably with **un véhicule**, *a vehicle* (pay attention to the spelling), although the latter noun can also apply to **un camion**, *a lorry*, **une camionnette**, *a van*, **un bus**, *a bus* or even **un deux-roues**, *a two-wheeler*. Other useful automotive words include **un pneu**, *a tyre* (an abbreviated and commonly used form of **un pneumatique** – note the pronunciation of the **pn** phoneme), **le capot**, *the bonnet*, **le coffre**, *the boot*, **une portière**, *a door*, **un phare**, *a headlight* (also *a lighthouse*), **le tableau de bord**, *the dashboard*, **un siège**, *a seat*, and **le réservoir (de carburant)**, *the (fuel) tank*. If you refuel your car, be careful to look for **l'essence** (f.), *petrol/gasoline*, or **le diesel**, *diesel*, and avoid **le fioul**, which is *fuel oil*. Any confusion could be disastrous! **Faire le plein**, "make the full", means *to fill the tank*.

→ **poste** is a dual-gender noun (see Module 18). The masculine, **un poste**, means either *a job* or *a post* (**Il a un nouveau poste dans l'entreprise**, *He has a new job in the company*), or *an office, station*, etc. (**un poste de police**, *a police station*). The feminine, **une poste**, means *the postal service* and, by extension, *a post office*. But if you're looking for somewhere to post a letter or parcel, it is preferable to use the full term: **Où se trouve le bureau de poste le plus proche, s'il vous plaît ?**, *Where's the nearest post office, please?*. (Remember also that you can buy a stamp, **un timbre**, in **un tabac**, see Module 23.)

→ **manquer**, *to miss, to lack*, can be an awkward verb. With the preposition **de**, it is straightforward: **Nous manquons de ressources**, *We lack resources*. But when we talk about missing someone or something, the word order is the opposite of English. **Tu me manques**, *I miss you* (literally "you are missing to me"). Likewise, **Est-ce que je te manque ?**: *Are you missing me? ("am I missing to you")*. To remember this reverse structure, always start the sentence with the most important person or thing (the one being missed). It's worth practising by repeating and memorising our two examples. (Another technique is to equate *to miss* with *to surprise*, as in *You surprise me*, where *me* is the person being surprised, and the subject of the sentence is the person causing the surprise.) The noun **un manque (de)** means *a lack (of)*.

CULTURE NOTES

France has one of the world's most extensive road networks, covering more than a million kilometres. More than 70% of the system is made up of *motorways*, **les autoroutes** (f.), which are operated by private companies. The country is also served by trunk roads, **les routes nationales** (f.), country roads, **les routes départementales** (f.) and smaller, one-track lanes, **les routes communales**. Each category is numbered and designated by its initial letter: **A, D** or **C**. Motorways charge tolls, which are collected (or paid by credit card) at booths or automatic machines, with the word **péage** (masc.) covering both the payment and the collection method. Some of these highways have evocative names, like **l'Autoroute du soleil**, or "sun motorway" (the A6/A7, from Paris to Lyon) and **l'Autoroute des deux mers**, "the two seas motorway" (the A61, from Narbonne to Toulouse). To break a long highway journey, many drivers stop at **une station-service**, *service station*, or **une aire de repos**, *rest area*. Motorways can get very crowded, especially during the summer driving season in July and August. Every year, the transport ministry issues a special map, known as **la carte Bison Futé** ("wily buffalo"), which indicates areas of congestion and recommends **les itinéraires bis**, *alternative itineraries*. Even so, it is almost impossible to avoid **le chassé-croisé**, *back and forth*, between **les juillétistes** and **les aoûtiens**, when holidaymakers returning home in *July* (**juillet**) cross paths with those departing in *August* (**août**). Visitors to France during this period are advised to take the train!

La Bourgogne, *Burgundy*, is one of the most beautiful regions of France, renowned as much for bucolic scenery as for food and wine. The main towns are the administrative capital, Dijon, the wine capital, Beaune, and the hilltop town of Vézelay, with an awe-inspiring 11th century basilica.

 GRAMMAR

MORE MULTI-WORD PREPOSITIONS

We have learned most of the common prepositions, including a couple comprising more than one word: **au milieu de**, *in the middle of* (Module 13) and **à cause de**, *because of* (Module 22). Here are some more very common multi-word prepositions:

au fond de	*at the end / bottom of*
au bord de	*at the edge / side of,* etc.
au bout de	*after* (see Module 10)
au-dessous de	*below*
au-dessus de	*above*

Le garage est au fond du jardin, *The garage is at the bottom of the garden.*
La ville de Menton est au bord de la Méditerranée, *The city of Menton is on the shores of Mediterranean.*
Au bout d'une heure, j'étais fatigué, *After an hour, I was tired.*
La température est passé au-dessous de zéro, *The temperature has gone below zero.*
Mettez le tableau au-dessus du lit, *Put the painting over the bed.*
To remember the difference between the last two prepositions, remember that **dessous** contains the *ou* of <u>s*ou*th</u>, which is below north. You will also come across **en dessous** and **en dessus** (with no hyphen). There is a slight difference of meaning, but in everyday French they are interchangeable.
Prepositions are important, so remember to revise them regularly.

COMPARATIVE OF EQUALITY: *AUTANT DE / QUE*

In the previous module, we saw the comparative of equality formed with **aussi …que** (*as* + adjective + *as*). We can also use the adverb **autant**, with **de** or **que**, to make a comparison.
Autant de is generally used with a noun: **Le Grand Paris a autant d'habitants que les Pays-Bas**, *Greater Paris has as many inhabitants as the Netherlands.*
Autant que is used with a verb: **Je travaille autant que lui mais je gagne moins,** *I work as much as he does but I earn less.*

Be careful not to confuse **autant que** with **aussi ... que**, which is used with an adjective or adverb (rather than a noun or verb).

Je suis aussi fort que toi, *I'm as strong as you* (not **autant fort**)

J'aime ce roman autant que toi, *I love that novel as much as you do* (not **aussi que**).

Lastly, **autant** can be used alone: **Elle travaille toujours autant,** *She is working as hard as ever.*

▲ CONJUGATIONS

THE SUBJUNCTIVE MOOD

We came across the subjunctive for the first time in the previous module. It is so-called because verbs in this mood rarely stand on their own but are "sub-joined" to another clause, which they depend on. Relatively infrequent in English (except in a phrase such as *I wish you were here*), the subjunctive is very common in everyday French. It expresses the speaker's attitude, especially their doubts, wishes, regrets or uncertainties.

To form the subjunctive of most verbs, take the third person plural of the present tense as a stem and add these endings:

je	-e	nous	-ions
tu	-es	vous	-iez
Il/elle	-e	ils/elles	-ent

Here are the three groups:

manger	finir	attendre
je mange	je finisse	j'attende
tu manges	tu finisses	tu attendes
il/elle mange	il/elle finisse	il/elle attende
nous mangions	nous finissions	nous attendions
vous mangiez	vous finissiez	vous attendiez
ils/elles mangent	ils/elles finissent	ils/elles attendent

We have already learned the irregular forms for **être** and **avoir**. Here are three more common irregular verbs: **faire**, **pouvoir** and **vouloir**:

faire	pouvoir	vouloir
je fasse	je puisse	je veuille
tu fasses	tu puisses	tu veuilles

il/elle fasse	il/elle puisse	il/elle veuille
nous fassions	nous puissions	nous voulions
vous fassiez	vous puissiez	vous vouliez
ils/elles fassent	ils/elles puissent	ils/elles veuillent

Several other common verbs also have irregular subjunctives, notably **aller**, **venir**, and **savoir**.

The negative is formed, as usual, with **ne ... pas: tu ne sois pas, ils ne puissent pas**, etc. For the interrogative, the third (inverted) form is the most common form: **Veux-tu que je t'attende ?**, etc.

A tell-tale word that announces a subjunctive clause is **que**, especially in impersonal expressions such as **il faut que, il est possible que, il est important que, il vaut mieux que** and **c'est dommage que**:

Il faut que tu sois patient, *You have to be patient.*

Il vaut mieux que nous louions une citadine, *We had better rent a mini.*

Il est possible que vous ne puissiez pas partir, *You may not be able to leave.*

Il est important que je fasse le plein, *It's important that I fill the tank.*

Remember, though, that **que** on its own does not necessarily announce a subjunctive. Moreover, with impersonal expressions, it is possible to avoid the subjunctive altogether by eliminating the relative and the pronoun, replacing them with the infinitive:

Il faut que tu sois patient → **Il faut être patient**

Il vaut mieux que nous louions une citadine → **Il vaut mieux louer une citadine**

Il est important que je fasse le plein → **Il est important de faire le plein**

⬣ EXERCISES

1. PUT THE VERBS BETWEEN BRACKETS INTO THE SUBJUNCTIVE MOOD

a. Il faut que nous (*faire*) une liste pour les courses.

b. Il vaut mieux que tu (*partir*) de bonne heure car demain est un jour férié.

c. Il n'est pas possible que votre papa (*pouvoir*) continuer à travailler comme ça. Il est trop âgé.

d. Il est important que vous (*attendre*) sa réponse avant de continuer.

e. C'est dommage que vous ne (*avoir*) pas attendu la fin du film.

VOCABULARY

consommer *to consume*
manquer *to miss, to lack*
proposer *to propose, to offer*
rouler *to drive* (see Module 22)
stationner *to park*
taper *to type, to enter*
vérifier *to check, to verify*

une aire (de repos) *a rest area*
une autoroute *a motorway*
une berline *a saloon* (car)
un(e) citadin(e) *a city dweller*
une (voiture) citadine *a city car, a mini*
un camion *a lorry*
une camionnette *a van*
une carte de crédit *a credit card*
un capot *a bonnet* (car)
un chemin *a track, a way* (itinerary)
un coffre *a boot* (car), *a safe*
un contrat *a contract*
un forfait *a set price, a package deal*
un jeton *a token*
la location *rental*
un péage *a toll, a toll booth*
un permis de conduire *a driving licence*
le personnel *staff*
un moteur *a motor, an engine*
un pneu *a tyre*
un poste *a job, an office*

une poste *a post office*
la pression *the pressure*
une rayure *a scratch*
un réservoir (de carburant) *a (petrol) tank*
une route *a road*
un timbre (or **timbre-poste**) *a (postage) stamp*
un véhicule *a vehicle*

avantageux/-euse *attractive (price), profitable*
économe *economical, thrifty*
en bon état *in good condition ("state")*
vide *empty*
au bord de *on / at the edge of*
autant que / de *as … as (comparison)*
au-dessous *below*
au-dessus *above*
au fond de *at the end / bottom of*

C'est clair ? *Is that clear?*
Tapez votre code *Enter your code (PIN)*
Tu me manques / Vous me manquez *I miss you*
Vous pourriez / Tu pourrais peut-être m'aider ? *Perhaps you can help me?*
Vous ne pouvez pas / Tu ne peux pas le manquer *You can't miss it.*

Congratulations! You've reached the end of this Target: Languages course. We hope you enjoyed it. But remember, as we said in the Introduction, this is where your work really begins. Take every opportunity to listen to, read and speak French on a regular basis. Or better still, visit France! Learning a language is like mastering any other skill: if you don't use it, you lose it. **Bonne chance !**

2. CHANGE THE SUBJUNCTIVE TO AN IMPERSONAL FORM BY REMOVING THE PERSONAL PRONOUNS

a. Il faut que vous soyez à l'heure pour l'avion.

b. Il faut que j'aie une réponse le plus rapidement possible.

c. Il faut que tu fasses le plein avant de partir.

d. Il faut que nous soyons nombreux.

e. Il vaut mieux que vous ayez une version récente du programme.

3. CHOOSE A PREPOSITION TO REPLACE THE ENGLISH WORDS (AND CHANGE THE DEFINITE ARTICLE WHERE NECESSARY)

a. La voiture est (*at the end of*) le parking. →

b. Je me suis endormi (*after*) dix minutes. →

c. Madeleine a laissé sa voiture (*on the side of*) la route. →

d. Le thermomètre est (*below*) deux degrés. →

e. La chambre est (*above*) le garage. →

4. TRANSLATE INTO FRENCH

28

a. Estelle left for Nîmes a month ago. I miss her.

b. You have to fill up straight away. The tank is almost empty.

c. Do you know* the fastest route? – Yes, you have to take the motorway.

d. You had better come next week. There will be fewer people.

e. Sandra works as hard as I do but she earns less than me. And she has as much experience as me.

* Use **vous** with the second and third interrogatives

ANSWER KEY

This section contains all the answers to the exercises at the end of each module. The recorded portions are indicated by the ◀ icon and the number of the streaming track. They are recorded on the same track as the module dialogue and have the same number.

1. INTRODUCTIONS

1. a. suis – est **b.** a **c.** sont **d.** êtes **e.** ont – a
2. a. Alain n'est pas français. **b.** Ils ne sont pas en retard. **c.** Virginie n'a pas deux sœurs. **d.** Lyon n'est pas une belle ville. **e.** Nous ne sommes pas à la Sorbonne. **f.** Je ne suis pas belge.
3. a. l' / une (fem.) **b.** la / une (fem.) **c.** le / un (masc.) **d.** la / une (fem.) **e.** le / un (masc.) **f.** la / une (fem.) **g.** la / une (fem.) **h.** le / un (masc.) **i.** le / un (masc.) **j.** le / un (masc.) **k.** la / une (fem.)

03 **4. a.** Salut Jean, tu vas bien ? – Très bien, merci. **b.** Vous êtes belge ? – Pas du tout. Je suis suisse. **c.** Lyon est une belle ville. **d.** Elle est en retard. – Moi aussi. **e.** Au revoir. – Attendez-moi !

2. GETTING TO KNOW YOU

1. a. faisons **b.** fais **c.** fait **d.** faites
2. a. une serveuse **b.** un journaliste **c.** une avocate **d.** une directrice **e.** un informaticien
3. a. gentilles **b.** petite **c.** malades **d.** spécialisé **e.** petite

04 **4. a.** Il enseigne les maths dans une école primaire. **b.** Est-ce que vous êtes mariée, Sophie ? – Oui, et j'ai un fils. **c.** Qu'est-ce que vous faites comme travail ? **d.** Vous avez combien d'élèves dans votre classe en ce moment ? **e.** Il est directeur d'une petite agence de voyages à Lyon.

3. IN BRITTANY

1. a. pouvons **b.** vais **c.** veulent **d.** peut **e.** veulent

2. a. Est-ce qu'il est / Est-il ? **b.** Est-ce qu'elles connaissent / Connaissent-elles **c.** Est-ce que vous prenez / Prenez-vous **d.** Est-ce que nous sommes / Sommes-nous **e.** Est-ce qu'ils font / Font-ils
3. a. Il n'est pas... **b.** Elles ne connaissent pas... **c.** Vous ne prenez pas... **d.** Nous ne sommes pas... **e.** Ils ne font pas...
4. a. quelle **b.** Quelle **c.** Quels **d.** Quelles **e.** du café ... de la ... des crêpes.

05 **5. a.** Est-ce que vous êtes / Es-tu de Nice ? – Non, je suis de Paris. **b.** L'hôtel est à deux kilomètres de l'école. **c.** Prenez cette carte. – Merci beaucoup de votre aide. **d.** Pouvez-vous / Peux-tu me donner un conseil ? – Bien sûr. **e.** Nous n'avons pas beaucoup de temps. – Vous pouvez partir en bus ce soir.

4. HOME AND FAMILY

1. a. habitent **b.** cherchons **c.** prépares **d.** cuisinez **e.** mange ... aime
2. a. ne trouve pas **b.** n'est pas **c.** n'habitent pas **d.** n'aidons pas **e.** ne parlez pas
3. a. Nos ... mon **b.** son **c.** ton **d.** vos **e.** Leurs ... leur

06 **4. a.** Les couteaux, les fourchettes et les cuillères sont toujours dans le lave-vaisselle. **b.** Ma sœur travaille à la Sorbonne à Paris mais elle va à Rennes. **c.** J'ai faim et j'ai soif. – Moi aussi ! **d.** Allez chercher les assiettes dans le placard dans le salon. **e.** Est-ce que je peux vous aider à faire quelque chose ? – Non merci. Tout est prêt.

5. WHERE IS...?

1. a. Pouvez-vous m'aider ? **b.** Nous ne les connaissons pas. **c.** Est-ce que Marie aime son travail ? – Elle l'adore ! **d.** Est-ce que tu l'achètes, cette carte ? **e.** Je t'attends au musée d'Orsay.

2. a. ne savons pas **b.** Continuez ... tournez **c.** vont **d.** coûtent **e.** sais – sais

3. a. à droite... angle **b.** ce pas **c.** Tout **d.** Combien **e.** mieux

07 🔊 **4. a.** quinze **b.** vingt-deux **c.** quarante-cinq **d.** trente-trois **e.** soixante-dix **f.** soixante et un **g.** douze **h.** vingt et un **i.** dix-sept

07 🔊 **5. a.** Il ne la comprend pas. Est-ce que tu peux l'aider ? **b.** J'aime ces tomates. Où est-ce que tu les achètes ? **c.** Combien coûtent les billets ? – Ils coûtent vingt-sept euros. **d.** Est-ce que vous savez / Savez-vous où je peux trouver un restaurant? **e.** Il vaut mieux prendre le métro. Le musée d'Orsay est assez loin.

6. WHAT TIME IS IT?

1. a. maigrit ... grossit **b.** réussit **c.** choisissez **d.** découvrons **e.** refroidir

2. a. ne remplis pas **b.** Est-ce que vous finissez **c.** ne réfléchissent pas **d.** ne choisissons pas **e.** Est-ce qu'ils reviennent

08 🔊 **3. a.** midi moins le quart / onze heures quarante-cinq **b.** six heures dix **c.** trois heures et quart / trois heures quinze **d.** dix heures moins vingt / neuf heures quarante **e.** huit heures et demie / huit heures trente **f.** quatre heures vingt-cinq **g.** deux heures moins vingt-cinq / une heure trente-cinq **h.** trois heures moins dix / deux heures cinquante **i.** neuf heures cinq

08 🔊 **4. a.** Voici votre table et voilà le menu, au mur. **b.** Qu'est-ce que vous allez choisir ? – Laissez-moi réfléchir. **c.** Nous n'avons pas / On n'a pas le temps de déjeuner ensemble. J'ai un rendez-vous. **d.** Est-ce qu'ils connaissent un bon endroit dans le quartier? **e.** Allons-y tout de suite. – Non, revenons après-demain.

7. AN APPOINTMENT

1. a. devons **b.** dois **c.** dois **d.** devez **e.** doivent

2. a. ne dois pas **b.** Est-ce que je dois **c.** ne devez pas **d.** Est-ce que tu dois

09 🔊 **3. a.** sous **b.** devant **c.** derrière **d.** jusqu'au **e.** depuis **f.** depuis

09 🔊 **4. a.** Pouvez-vous épeler votre nom, s'il vous plait ? – R.O.M.A.I.N. T.A.R.D.Y **b.** Allumez la lumière avant d'entrer dans la cuisine. **c.** Il y a une trentaine de personnes devant le musée. **d.** Nous devons partir à cinq heures / dix-sept heures au plus tard. **e.** Monsieur Desprats a envie de vous rencontrer. – Il est très gentil, mais je dois partir.

8. THIS WEEKEND

1. a. ne recevons* **b.** voyez **c.** pleut **d.** ne veulent pas **e.** déçois*

Remember the rule concerning the use of the cedilla under the letter "c" before "a", "o" and "u". See Pronunciation.

2. a. Je ne les aime plus **b.** Nous n'allons jamais au travail en voiture. **c.** Tu ne comprends rien. **d.** Mes grand-parents ne viennent jamais à Paris. **e.** Je ne fume plus.

3. a. soixante-dix-sept **b.** quatre-vingt-neuf **c.** quatre-vingt-treize **d.** soixante-quatorze **e.** quatre-vingt **f.** soixante et onze **g.** quatre-vingt-douze **h.** soixante-dix-huit **i.** quatre-vingt-cinq **j.** quatre-vingt-onze **k.** quatre-vingt-dix-neuf **l.** quatre-vingt-huit

4. a. Simon est très occupé en ce moment. – Comme d'habitude ! **b.** Quel temps fait-il à Marseille cette semaine ? – Il fait beau et très chaud. **c.** Je ne bois pas de café l'après-midi. – Moi non plus. Ça m'empêche de dormir. **d.** Il n'y a plus de trains directs. – C'est vrai ? **e.** Qu'est-ce que tu deviens / vous devenez ? – Je suis obligé de louer une voiture et descendre dans le Midi ce week-end.

9. HOLIDAYS

1. a. pourrions **b.** Est-ce que tu voudrais **c.** ne pourrait pas **d.** Est-ce que vous voudriez **e.** Est-ce que vous pourriez

2. a. Comment pouvons-nous prendre rendez-vous ? **b.** Combien peux-tu payer ? **c.** Où habitent-ils ? **d.** Pourquoi veut-elle partir en mai ?

e. Quand voulez-vous venir ?

3. a. français **b.** dernière **c.** gentilles **d.** complète **e.** seule **f.** chères **g.** neuve **h.** ancienne **i.** heureux **j.** complets

4. a. L'hôtel est complet en juin, juillet et août, et il ferme de novembre à mars. **b.** À quoi pensez-vous ? – Les ponts dans la deuxième quinzaine de mai. **c.** Comment est-ce que nous pouvons prendre rendez-vous ? **d.** Elle a raison, c'est bon marché : un séjour en Corse pour cinq cents euros. **e.** Combien ça coûte / Combien est-ce que ça coûte ? – Deux cent cinquante euros. – Ça me va.

10. RELAXING

1. a. se réveillent … se rasent … s'habillent **b.** se disputent **c.** me lève … me couche **d.** nous dépêchons … nous occupons **e.** vous reposez … vous amusez.

2. a. te rases **b.** ne nous disputons pas **c.** ne vous dépêchez pas **d.** occuper **e.** ne me couche jamais

3. a. doucement **b.** facilement **c.** rarement **d.** vraiment **e.** complètement

4. a. Qu'est-ce que vous pensez de tout ça ? – Je m'amuse énormément. **b.** Il s'ennuie facilement et parfois il s'endort avant la fin de l'émission. **c.** Mes amis arrivent à la gare aux alentours de dix heures. Ils sont épuisés. **d.** On ne se dispute jamais parce qu'on se parle rarement. **e.** Elle doit s'occuper de sa fille, qui se réveille toujours de bonne heure.

11. SHOPPING

1. a. Ces **b.** ceux **c.** celles-ci ... celles-là **d.** celle **e.** Ce ... celles-là
2. a. *vieille* maison **b.** robe *bleue* **c.** *joli* pantalon **d.** *petit* magasin **e.** l'art *moderne*. **f.** *gros* pull
3. a. de *beaux* manteaux **b.** de *vieux* villages **c.** de *jeunes* informaticiens **d.** de *gentilles* collègues **e.** de *mauvais* films
13 🔊 **4. a.** Je cherche un nouveau manteau. – Quelle taille faites-vous ? / Quelle est votre taille ? **b.** Et de nouvelles chaussures. – Quelle pointure faites-vous ? / Vous chaussez du combien ? **c.** Celui-ci / Celle-ci est un excellent choix. Il / Elle vous va très bien. **d.** Est-ce que tu fais du shopping / des courses ? – Non, je fais du lèche-vitrines. **e.** Elle veut acheter un pantalon, un jean, un collant, deux chemises de nuit, un tailleur et trois shorts.

12. PHONE CONVERSATION

1. a. apprenez-vous **b.** ne dites pas **c.** vendent **d.** lis **e.** connais ... sais
2. a. qui **b.** que **c.** qui **d.** qui **e.** qui ... que
3. a. connais **b.** sais **c.** sait **d.** sais ... connais
14 🔊 **4. a.** Ne quittez pas, j'ai un autre appel. Désolé, je vais vous laisser. **b.** Parlez plus fort s'il vous plaît. Je ne vous entends pas. **c.** Elle est un peu inquiète pour son frère. – Le frère que je connais ? **d.** Je connais une société qui cherche des gens qui parlent l'arabe. **e.** Pas de problème. Il te rappelle plus tard si tu veux.

13. TALKING ABOUT THE HOLIDAY

1. a. avons réservé **b.** n'ai pas nagé ... j'ai fait **c.** Où est-ce que vous avez / Où avez-vous passé **d.** avez aimé **e.** n'avons pas trouvé
2. a. fatigués **b.** compliquées **c.** terminé **d.** aimées **e.** visité
3. a. plus intéressant que **b.** moins grand que **c.** n'est pas plus cher que **d.** aussi difficile que
15 🔊 **4. a.** C'était comment, Bastia? – C'est une belle ville mais moins belle que Calvi. **b.** Nous faisons du ski chaque année en janvier. C'est très chouette. **c.** Il y a beaucoup de monde sur la plage ce matin. – Oui, tout le monde aime nager. **d.** L'agent de voyage a-t-il téléphoné hier ? – Non, malheureusement. **e.** Vous connaissez bien / Est-ce que vous connaissez bien la Corse ?– Non, je ne voyage jamais. C'est trop fatiguant.

14. FINDING A FLAT

1. a. fourni **b.** n'ai pas réussi **c.** Est-ce que vous avez / Avez-vous rempli **d.** ont converti **e.** Est-ce que tu as réfléchi / As-tu réfléchi
2. a. As-tu fini **b.** Ont-ils réussi **c.** Avons-nous réfléchi **d.** Ont-elles fourni
3. a. meilleur **b.** le plus cher **c.** pires **d.** moins grandes ... plus rapides. **e.** le pire
16 🔊 **4. a.** Les résultats de leur équipe sont pires que la semaine dernière. – Tant pis. **b.** Vous avez / Tu as quelque chose à faire la semaine prochaine, Madeleine ? – Je ne suis pas tout à fait prête. **c.** Le studio au

rez-de-chaussée est plus bruyant et moins clair que l'appartement au deuxième étage. **d.** Tout cela est très bien mais est-ce que vous avez / avez-vous fini vos études ? **e.** Il y a une épicerie et deux supermarchés dans les environs. – Tu n'es pas loin du centre-ville, j'espère ?

15. LISTENING TO MUSIC

1. a. a appris **b.** As-tu répondu ... J'ai répondu **c.** n'ai pas lu **d.** est-ce que vous avez connu **e.** J'ai appris ... je n'ai pas compris
2. a. la mienne **b.** le mien **c.** les tiennes **d.** les nôtres **e.** les leurs
3. a. vieux copain **b.** femme intelligente ... mari sympathique **c.** mauvaise nouvelle ... grand musicien **d.** petits verres ... placard rouge **e.** deuxième disque ... meilleur

17 🔊 **4. a.** Où est-ce qu'il a mis sa tablette ? – La voilà. – Mais ce n'est pas la sienne ; c'est la mienne. **b.** Qu'est-ce qu'il t'a dit ?– Qu'il a perdu sa mère il y a vingt ans. **c.** Armand est bibliothécaire pendant la semaine mais il travaille dans une librairie le samedi et le dimanche. **d.** Et que fait sa femme ? – C'est une excellente comédienne. **e.** J'ai vu sa première pièce de théâtre la semaine dernière mais je n'ai pas vraiment compris le message.

16. A LIFE STORY

1. a. sont sorties ... ne sont pas rentrées **b.** est parti ... est parti **c.** sont nées ... sont mortes **d.** sommes sortis ... ne sommes pas allés **e.** sont arrivés

... sont déjà partis.
2. a. toute ... tout **b.** tout ... tout **c.** Tous ... toutes **d.** toutes ... Tout **e.** Tous ... tout
3. a. mil neuf cent quatre-vingt-quatre / dix-neuf cent quatre-vingt-quatre **b.** huit cent vingt-sept **c.** mil huit cent trente-deux / dix-huit cent trente-deux **d.** deux mille dix neuf **e.** mil cent / onze cent **f.** mil neuf cent quatre-vingt-dix-neuf / dix-neuf cent quatre-vingt-dix-neuf **g.** mil cinq cent cinquante-cinq / quinze cent cinquante-cinq **h.** mil soixante-six **i.** mil six cent / seize cent **j.** deux mille

18 🔊 **4. a.** Je pense que tous les étudiants ont le droit de prendre des vacances à Noël. – Tout à fait. **b.** Elle a étudié le droit et elle est devenue l'une des plus jeunes avocates de France. **c.** Nous sommes tombés amoureux, et nous sommes restés ensemble pendant une vingtaine d'années. **d.** Avez-vous entendu la nouvelle ? La comédienne Jeanne Morteau est morte à l'âge de quatre-vingt-douze ans. **e.** Elle a obtenu sa maîtrise en moins de trois ans. – Elle est vraiment douée !

17. LET'S GO TO THE MARKET

1. a. nous y allons **b.** il n'y habite plus **c.** ils y pensent **d.** Ils y passent **e.** je peux y aller
2. a. J'en veux deux **b.** ils en ont **c.** vous pouvez m'en parler **d.** J'en ai besoin **e.** Tout le monde en parle
3. a. lui **b.** leur **c.** lui **d.** nous **e.** m'

19 🔊 **4. a.** Pouvez-vous me donner vos coordonnées s'il vous plait ? **b.** Est-ce que Bruno vous a écrit ? Répondez-moi ! Sinon, téléphonez-lui vite ! **c.** Ils ont perdu le match de football. – Quel dommage ! **d.** Est-ce que je peux vous accompagner au marché ? – Bien sûr, tout le monde y va le week-end. **e.** Pas de nouvelles, bonnes nouvelles.

18. DIETS

1. a. prendrai **b.** mangera **c.** perdrons **d.** passeront **e.** aiderez
2. a. Est-ce que tu seras **b.** Nous n'aurons pas **c.** Est-ce que Émilie pourra **d.** ils ne feront pas **e.** Est-ce que vous irez
3. a. J'ai passé **b.** n'est pas retournée **c.** sont rentrés **d.** avons sorti **e.** sont entrés ... ont entré

20 🔊 **4. a.** La femme de Fabien a retourné toute la maison pour trouver son (téléphone) portable. **b.** Dans notre nouveau quartier, nous aurons deux fromageries, trois boulangeries et une boucherie. **c.** Je pense que tu n'es pas contente/heureuse, Marion. – Si, si, tout va très bien, merci. **d.** Mettez vos clés dans votre poche, sinon vous les perdrez. **e.** Benjamin dit qu'il n'achètera plus de chocolat. – Il fait des économies de bout de chandelle !

19. BOOKING

1. a. *À combien* sont les oignons ? **b.** *À quelle heure* arrive Marion ? **c.** *À qui* veulent-elles parler ? **d.** *De combien* de places avez-vous besoin ? **e.** *À quoi* pensez-vous ?
2. a. Ce mail vient de qui ? **b.** Il veut parler à qui ? **c.** Ils ont besoin de quoi ? **d.** Vous pensez à quoi ? **e.** Ils arrivent d'où ?
3. a. chaque **b.** Chacun **c.** chacune **d.** Chacun **e.** chacun

21 🔊 **4. a.** Cette caméra coûte seulement deux cents euros. – C'est une bonne affaire ! **b.** Sophie m'a demandé de l'appeler à dix heures. – Appelle-la, tu es en retard. **c.** Il faut deux heures pour aller de Paris à Bordeaux en train. – C'est tout ? **d.** Qui est à l'appareil ? – C'est moi, Arnaud. – Je te rappellerai dans une demi-heure. **e.** J'ai encore des chambres, mais il faut faire vite. – Pas de soucis.

20. SPORT

1. a. du ... le **b.** à **c.** sur **d.** te ... au **e.** (no preposition) ... de **f.** au ... de **g.** de
2. a. un animal → des animaux **b.** un bateau → des bateaux **c.** un journal → des journaux **d.** un tuyau → des tuyaux **e.** un genou → des genoux
3. a. nous demandons / demandons **b.** Avez-vous trouvé / se trouve **c.** t'entends / m'entends **d.** Passez / se passe

22 🔊 **4. a.** Je ne m'y connais pas en rugby mais je ferai un effort si ça te/vous fait plaisir. **b.** Il faut apprendre à être patient. – Il n'en est pas question. **c.** Ça te / vous dit de voir un film ce soir ? Ça vaut la peine d'arriver de bonne heure au cinéma. **d.** Peux-tu /

Pouvez-vous m'aider à finir ce travail ? – Je ne peux pas faire trente-six / trente-six mille choses à la fois. **e.** Vous cherchez le métro ? – Non, nous attendons le bus. – Venez-avec moi. – Ça marche !

21. SICKNESS

1. a. lui **b.** leur **c.** nous **d.** en **e.** leur
2. a. la lui **b.** n'y **c.** m'en **d.** la lui **e.** les leur
3. a. mieux **b.** meilleurs **c.** mieux **d.** le meilleur **e.** les meilleures
23 🔊 **4. a.** Je n'ai pas l'adresse de Marie avec moi. – Je vous/te la donnerai quand je vous/te verrai demain. **b.** Comment ça, ils ont refusé mon invitation ? Ça ne se fait pas. **c.** Qu'est-ce qu'elle a ? Elle se sent malade ? – Il parait qu'elle a de la fièvre. **d.** Est-ce que tu as envoyé le rapport à ton médecin ? – Oui, je le lui ai envoyé sans attendre. **e.** Vous avez l'air en forme. – N'importe quoi ! Je suis très malade.

22. WORKING LIFE

1. a. vivions ... travaillais **b.** voulais **c.** pensait ... j'étais **d.** étaient ... étaient **e.** habitaient
2. a. étions **b.** allions **c.** promenions **d.** mangions **e.** regardions **f.** louait
3. a. à ... au **b.** en ... aux **c.** en ... en **d.** à (no preposition) **e.** du ... (no preposition)
24 🔊 **4. a.** Emmanuelle et ses amis travaillent pour une grosse boîte aux Ulis. – Ils se débrouillent bien. **b.** Michelle s'est levée à dix heures

et son mari s'est levé à midi. – Ah bon ? **c.** Elle est devenue riche très vite, et elle a acheté une maison au Mans. **d.** Ils sont partis au Canada quand ils étaient très jeunes. – Tant mieux pour eux ! **e.** Est-ce que tu pensais que ces émissions auraient du succès ? – Pas vraiment.

23. PARTYING

1. a. viennent ... viendront **b.** pourras ... l'as perdu **c.** allez ... prenez **d.** irons ... fait **e.** invites ... viendra
2. a. Ce qui **b.** ce que **c.** ce qui **d.** Ce que **e.** ce qui
3. a. On est très contents de vous avoir ici avec nous. **b.** Ce n'est pas grave, on s'amusera quand même. **c.** On ne l'a pas vu ... on lui a parlé **d.** Nous préférons ... nous attendons **e.** Ce qu'on pense ... qu'on doit
25 🔊 **4. a.** Ils ont sauté au plafond quand on leur a donné la mauvaise nouvelle. C'est pour cette raison qu'ils sont de mauvaise humeur. **b.** Est-ce que vous êtes au courant que les magasins seront fermés demain et lundi ? **c.** On a / nous avons du pain sur la planche : on doit / nous devons organiser la fête de Nelly. **d.** Qu'est-ce qui ne vas pas, Monique ? – J'ai le cafard parce que mon ex sort avec ma meilleure amie. **e.** Je vais peut-être les inviter. – Tu peux toujours essayer. Ça ne mange pas de pain.

24. THE LOTTERY

1. a. ferais ... gagnais **b.** n'achèterai pas **c.** voudrais ... avais ... ferait

d. démissionnerait ... n'irait plus **e.** n'habiterais pas ... pouvais **2. a.** Elle n'aime pas beaucoup ses films car ils sont beaucoup trop tristes. **b.** Tu es égoïste : tu ne penses jamais à moi. **c.** Il m'a dit qu'il va certainement partir demain. **d.** J'ai toujours pensé qu'ils étaient nos amis mais j'avais tort. **e.** Nous l'avons souvent vu à la télévision : c'est une star ! **3. a.** les yeux de la tête **b.** par la fenêtre **c.** te *changer* les idées **d.** sur l'or **e.** le coup de foudre

26 🔊 **4. a.** Ça vous / te dit de passer la soirée avec nous ? – À vrai dire / À dire vrai, je n'ai pas beaucoup de temps. **b.** Je suis convaincu que vous feriez / tu ferais pareil si vous étiez / tu étais à notre place. **c.** Je me suis rendu compte que leur nouveau quartier est très branché. – Franchement, nous n'y avons / on n'y a jamais pensé. **d.** Il partirait demain s'il pouvait, juste pour se changer les idées. **e.** Les deux magasins sont pareils : assez chic et très cher.

25. POLITICS

1. a. aussi vite que **b.** plus rapidement que **c.** moins que **d.** le plus fort **e.** plus (S) / moins (I) souvent qu' **2. a.** Il semble que **b.** Il suffit d' **c.** Il arrive que **d.** Il est important de **e.** Il faut que **3. a.** soyez **b.** j'aie **c.** soyons **d.** aies **e.** soient

27 🔊 **4. a.** Depuis combien de temps m'attendez-vous / est-ce que vous m'attendez ? – Je suis ici depuis deux heures. **b.** Vous savez / Tu sais aussi bien que moi que le chômage monte plus vite qu'avant. **c.** Pour combien de temps êtes-vous à Paris ? – Le plus longtemps possible. **d.** Il faut que nous soyons enthousiastes et optimistes. – Jusqu'à quand ? **e.** « La politique est une chose beaucoup trop sérieuse pour être confiée aux politiciens. » Charles de Gaulle

26. RENTING A CAR

1. a. fassions **b.** partes **c.** puisse **d.** attendiez **e.** n'ayez **2. a.** Il faut *être* **b.** Il faut *avoir* **c.** Il faut *faire* **d.** Il faut *être* **e.** Il vaut mieux *avoir* **3. a.** au fond du **b.** au bout de **c.** au bord de **d.** au-dessous de **e.** au-dessus du

28 🔊 **4. a.** Estelle est partie à Nîmes il y a un mois. Elle me manque. **b.** Il faut que vous fassiez le plein tout de suite. Le réservoir est presque vide. **c.** Connaissez-vous / Est-ce que vous connaissez le chemin le plus rapide ? – Oui, il faut prendre l'autoroute. **d.** Il vaut mieux que vous veniez la semaine prochaine. Il y aura moins de monde. **e.** Sandra travaille autant que moi mais elle gagne moins que moi. Et elle a autant d'expérience que moi.

REFERENCE: CONJUGATIONS

◆ VERBS

There are three main groups of verbs, identified by their infinitive endings. They are:
-er (the most common), **-ir** and **-re**.
Here is an example of each, using the tenses and the moods we have seen:

1) *-ER* VERBS

Most of these are regular. Any new verbs added to the language, for example, **textoter**,
to text, come into this category.
• **penser**, *to think*
Present participle: **pensant**; past participle: **pensé**
Present tense

je pense	I think	nous pensons	we think
tu penses	you think	vous pensez	you think
il/elle pense	he/she/it thinks	ils/elles pensent	they think

Future tense

je penserai	I will think	nous penserons	we will think
tu penseras	you will think	vous penserez	you will think
il/elle pensera	he/she/it will think	ils/elles penseront	they will think

Perfect tense (**passé composé**)

j'ai pensé	I thought	nous avons pensé	we thought
tu as pensé	you thought	vous avez pensé	you thought
il/elle a pensé	he/she/it thought	ils/elles ont pensé	they thought

Imperfect

je pensais	I was thinking	nous pensions	we were thinking
tu pensais	you were thinking	vous pensiez	you were thinking
il/elle pensait	he/she/it was thinking	ils/elles pensaient	they were thinking

Conditional

je penserais	I would think	nous penserions	we would think
tu penserais	you would think	vous penseriez	you would think
il/elle penserait	he/she/it would think	ils/elles penseraient	they would think

Subjunctive

je pense	I think	nous pensions	we think
tu penses	you think	vous pensiez	you think
il/elle pense	he/she/it think	ils/elles pensent	they think

2) -IR VERBS

• **finir**, *to finish*
Present participle: **finissant**; past participle: **fini**
Present tense

je finis	I finish	nous finissons	we finish
tu finis	you finish	vous finissez	you finish
il/elle finit	he/she/it finishes	ils/elles finissent	they finish

Future tense

je finirai	I will finish	nous finirons	we will finish
tu finiras	you will finish	vous finirez	you will finish
il/elle finira	he/she/it will finish	ils/elles finiront	they will finish

Perfect tense (**passé composé**)

j'ai fini	I finished	nous avons fini	we finished
tu as fini	you finished	vous avez fini	you finished
il/elle a fini	he/she/it finished	ils/elles ont fini	they finished

Imperfect

je finissais	I was finishing	nous finissions	we were finishing
tu finissais	you were finishing	vous finissiez	you were finishing
il/elle finissait	he/she/it was finishing	ils/elles finissaient	they were finishing

Conditional

je finirais	I finished	nous finirions	we finished
tu finirais	you finished	vous finiriez	you finished
il/elle finirait	he/she/it finished	ils/elles finiraient	they finished

Subjunctive

je finisse	I finish	nous finissions	we finish
tu finisses	you finish	vous finissiez	you finish
il/elle finisse	he/she/it finish	ils/elles finissent	they finish

3) -RE VERBS

This group is composed of irregular verbs. It has two sub-sets: those ending in **-oir** and those ending in **-ir** that do not have a present participle with an **-issant** termination.

• **apprendre**, *to learn*
Present participle: **apprenant**; past participle: **appris**
Present tense

j'apprends	I learn	nous apprenons	we learn
tu apprends	you learn	vous apprenez	you learn
il/elle apprend	he/she/it learns	ils/elles apprennent	they learn

Future tense

j'apprendrai	I will learn	nous apprendrons	we will learn
tu apprendras	you will learn	vous apprendrez	you will learn
il/elle apprendra	he/she/it will learn	ils/elles apprendront	they will learn

Perfect tense (**passé composé**)

j'ai appris	I learned	nous avons appris	we learned
tu as appris	you learned	vous avez appris	you learned
il/elle a appris	he/she/it learned	ils/elles ont appris	they learned

Imperfect

j'apprenais	I was learning	nous apprenions	we were learning
tu apprenais	you were learning	vous appreniez	you were learning
il/elle apprenait	he/she/it was learning	ils/elles apprenaient	they were learning

Conditional

j'apprendrais	I would learn	nous apprendrions	we would learn
tu apprendrais	you would learn	vous apprendriez	you would learn
il/elle apprendrait	he/she/it would learn	ils/elles apprendraient	they would learn

Subjunctive

j'apprenne	I learn	nous apprenions	we learn
tu apprennes	you learn	vous appreniez	you learn
il/elle apprenne	he/she/it learn	ils/elles apprennent	they learn

• **boire**, *to drink*

Present participle: **buvant**; past participle: **bu**

Present tense

je bois	I drink	nous buvons	we drink
tu bois	you drink	vous buvez	you drink
il/elle boit	he/she/it drinks	ils/elles boivent	they drink

Future tense

je boirai	I will drink	nous boirons	we will drink
tu boiras	you will drink	vous boirez	you will drink
il/elle boira	he/she/it will drink	ils/elles boiront	they will drink

Perfect tense (**passé composé**)

j'ai bu	I drank	nous avons bu	we drank
tu as bu	you drank	vous avez bu	you drank
il/elle a bu	he/she/it drank	ils/elles ont bu	they drank

Imperfect

je buvais	I was drinking	nous buvions	we were drinking
tu buvais	you were drinking	vous buviez	you were drinking
il/elle buvait	he/she/it was drinking	ils/elles buvaient	they were drinking

Conditional

je boirais	I would drink	nous boirions	we would drink
tu boirais	you would drink	vous boiriez	you would drink
il/elle boirait	he/she/it would drink	ils/elles boiraient	they would drink

Subjunctive

je boive	I drink	nous buvions	we drink
tu boives	you drink	vous buviez	you drink
il/elle boive	he/she/it drink	ils/elles boivent	they drink

• **lire**, *to read*
Present participle: **lisant**, past participle: **lu**
Present tense

je lis	I read	nous lisons	we read
tu lis	you read	vous lisez	you read
il/elle lit	he/she/it reads	ils/elles lisent	they read

Future tense

je lirai	I will read	nous lirons	we will read
tu liras	you will read	vous lirez	you will read
il/elle lira	he/she/it will read	ils/elles liront	they will read

Perfect tense (**passé composé**)

j'ai lu	I read	nous avons lu	we read
tu as lu	you read	vous avez lu	you read
il/elle a lu	he/she/it read	ils/elles ont lu	they read

Imperfect

je lisais	I was reading	nous lisions	we were reading
tu lisais	you were reading	vous lisiez	you were reading
il/elle lisait	he/she/it was reading	ils/elles lisaient	they were reading

Conditional

je lirais	I would read	nous lirions	we would read
tu lirais	you would read	vous liriez	you would read
il/elle lirait	he/she/it would read	ils/elles liraient	they would read

Subjunctive

je lise	I read	nous lisions	we read
tu lises	you read	vous lisiez	you read
il/elle lise	he/she/it read	ils/elles lisent	they read

4) AUXILIARIES

Here are the main irregular verbs. First, the two auxiliaries **être** and **avoir**.

• **être**, *to be*

Present participle: **étant**; past participle: **été**

Present tense

je suis	I am	nous sommes	we are
tu es	you are	vous êtes	you are
il/elle est	he/she/it is	ils/elles sont	they are

Future tense

je serai	I will be	nous serons	we will be
tu seras	you will be	vous serez	you will be
il/elle sera	he/she/it will be	ils/elles seront	they will be

Perfect tense (**passé composé**)

j'ai été	I was	nous avons été	we were
tu as été	you were	vous avez été	you were
il/elle a été	he/she/it was	ils/elles ont été	they were

Imperfect

j'étais	I was being	nous étions	we were being
tu étais	you were being	vous étiez	you were being
il/elle était	he/she/it was being	ils/elles étaient	they were being

Conditional

je serais	I would be	nous serions	we would be
tu serais	you would be	vous seriez	you would be
il/elle serait	he/she/it would be	ils/elles seraient	they would be

Subjunctive

je sois	I be	nous soyons	we be
tu sois	you be	vous soyez	you be
il/elle soit	he/she/it be	ils/elles soient	they be

• **avoir**, *to have*
Present participle: **ayant**; past participle: **eu**
Present tense

j'ai	I have	nous avons	we have
tu as	you have	vous avez	you have
il/elle a	he/she/it has	ils/elles ont	they have

Future tense

j'aurai	I will have	nous aurons	we will have
tu auras	you will have	vous aurez	you will have
il/elle aura	he/she/it will have	ils/elles auront	they will have

Perfect tense (**passé composé**)

j'ai eu	I had	nous avons eu	we had
tu as eu	you had	vous avez eu	you had
il/elle a eu	he/she/it had	ils/elles ont eu	they had

Imperfect

j'avais	I was having	nous avions	we were having
tu avais	you were having	vous aviez	you were having
il/elle avait	he/she/it was having	ils/elles avaient	they were having

Conditional

j'aurais	I would have	nous aurions	we would have
tu aurais	you would have	vous auriez	you would have
il/elle aurait	he/she/it would have	ils/elles auraient	they would have

Subjunctive

j'aie	I have	nous ayons	we have
tu aies	you have	vous ayez	you have
il/elle ait	he/she/it have	ils/elles aient	they have

5) MODALS

A modal is a verb used with another verb to talk about a possibility not expressed in the first one. Whereas English has ten modals (*could*, *may*, *might*, etc.), French has only three, all irregular: **devoir**, **pouvoir** and **vouloir**:

• **devoir**, *must, to have to*

Present participle: **devant**; past participle: **dû**

Present tense

je dois	I must	nous devons	we must
tu dois	you must	vous devez	you must
il/elle doit	he/she/it must	ils/elles doivent	they must

Future tense

je devrai	I will have to	nous devrons	we will have to
tu devras	you will have to	vous devrez	you will have to
il/elle devra	he/she/it will have to	ils/elles devront	they will have to

Perfect tense (**passé composé**)

j'ai dû*	I had to	nous avons dû	we had to
tu as dû	you had to	vous avez dû	you had to
il/elle a dû	he/she/it had to	ils/elles ont dû	they had to

* *must* is a defective verb, i.e. its conjugation is incomplete. In this case, there is no precise English equivalent for the French imperfect tense.

Imperfect

je devais	I had to	nous devions	we had to
tu devais	you had to	vous deviez	you had to
il/elle devait	he/she/it had to	ils/elles devaient	they had to

Conditional

je devrais	I had to	nous devrions	we had to
tu devrais	you had to	vous devriez	you had to
il/elle devrait	he/she/it had to	ils/elles devraient	they had to

Subjunctive

je doive	I must	nous devions	we must
tu doives	you must	vous deviez	you must
il/elle doive	he/she/it must	ils/elles doivent	they must

• **pouvoir**, *can, to be able to*
Present participle: **pouvant**; past participle: **pu**
Present tense

je peux	I can	nous pouvons	we can
tu peux	you can	vous pouvez	you can
il/elle peut	he/she/it can	ils/elles peuvent	they can

Future tense

je pourrai	I will be able to	nous pourrons	we will be able to
tu pourras	you will be able to	vous pourrez	you will be able to
il/elle pourra	he/she/it will be able to	ils/elles pourront	they will be able to

Perfect tense (**passé composé**)

j'ai pu	I was able to	nous avons pu	we were able to
tu as pu	you were able to	vous avez pu	you were able to
il/elle a pu	he/she/it was able to	ils/elles ont pu	they were able to

Imperfect*

je pouvais	I was able to	nous pouvions	we were able to
tu pouvais	you were able to	vous pouviez	you were able to
il/elle pouvait	he/she/it was able to	ils/elles pouvaient	they were able to

* *to be able to* is a defective verb, i.e. its conjugation is incomplete. In this case, there is no precise English equivalent for the French imperfect tense.

Conditional

je pourrais	I could	nous pourrions	we could
tu pourrais	you could	vous pourriez	you could
il/elle pourrait	he/she/it could	ils/elles pourraient	they could

Subjunctive

je puisse	I be able to	nous puissions	be able to
tu puisses	you be able to	vous puissiez	you be able to
il/elle puisse	he/she/it be able to	ils/elles puissent	they be able to

• **vouloir**, *to want*

Present participle: **voulant**; past participle: **voulu**

Present tense

je veux	I want	nous voulons	we want
tu veux	you want	vous voulez	you want
il/elle veut	he/she/it want	ils/elles veulent	they want

Future tense

je voudrai	I will want	nous voudrons	we will want
tu voudras	you will want	vous voudrez	you will want
il/elle voudra	he/she/it will want	ils/elles voudront	they will want

Perfect tense (**passé composé**)

j'ai voulu	I wanted	nous avons voulu	we wanted
tu as voulu	you wanted	vous avez voulu	you wanted
il/elle a voulu	he/she/it wanted	ils/elles ont voulu	they wanted

Imperfect

je voulais	I wanted	nous voulions	we wanted
tu voulais	you wanted	vous vouliez	you wanted
il/elle voulait	he/she/it wanted	ils/elles voulaient	they wanted

Conditional

je voudrais	I would want	nous voudrions	we would want
tu voudrais	you would want	vous voudriez	you would want
il/elle voudrait	he/she/it would want	ils/elles voudraient	they would want

Subjunctive

je veuille	I want	nous voulions	we want

tu veuilles	you want	vous vouliez	you want
il/elle veuille	he/she/it want	ils/elles veuillent	they want

6) DEFECTIVE VERBS

Another highly irregular and very common verb is **falloir**, which is defective (i.e. is only used in certain forms):

No present participle; past participle: **fallu**

Present tense

il faut	it is necessary

Future tense

il faudra	it will be necessary to

Perfect tense (**passé composé**)

il a fallu	it was necessary to

Imperfect

il fallait	it was necessary to

Conditional

il faudrait	it would be necessary to

Subjunctive

il faille	it be necessary to

7) OTHER IRREGULAR VERBS

Lastly, two very irregular – but very useful – verbs are **aller** and **savoir**:

• **aller**, to go

Present participle: **allant**; past participle: **allé**

Present tense

je vais	I go	nous allons	we go
tu vas	you go	vous allez	you go
il/elle va	he/she/it goes	ils/elles vont	they go

Future tense

j'irai	I will go	nous irons	we will go
tu iras	you will go	vous irez	you will go
il/elle ira	he/she/it will go	ils/elles iront	they will go

Perfect tense (**passé composé**)

je suis allé/allée	I went	nous sommes allés/allées	we went
tu es allé/allée	you went	vous avez êtes allés/allées	you went
il/elle est allé/ allée	he/she/it went	ils/elles sont allés/allées	they went

Imperfect

j'allais	I was going	nous allions	we were going
tu allais	you were going	vous alliez	you were going
il/elle allait	he/she/it was going	ils/elles allaient	they were going

Conditional

j'irais	I would know	nous irions	we would know
tu irais	you would know	vous iriez	you would know
il/elle irait	he/she/it would know	ils/elles iraient	they would know

Subjunctive

j'aille	I go	nous allions	we go
tu ailles	you go	vous alliez	you go
il/elle aille	he/she/it go	ils/elles aillent	they go

• **savoir**, *to know*
Present participle: **sachant**; past participle: **su**
Present tense

je sais	I know	nous savons	we know
tu sais	you know	vous savez	you know
il/elle sait	he/she/it knows	ils/elles savent	they know

Future tense

je saurai	I will know	nous saurons	we will know
tu sauras	you will know	vous saurez	you will know
il/elle saura	he/she/it will know	ils/elles sauront	they will know

Perfect tense (passé composé)

j'ai su	I knew	nous avons su	we knew
tu as su	you knew	vous avez su	you knew
il/elle a su	he/she/it knew	ils/elles ont su	they knew

Imperfect

je savais	I was knowing	nous savions	we were knowing
tu savais	you were knowing	vous saviez	you were knowing
il/elle savait	he/she/it was knowing	ils/elles savaient	they were knowing

Conditional

je saurais	I would know	nous saurions	we would know
tu saurais	you would know	vous sauriez	you would know
il/elle saurait	he/she/it would know	ils/elles sauraient	they would know

Subjunctive

je sache	I know	nous sachions	we know
tu saches	you know	vous sachiez	you know
il/elle sache	he/she/it know	ils/elles sachent	they know

8) NOTES AND REMINDERS

– The French present tense translates both the simple (*I eat*) and the continuous (*I am eating*) forms of the English present.

– The perfect tense translates the past simple and the present perfect tenses in English.

– The past participle is used with the auxiliaries **avoir** or **être** to form the perfect tense. With **avoir**, the participle agrees with a direct object that comes before the verb. **J'ai envoyé les lettres** but **Les lettres que j'ai envoyées.** When **être** is the auxiliary, the participle agrees with the subject: **Il est allé, Elle est allée, Ils sont allés**, etc.

– All reflexive verbs form their past tense with **être** (**Elle s'est assise par terre**, *She sat on the floor*; **Nous nous sommes rencontrés il y a vingt ans**, *We met 20 years ago*.)

– Present and past participles can be used as adjectives, in which case they always agree in number and gender (**une personne intéressante**, *an interesting person*; **les clés perdues**, *lost keys*).

Graphic design, cover and layout: Sarah Boris
Sound engineer: Leonard Mule @ Studio du Poisson Barbu

© 2019, Assimil.
Legal deposit: January 2019
Edition number: 4280 - August 2023
ISBN: 978-2-7005-0970-0
www.assimil.com

Printed in Spain by Ganboa